D0983909

Responsibility and the Moral Sentiments

Responsibility and the Moral Sentiments

※

R. Jay Wallace

Harvard University Press
Cambridge, Massachusetts
London, England
1994

BJ
1451
.W27
1994

Copyright © 1994 by the President and Fellows of Harvard College
All rights reserved
Printed in the United States of America

This book is printed on acid-free paper, and its binding
materials have been chosen for strength and durability.

Library of Congress Cataloging-in-Publication Data
Wallace, R. Jay.
Responsibility and the moral sentiments / R. Jay Wallace.
p.   cm.
Includes bibliographical references (p.   ) and index.
ISBN 0-674-76622-9
1. Responsibility.   2. Agent (Philosophy).   3. Social ethics.
4. Free will and determinism.   5. Emotions—Moral and ethical aspects.
I. Title.
BJ1451.W27   1994
170—dc20
94-17255
CIP

LONGWOOD COLLEGE LIBRARY
FARMVILLE, VIRGINIA 23901

For Katharina

Preface

꧁꧂

I began thinking about the problems discussed in this book ten years ago, in a seminar for first-year graduate students given by T. M. Scanlon at Princeton. Scanlon was a marvelous guide to this terrain; he managed to convey quite memorably both the normative significance of the issues and the unusual difficulty of giving an adequate account of them. I almost certainly would not have become sufficiently obsessed by the problems of freedom and responsibility to write a book about them had it not been for his gripping introduction to the subject.

Though I continued to be haunted by these problems during the rest of my graduate career, they receded into the background while I finished my course work and produced a dissertation on a different set of issues (concerning practical reason). It was not until my arrival at the University of Pennsylvania in the fall of 1988 that I returned to working systematically on responsibility, galvanized—as only beginning teachers can be—by the need to think of something to say to the students in the course on free will that I had inherited.

The stimulus provided by this teaching assignment eventually resulted in a paper on freedom and responsibility that first set out some of the ideas developed in this book, and that was read to audiences at Penn and Columbia during the 1990–91 academic year. I am grateful to both audiences for expressing interest in my views, and for convincing me that more would need to be said for others to be able to make them out. I owe a special debt to Akeel Bilgrami, who took the trouble to write up his detailed thoughts about where I had gone wrong in my interpretation of Strawson; I learned much from the exchange (though he will probably find that I did not learn enough).

The first draft of this book was written during the summer and fall of 1991, when I enjoyed the benefit of an academic leave. I am very grateful to the University of Pennsylvania for making possible this release from my teaching duties, without which I would certainly not have been able to launch this project so expeditiously.

I am especially grateful to the friends and colleagues who worked their way through the first draft I showed them when my leave was over. Rüdiger Bittner's extensive written comments were the first response to the manuscript I received; in addition to providing many excellent points of substantive criticism and advice, those comments also helped to reassure me that the manuscript might eventually make a decent book—an equally valuable service. Later in the spring of 1992 I had a series of extremely helpful conversations about the first draft with Samuel Freeman, who saved me from countless large and small mistakes; his influence on my thinking about moral philosophy has been profound and salutary since my arrival at Penn, and undoubtedly shows up in the book in many ways I am no longer able to identify. Further conversations that spring with Gary Ebbs, Paul Guyer, and Wolfgang Mann made clear to me the need for major changes both in the details of my argument and in the way it was structured and presented in the first draft.

Spurred on by these critical responses, I thoroughly reorganized and rewrote the manuscript during the summer of 1992. The Research Foundation of the University of Pennsylvania provided a generous research grant that made it possible for me to devote the summer exclusively to this project.

The revised draft served as the centerpiece in a graduate seminar I taught on responsibility during the fall semester of 1992. I owe many thanks to the students in that seminar for their questions and objections, which eventually made me realize that clarity had not yet been attained. Later during the 1992–93 academic year I received four wonderful and detailed sets of written comments on the draft, provided by readers for Princeton University Press and Harvard University Press. These were models of the kind of critical feedback an author needs during the process of revision, pointing out innumerable errors, raising large and small objections from a variety of critical perspectives, and offering sage advice about how I might make my points more effectively. I am very glad to be able to thank Gary Watson by name, who identified himself to me as one of the readers for Harvard University Press, and whose trenchant and thoughtful comments stood out even in the company of an excellent group of reader's reports. He more than anyone forced me to rethink the fundamental terms of my position, in a way that eventually led me to understand better what I was really trying to say. Gary

Ebbs, Samuel Freeman, and Stephen J. Morse also allowed me to try out on them parts of the penultimate draft, and provided (once again) extremely constructive advice.

Although this may seem a strange place to mention them, I have to thank Ann Wald and Walter Lippincott of Princeton University Press for their enthusiasm about this project, which gave me quite a boost. Lindsay Waters of Harvard University Press has been a pleasure to work with. I am especially grateful to him for the deft way in which he urged on me the virtues of concision; taking his advice to heart has, I think, greatly improved the book.

The final draft of the book was written during the spring and summer of 1993. A second (and surprising) summer research grant from the Research Foundation of the University of Pennsylvania made it possible for me to work on the project uninterruptedly during this period. Julie Ericksen Hagen's meticulous copyediting of the final manuscript resulted in many stylistic improvements.

On a more personal note I would like to thank my parents-in-law, Ursula and Bruno Kaiser, for generously making available to us a comfortable retreat in Hamburg, Germany, where almost all of the writing and rewriting of this book was done; I doubt I would have been able to concentrate so effectively on this project had I not been able to remove myself during the summers to the cool and leafy environs of the Schlüterstraße. Thanks above all to my wife, Katharina, who has put up with me so patiently during the past three years.

Contents

❧

1

Introduction

❧

This is a book about moral responsibility. In the most basic terms, it sets out to provide an account of the kind of moral agency in virtue of which people are morally responsible for the things they do. The approach I advocate gives a central place to distinctively rational powers among the conditions of responsibility. Being a responsible moral agent, I believe, is not really a matter of having freedom of the will. Rather it primarily involves a form of normative competence: the ability to grasp and apply moral reasons, and to govern one's behavior by the light of such reasons.

The book moves indirectly toward this target. My starting point is not the question, What is it to be a morally responsible agent? but rather, What is it to treat someone as a morally responsible agent, or to hold a person morally responsible? This way of proceeding reflects a conviction that the question of what it is to be a morally responsible agent should be given what I call a normative interpretation. If we wish to make sense of the idea that there are facts about what it is to be a responsible agent, it is best not to picture such facts as conceptually prior to and independent of our practice of holding people responsible. Instead, I propose that we begin by examining that practice itself, focusing on the distinctive stance of holding someone morally responsible—the stance characteristic of the moral judge, rather than the agent who is judged. An account of moral agency can then be accepted or rejected, depending on whether the conditions it describes make it fair to adopt this stance. I hope to show that the conditions of rational power just mentioned satisfy this constraint: that it is fair to hold people morally responsible if they possess the rational power to grasp and apply moral reasons, and to control their behavior by the light of those reasons.

This presupposes, of course, an account of what it is to hold a person morally responsible; a further aim of the book will be to develop such an account. I postulate a close connection between holding someone responsible and a central class of moral sentiments, those of resentment, indignation, and guilt. To hold someone responsible, I argue, is essentially to be subject to emotions of this class in one's dealings with the person. Both the plausibility and the implications of this proposal depend crucially on how the moral sentiments in question are understood. A central thesis of the book is that these emotions are distinguished by their connection with expectations. Understanding this connection will help to make plausible the suggestion that holding someone responsible involves a susceptibility to these moral sentiments. It will also point toward the conditions of responsibility, helping us to see why moral agency essentially involves the powers of reflective self-control.

The book may thus be thought of as having two main parts. One is an account of what it is to hold people morally responsible, in terms of the moral sentiments. The other is an account of the conditions of moral agency, in terms of the rational power to grasp moral reasons and to control one's behavior by the light of them. The leading idea of the book is that these two parts illuminate and reinforce each other, producing together a unified and compelling interpretation of moral responsibility and its conditions.

1.1   The Problem

The traditional problem of freedom of the will is the problem of the compatibility of freedom with determinism. Philosophers who affirm that freedom is compatible with determinism are usually called compatibilists, while those who deny this are referred to as incompatibilists.

But compatibilism and incompatibilism, construed in this way, do not seem to be well-defined positions. Surely there are some conceptions of freedom of the will that are compatible with determinism and others that are not so compatible. The interesting question is how much freedom we need to make sense of the various ways in which we tend to think of ourselves: as persons, as subjects of certain ways of experiencing our own actions, as autonomous pursuers of the good, as morally responsible agents. To be sure, philosophers sometimes write as if freedom were something intrinsically valuable, suggesting that we desire freedom of the will for its own sake (as it were). But such claims ring false, to my ear. What we want is not freedom of the will per se, but the kind of freedom that makes us persons, or deliberators, or autonomous valuers, or morally accountable agents; a desire for freedom that floated loose from all such contexts would be a kind of fetish. In discussing the relation between freedom of the will and determinism, it is therefore important to keep in mind what we want freedom for. Only then will we be addressing a serious question when we ask whether an incompatibilist conception of freedom is or is not adequate.

My larger interest, in this book, is in our conception of ourselves as morally responsible agents, and in determining the kind of freedom or ability that is required to make sense of this conception. For purposes of addressing this issue, we may assume that there is a notion of freedom of the will—call it "strong" freedom of the will—that is not compatible with determinism. This kind of freedom involves, roughly speaking, the availability of a range of alternate possibilities, holding fixed the laws of nature and the facts about the past; determinism would plausibly deprive us of alternate possibilities, construed in this way. A central problem is then the following: does moral responsibility require that agents have freedom of the will, in this strong sense, or is it instead to be understood in terms of abilities that do not involve strong freedom of the will? Departing somewhat from standard usage, I shall call an account of moral responsibility "incompatibilist" if it affirms that moral responsibility requires that agents be strongly free, and "compatibilist" if it denies this.

In focusing on the compatibility of responsibility and determinism, I do not mean to suggest that moral responsibility is the only context in which questions about freedom arise. As I mentioned, it is also natural to suppose that our status as persons, our status as autonomous valuers, and our status as deliberators all require freedom of a sort, and the question may be posed as to whether these sorts of freedom are compatible with determinism. For what it's worth, though, it seems to me that concerns about moral responsibility are by far the most troubling sources for the thought that we need a kind of freedom that is incompatible with determinism. The experience of agency, for instance, evidently requires that our actions should be unpredictable by us, while we are deliberating about what to do;[1] otherwise there would be no room for deliberation and for the related phenomenon of acting as the result of decision or choice, on the basis of reasons. We act "under the

---

1. Deliberation is compatible with a high degree of antecedent confidence about what we are going to do. But we do not seriously deliberate about what we already *know* we are going to do.

idea of freedom," in Kant's memorable phrase. But there is little reason to suppose that determinism would deprive us of this kind of unpredictability: if the particular movements of our bodies are governed (at some level of description) by deterministic laws, it will almost certainly *not* follow that human beings are ever in a position simply to predict what they are going to do, on the basis of knowledge of these laws.

Even if epistemic indeterminacy is sufficient for deliberation and the experience of agency, however, doubts are bound to persist about whether it is really enough for moral responsibility. Responsibility, or distinctively *moral* agency, it will be thought, requires not merely that alternatives be open to us "for all we know"; it requires genuine alternatives, or strong freedom of the will. Until compatibilist philosophers find an effective response to this thought, they will not have come to terms with a deep source—perhaps the deepest source—of the desire for strong freedom of will. Yet for all the attention it has received, discussions of this issue do not seem to have advanced very far. Even very sophisticated compatibilists continue to fall back on the tired strategy of staking their position to a broadly utilitarian account of responsibility, praise, and blame.[2] On this approach, moral praise and blame are essentially seen as forward-looking techniques of education and deterrence; it is then pointed out that the truth of determinism would not make these techniques any less effective at promoting their forward-looking aims, and the conclusion is reached that determinism is compatible with the practice of holding people morally responsible. Incompatibilists have rightly objected that the exclusively forward-looking account does not capture all that we are doing when we hold people responsible. Instead of developing a superior account of moral responsibility, however, they tend merely to assert that responsibility requires genuine alternatives; attention is then lavished on the project of showing in detail why and how determinism is incompatible with the possession of such genuine alternatives, thereby depriving us of the kind of freedom that responsibility demands.[3]

2. Exemplary in this connection is Daniel C. Dennett's *Elbow Room: The Varieties of Free Will Worth Wanting* (Cambridge, Mass.: MIT Press, 1984). See Gary Watson's review of *Elbow Room* in *Journal of Philosophy* 83 (1986), pp. 517–522.

3. See, for example, David Wiggins, "Towards a Reasonable Libertarianism," in Ted Honderich, ed., *Essays on Freedom of Action* (London: Routledge and Kegan Paul, 1973), pp. 33–61, and Peter van Inwagen, *An Essay on Free Will* (Oxford: Clarendon Press, 1983). (Van Inwagen considers the importance of alternate possibilities to moral responsibility in chap. 5 of his book, but most of his discussion is devoted to refuting counterexamples that have been brought against the claim that responsibility requires alternate possibilities. Positive support for this claim is presented only on p. 161, and consists in little more than an appeal to direct intuition.)

I believe that progress with this debate requires that we step back and try to take in a wider view. Before proceeding to consider whether alternate possibilities are or are not compatible with determinism, and before offering detailed analyses of "can" and "could have done otherwise," we should pause to consider why philosophers have insisted that alternate possibilities matter to moral responsibility in the first place. In support of this claim it is often said, for instance, that ought implies can; but this suggestion raises more questions than it answers. What does the principle mean, that ought implies can? What kind of implication is at issue? Is the principle a logical or grammatical principle, or should it rather be understood as a kind of moral principle? We need answers to questions such as these if we are to understand what is meant in saying that responsibility requires alternate possibilities. But we shall need still more if we are not only to understand but also to assess this claim. To decide whether responsibility really does require alternate possibilities—and what kind of possibilities (or "cans") might matter—we must first try to get clear about what is involved in holding someone morally responsible. For unless we know what it is to hold someone morally responsible, debates about whether strong freedom of the will is a condition of responsibility are apt to remain inconclusive. We will lack a clear framework for conducting and resolving those debates.

These themes determine the structure of my argument, so it will be helpful to set them out a bit more systematically. I propose that we interpret the debate about moral responsibility in normative terms. The primary issue is not whether our practice of holding people responsible answers to facts about responsibility that are prior to and independent of that practice as a whole. It turns, rather, on the following question: What are the conditions that make it morally fair for us to adopt the stance of holding people responsible? Philosophers have often suggested that freedom matters to responsibility because it would be unfair to hold people responsible in the absence of freedom of will. I take this thought much more seriously than it has been taken heretofore, and work it up into an interpretation of what is at stake in the debate between compatibilists and incompatibilists. This normative interpretation has two important consequences. First, we cannot establish what it is to be a morally responsible agent unless we first understand the stance of holding someone responsible—the stance of the moral judge, rather than of the agent who is judged. Second, determining what the conditions of responsibility are will require an excursion into normative moral theory; we will need to investigate our principles of fairness, to see what they entail about the conditions under which it would be fair to hold people responsible. These two conclusions set my agenda in this book, which begins with an account of what we are doing when we hold people responsible, and concludes with a normative examination of the conditions under which it would be fair to adopt that stance. In pursuing this agenda, I hope to develop a version of compatibilism that is grounded in a recognizable interpretation of our practice of holding people responsible, and that engages rather than ignores the concerns that have traditionally made incompatibilist accounts seem attractive.

Any treatment of issues as complex as those of responsibility and freedom must take some things for granted; otherwise progress would be impossible. Among the things I simply assume, for purposes of discussion in this book, are the existence and explanatory efficacy of such propositional attitudes as beliefs, desires, and emotions. These are, of course, large assumptions, since difficult questions arise about how intentional explanations can be reconciled with our membership in a world of natural objects subject to mechanistic explanations.[4] But no work in moral philosophy would get very far off the ground if it were required to first address and resolve these questions. My main concern is with moral responsibility, a kind of status that presupposes intentionality, but that goes beyond it somehow.[5] Thus an agent might be subject to propositional attitudes that explain its actions and thoughts without its being morally responsible—consider, for instance, children, the insane, and (perhaps) certain animals. It is natural to suppose that the extra ingredient that makes an agent responsible is some sort of freedom or ability. Determinism has accordingly been seen as a special threat to responsibility, not because it would undermine all intentional explanations of what we do,[6] but because it seems to undermine the condition of freedom or ability that sets responsible agents apart from other kinds of intentional creatures. To focus effectively on the specific issue of what it is to be morally responsible, we therefore would do best to take for granted the basic legitimacy of intentional explanations.

Another question I do not attempt to resolve is the question of whether determinism is true. At various points in my discussion, I call

4. For discussion of this issue, with special attention to its implications for deliberation and action, see Dennett, *Elbow Room,* chaps. 2–6.

5. Compare the distinction between the intentional and the personal stance drawn by Daniel C. Dennett in "Mechanism and Responsibility," as reprinted in Gary Watson, ed., *Free Will* (Oxford: Oxford University Press, 1982), pp. 150–173, at pp. 157–158.

6. In fact determinism per se, as distinguished from mechanism or naturalism more generally, would not seem to pose a special threat to such explanations; on this point, see Gary Watson, "Introduction," in Watson, ed., *Free Will,* pp. 1–14, at pp. 13–14.

on a fairly standard—and fairly crude—interpretation of what determinism would involve, but I do not have anything to say about the plausibility of determinism so construed.[7] This restriction of focus is partly a reflection of my own limited qualifications as an interpreter of modern science, but it also reflects a conviction that the particular issue that divides compatibilists and incompatibilists would retain much of its grip on us even if we knew determinism to be false. The real interest of the debate—admittedly sometimes obscured behind the haze of technical detail that it has tended to generate—lies in what it promises to tell us about the conditions of responsibility. We want to know what it would take to be a morally responsible agent. Is it a matter of having freedom of the will, or alternate possibilities? If so, how are we to understand the kind of freedom that is required? And if not, what does (or would) make us morally responsible agents, and why have we been led to think that freedom and alternate possibilities are important? Determinism is a crux that helps us to sharpen these questions, and to refine our answers to them.[8] The possibility that determinism might be true gives an extra immediacy to the issue of whether it is compatible with moral responsibility, but the reason for considering this issue—my reason, at least—is to obtain an improved understanding of the conditions of responsibility, the conditions that must obtain if we are to be morally accountable for what we do.[9]

1.2   The Solution

The position for which I argue in this book is a compatibilist one. It holds that the conditions of responsibility do not involve freedom of the will, but primarily include the possession of certain rational powers: the power to grasp and apply moral reasons, and the power to control one's behavior by the light of such reasons. The "can" that matters in

7. On the interpretation of determinism and its complicated relations to Newtonian and modern physics, see John Earman, *A Primer on Determinism* (Dordrecht: D. Reidel, 1986).

8. Consideration of the relation between responsibility and divine foreknowledge is less useful for this purpose, in my view. The postulation of a God who is at once all-knowing and the ultimate moral judge threatens to distort rather than illuminate the standard conditions of responsibility. The kind of freedom we need to be held responsible by an omniscient God—who both created us and stands in judgment over us—may be different from the freedom we need to be held morally responsible by ordinary mortals.

9. Another salient issue that I do not have the space to address, but that clearly has some bearing on questions of moral responsibility, concerns the conditions of personal identity over time. Taking for granted the familiar idea that persons persist through a variety of physical and psychological changes, my aim is to identify the special conditions that persons have to satisfy to count as morally responsible agents.

moral responsibility is thus not the "can" of alternate possibilities, or strong freedom of the will, but rather the "can" of general rational power. In support of this position, I draw on a particular account of what we are doing when we hold people morally responsible. According to this account, to hold someone morally responsible is essentially to be subject to a distinctive range of moral sentiments in one's interactions with the person. Once we grasp this, and understand the kind of sentiments involved, I believe we will be able to see why the conditions of responsibility should be understood in terms of general rational powers rather than in terms of freedom of the will, in the strong sense.

That is the broad shape of the compatibilist position I defend. It is distinctive in that it weaves together two prominent strands in philosophical writing about responsibility that have previously been treated largely in isolation from each another. One of these might be called the Strawsonian strand, in reference to P. F. Strawson's famous and influential British Academy lecture "Freedom and Resentment."[10] Strawson urges that responsibility needs to be understood in the context of a central range of sentiments that we are subject to in our dealings with each other, which he calls the reactive attitudes. As Strawson understands them, these attitudes include gratitude, resentment, forgiveness, love, hurt feelings, and, in the specifically moral case, indignation and disapprobation.[11] To treat someone as morally responsible, Strawson suggests, is to be disposed to respond to the person with the distinctively moral reactive attitudes; but Strawson thinks it very important that this stance of holding people responsible be seen as part of the broader network of feelings that provides the emotional context of our interpersonal relations. Appreciating this point, Strawson suggests, can help us to see why determinism (whatever that might come to) is not a genuine threat to our practice of holding people responsible.

Thus we may distinguish the question of whether we *would* stop holding people responsible, if we knew determinism to be true, from the question of whether we *should* stop holding people responsible if

---

10. Originally published in *Proceedings of the British Academy* 48 (1962), pp. 1–25; references in this book to "Freedom and Resentment" are to the accessible reprinting in Watson, ed., *Free Will*, pp. 59–80. The approach could with perhaps equal justice be called "Butlerian," in reference to Joseph Butler's sermon "Upon Resentment" (sermon 8, from the *Fifteen Sermons Preached at the Rolls Chapel*), which develops similar ideas about the connection between responsibility and the moral sentiments.

11. Strawson, "Freedom and Resentment," pp. 62, 70.

we knew determinism to be true. Strawson believes that both questions receive a clearly negative answer when we properly situate responsibility in the context of the reactive attitudes. To suppose that we would give up holding people responsible in the face of determinism presupposes that it is possible for us to give up this practice. But Strawson argues that the connection of responsibility with the reactive attitudes calls into question the assumption that it is a live option for us to stop holding people responsible.[12] The reactive emotions are *natural* sentiments, inevitably given to us with our participation in interpersonal relationships. Hence it is not a real possibility for us to give up, across the board, the reactive attitudes, or the stance of holding people responsible with which those attitudes are connected—regardless of whether determinism does or does not obtain. Of course, we do sometimes retreat from interpersonal involvement, relinquishing the reactive attitudes in favor of a kind of objectivity of stance.[13] This objective stance is available to us only intermittently, however, for purposes of scientific investigation or psychological treatment or momentary personal relief; there is no question of our adopting it all the time.

As to the question of whether we *should* give up holding people responsible in the face of determinism, Strawson interprets this as a question about the rationality of holding people responsible in a deterministic world. Given (again) the connection between responsibility and the reactive attitudes, this becomes the question of whether it would be rational to relinquish the reactive attitudes in a deterministic world, in favor of a thoroughgoing objectivity of attitude (supposing this to be—*per impossibile*—a real option for us). Strawson implicitly distinguishes two standards of rationality by reference to which we might answer this question.[14] By the standards internal to our moral practices, it would not be rational to give up holding people responsible in a deterministic world, for the considerations that prompt us to withdraw the reactive attitudes in practice are quite different from the sorts of considerations that determinism would introduce. But if we abstract from the standards internal to our moral practices, Strawson suggests, the only criteria of rationality to which we might appeal are *pragmatic* criteria, concerning the gains and losses of the reactive attitudes for human life. By these criteria, we clearly should not give up responsi-

---

12. Strawson, "Freedom and Resentment," pp. 68–69, 74.
13. Strawson, "Freedom and Resentment," pp. 66–67.
14. Strawson, "Freedom and Resentment," pp. 69–70, 74–75.

bility and the reactive attitudes in a deterministic world, for those attitudes immeasurably enrich human life: independently of whether determinism is or is not true, we know that a life without those attitudes, and without the forms of interpersonal relationship they make possible, would be impoverished and barren.

This is a complex and highly suggestive argument. It may fairly be said to have transformed contemporary discussion of the problems of freedom and responsibility, inspiring a wide following and even wider critical discussion.[15] The very complexity of Strawson's position, however, virtually ensured that its legacy would be similarly complex and multifaceted. Thus there is no fixed and stable view that might be labeled the Strawsonian account of responsibility. Strawson's original lecture contains a wealth of ideas, and the many philosophers who have been influenced by the lecture have naturally chosen to develop and defend different ones among them, and to develop them in different ways. For my part, what I find promising in Strawson's position are not so much the official answers he provides to the question of the compatibility of responsibility with determinism, as the suggestions he makes about the connection between responsibility and the moral sentiments. The naturalist and pragmatic arguments I have sketched do not seem to me convincing responses to incompatibilist concerns, but the interpretation of responsibility, as distinctively linked with our moral sentiments, provides the framework within which a more satisfactory response may be devised.

To understand the connection between responsibility and the moral sentiments, however, we will need an interpretation of the reactive attitudes that departs quite radically from Strawson's own interpretation. As I have noted, Strawson takes the reactive attitudes to include the full range of feelings we are susceptible to in virtue of participating with people in interpersonal relationships; he then attempts to situate responsibility inextricably within this web of interpersonal emotions. This may be seen as a dramatic attempt to raise the stakes in the debate about the

15. Substantial discussions of Strawson's position include A. J. Ayer, "Free-will and Rationality," in Zak van Straaten, ed., *Philosophical Subjects: Essays Presented to P. F. Strawson* (Oxford: Clarendon Press, 1980), pp. 1–13; Jonathan Bennett, "Accountability," in van Straaten, ed., *Philosophical Subjects,* pp. 14–47; Paul Benson, "The Moral Importance of Free Action," *Southern Journal of Philosophy* 28 (1990), pp. 1–18; Ulrich Pothast, *Die Unzulänglichkeit der Freiheitsbeweise: Zu einigen Lehrstücken aus der neueren Geschichte von Philosophie und Recht* (Frankfurt am Main: Suhrkamp Verlag, 1987), chap. 4; Michael S. Pritchard, *On Becoming Responsible* (Lawrence: University of Kansas Press, 1991); T. M. Scanlon, "The Significance of Choice," in Sterling M. McMurrin, ed., *The Tanner Lectures on Human Values,* vol. 8 (Salt Lake City: University of Utah Press, 1988), pp. 149–

bearing of determinism on responsibility. The suggestion is that if determinism threatens responsibility, it must equally threaten to tear away the whole emotional fabric of our interpersonal lives. This idea has been widely adopted, becoming perhaps the most influential of Strawson's contributions to the debate about freedom and responsibility.[16] Even philosophers who otherwise show little evidence of having been influenced by Strawson routinely speak as if the discussion about compatibilism touches not only on the legitimacy of holding people morally responsible, but also on the appropriateness of the range of emotions we feel toward those with whom we participate in interpersonal relations.[17] Incompatibilists have found that they may accept this point, but they conclude that—instead of helping to protect responsibility from the depredations of determinism—it only goes to show how extensively our ordinary lives would be called in question by the discovery that determinism is true.[18]

It seems to me a mistake, however, to interpret the reactive emotions in this encompassing manner. The general difficulty is that the wider we stretch the class of reactive attitudes, making them coextensive with the emotions we feel toward people with whom we participate in interpersonal relations, the less plausible the claim becomes that holding people responsible is inextricably a part of this web of attitudes. The reason for this is that the inclusive interpretation of the reactive attitudes frustrates any attempt to provide an informative account of what unifies this set of emotions as a class. More specifically, on this approach it becomes extremely difficult to characterize the reactive attitudes as having distinctive propositional objects; consequently the claim that responsibility is to be understood in terms of such attitudes picks up a noncognitivist animus, which makes the claim hard to accept. Holding someone responsible comes to be interpreted as a susceptibility to

216; Lawrence Stern, "Freedom, Blame, and Moral Community," *Journal of Philosophy* 71 (1974), pp. 72–84; Galen Strawson, *Freedom and Belief* (Oxford: Clarendon Press, 1986), chap. 5; Gary Watson, "Responsibility and the Limits of Evil: Variations on a Strawsonian Theme," in Ferdinand Schoeman, ed., *Responsibility, Character, and the Emotions: New Essays in Moral Psychology* (Cambridge: Cambridge University Press, 1987), pp. 256–286; and Susan Wolf "The Importance of Free Will," *Mind* 90 (1981), pp. 386–405.

16. See, for instance, the prominence ascribed to the idea by Wolf, in "The Importance of Free Will."

17. See, for example, John Martin Fischer, "Introduction: Responsibility and Freedom," in Fischer, ed., *Moral Responsibility* (Ithaca, N.Y.: Cornell University Press, 1986), pp. 9–61, at pp. 11–14, and Ted Honderich, *The Consequences of Determinism*, vol. 2 of *A Theory of Determinism* (Oxford: Clarendon Press, 1990), pp. 32–41.

18. See, for instance, Wiggins, "Towards a Reasonable Libertarianism," pp. 55–56.

feelings that have no privileged connection with beliefs about the person who is held responsible. But this seems false, given the characteristic focus of the stance of holding people responsible. That stance is essentially a disposition to respond in certain ways to the moral wrongs that people commit, but we can make sense of this defining connection between the stance and moral wrongs only if we suppose that the reactive emotions in terms of which the stance is understood have their own propositional objects.

I therefore follow a different strategy for developing the Strawsonian approach. Instead of interpreting the reactive attitudes simply as those emotions implicated in interpersonal relations, I construe them more narrowly, taking the paradigms to be resentment, indignation, and guilt. Interpreting the reactive emotions in this narrow way permits us to understand how these emotions hang together as a class. The key, I argue, lies in their distinctive connection with expectations. Thus, episodes of guilt, resentment, and indignation are caused by the belief that an expectation to which one holds a person has been breached; the connection with expectations gives the reactive emotions common propositional objects, tying them together as a class. Once this interpretation of the reactive emotions is in place, we can draw on it to account for the stance of holding people morally responsible. That stance is characterized by the responses of blame and moral sanction; to understand the stance, we therefore need an interpretation of blame and moral sanction. I propose that blame involves a susceptibility to the reactive emotions, and that the responses of moral sanction serve to express these emotions. Because of the connection of the reactive emotions with expectations, this account makes sense of the backward-looking character of blame and moral sanction, which are essentially reactions to a moral wrong. The connection to expectations also serves to situate moral responsibility in relation to the notion of moral obligation, and helps us see that the stance of holding people responsible involves a commitment to moral justifications, which support the obligations we expect people to comply with. By illuminating these points, the Strawsonian approach, as I develop it, sets the stage for an investigation of what it is to be a morally responsible agent.

To complete this investigation, however, it will be necessary to draw on a quite different source from the tradition of philosophical reflection on responsibility. I shall refer to this second source as the broadly Kantian approach, in reference to Kant's conception of the nature of moral agency. According to this conception, to be an accountable agent—an agent who is subject to moral requirements, and who may appropriately be held responsible for failing to comply with such requirements—it is not enough merely to be subject to desires and capable of acting to promote the ends set by such desires. Moral agency requires, in addition, the capacity to step back from one's given desires and to assess the ends they incline one to pursue in light of moral principles.[19] This capacity is critical, insofar as it involves the ability to assess the ends proposed by one's given desires, and to endorse, reject, or adjust them as the result of critical reflection. It is also distinctively rational, involving the capacity to reason morally by grasping and applying moral principles in particular situations of decision.

Now, Kant himself seemed to think that moral agency, on this conception of it, goes together with freedom of the will. That is, he evidently supposed that the capacity to step back from our desires, and to reflect critically on the ends they propose—what Kant himself sometimes called "practical freedom"—requires "transcendental" freedom of the will, a capacity for absolute spontaneity or self-determination.[20] He also (and notoriously) thought that moral agency so conceived, combining practical and transcendental freedom, could be shown to be compatible with determinism by calling on the resources of his own transcendental idealism. I, too, wish to put a broadly Kantian conception of moral agency to work in the service of a compatibilist account of responsibility. But to this end I do not claim that transcendental freedom is somehow compatible with determinism; rather, I try to prise apart the two elements of practical and transcendental freedom that Kant himself welded together in his account of moral agency. These two elements apparently fit with each other to make a coherent package. In particular, it is tempting to suppose that the possession of transcendental freedom is what gives a moral agent the rational powers of reflective self-control that are collected under the heading of practical freedom. On this picture, each basic action of a responsible moral agent involves a moment of spontaneity or self-determination in which some given

19. The most developed statement of this picture is found in bk. 1 of Kant's *Religion within the Limits of Reason Alone*.

20. On practical and transcendental freedom, see for instance the discussion of the resolution of the third antinomy, in Kant's *Critique of Pure Reason,* pp. A 532–534/B 560–562. (My gloss on practical freedom is deliberately tendentious, and it ignores questions about ambiguities or changes in Kant's conception of practical freedom and its relation to transcendental freedom, raised for instance by the passage at p. A 803/B 831 of the "Canon" in the first critique.)

incentive is "taken into" the agent's maxim;[21] the ubiquitous role of such spontaneity ensures that the moral agent always retains the ability to step back from received desires, in critical reflection on their ends. But this tempting picture can and should be resisted: it is possible that agents might have the general powers of reflective self–control without having strong freedom of the will, and so it is open to us to affirm that practical freedom is a condition of responsibility, while denying that transcendental freedom is such a condition.

That is the position for which I argue. Because the resulting picture departs from Kant's own account, while still being broadly inspired by that account, it seems fitting to refer to it as a broadly Kantian conception of moral agency. So construed, the broadly Kantian conception captures a compelling idea about what sets responsible agents apart from other kinds of creatures who are capable of purposive action. To be a moral agent, bound by moral requirements and therefore subject to blame or moral sanction for failing to comply with those requirements, it is not sufficient that one should be prone to desires and capable of acting to achieve the ends set by those desires. Animals and young children may be agents in this minimal sense, but that does not entitle us to regard them as morally responsible for what they do. Responsibility requires, in addition, the further powers to step back from one's desires, to reflect on the ends they incline one to pursue in light of moral principles, and to adjust or revise one's ends as a result of such reflection.[22]

The account of responsible moral agency I defend is not the only aspect of my discussion that has a Kantian cast. Other Kantian themes emerge in my development of the Strawsonian approach to responsibility. That approach treats the stance of holding people responsible in terms of the reactive emotions, but my interpretation of the reactive emotions connects them with moral *obligations,* and these in turn are supported by principled *justifications* and are focused on the *choices*

---

21. See, for instance, Immanuel Kant, *Religion within the Limits of Reason Alone,* trans. Theodore M. Greene and Hoyt H. Hudson (New York: Harper and Row, 1960), p. 19 (p. 24 in the Akademie edition).

22. Related ideas have assumed a prominent place in the contemporary debate about freedom of the will. Consider, for instance, Harry Frankfurt's influential suggestion that persons are distinguished by their susceptibility to higher-order volitions, in "Freedom of the Will and the Concept of a Person," as reprinted in his *The Importance of What We Care About: Philosophical Essays* (Cambridge: Cambridge University Press, 1988), pp. 11–25. Much of the appeal of this suggestion stems, I think, from its appropriation of important elements in the broadly Kantian conception, in particular the idea that we are able to step back from our given desires, and to reflect critically on them. Similar remarks apply to Gary Watson's account of freedom in "Free Agency," as reprinted in Watson, ed., *Free Will,* pp. 96–110. But both Frankfurt and Watson are interested primarily in

expressed in what people do. These too are recognizably Kantian ideas.[23] Traditionally, theories of the moral sentiments have been associated with empiricist approaches to ethics, and have been set against Kantian accounts, with their emphasis on the primacy of reason in moral personality. But this contrast is overdrawn. There is a class of moral sentiments—the reactive emotions—that can properly be understood only when seen in relation to the notions of moral obligation, justification, and choice. Appreciating these connections will help us to recover a commitment to some of the central concepts of Kantian moral theory, describing a foothold for those concepts in our emotional lives. It will also enable us to grasp the complexity of the stance of holding someone morally responsible, something that is crucial if we are to move away from one-dimensional treatments of that stance, in terms of either vengeance or forward-looking, deterrent concerns.

These introductory remarks are intended to orient the reader, by locating the account that follows in relation to other ways of treating the problems of freedom and responsibility. In the end, of course, the position I develop will have to be judged on its own merits. It is meant as a free-standing interpretation of responsibility, and not merely as a commentary on Strawsonian and Kantian texts and themes (in fact there are very few direct references to Kant in the following pages, and more often than not Strawson is mentioned to call attention to a point of contrast rather than affinity with my approach). If the interpretation I offer is found to have promise, this will have to be because the way I develop selected Strawsonian and Kantian themes, and bring them into relation with each other, is independently compelling. Here, a very large role will be played by the normative interpretation of the debate about responsibility that I put forward. On that interpretation—which has no clear analogue in either Strawson or Kant—conditions of responsibility are to be construed as conditions that make it fair to adopt the stance of holding people responsible. Accordingly, I try to show

the problem of autonomy rather than that of responsibility (see sec. 3.1 for this distinction). For the purpose of understanding moral responsibility, what matters is not so much the issue—central to both Frankfurt and Watson—of whether and how we *exercise* the powers of reflective self-control, but the more basic issues of whether we *possess* those powers, and whether they are sufficiently developed to render us competent to grasp and comply with moral reasons.

23. Of course, they are not exclusively Kantian ideas but may also find a place in other approaches to morality. Note too that there are a number of prominent Kantian themes that I do *not* make use of in this book. These include—in addition to the idea of transcendental freedom—the following ideas: that the categorical imperative is the supreme principle of morality; that moral requirements are distinctively requirements of reason; and that acting from the motive of duty involves a form of autonomy that is supremely valuable.

that once we correctly understand the stance of holding people responsible in terms of the reactive emotions, we will be able to see that the condition that makes it fair to adopt this stance is not freedom of the will in the strong sense; rather it is the kind of normative competence in virtue of which one is able to grasp moral reasons and to control one's behavior by their light.

1.3   Prospectus

At the beginning of the present chapter I suggested that the argument of this book may be thought of as having two parts: an account of what it is to hold someone morally responsible, and an account of the conditions of moral agency. Very roughly, the first of these parts takes up Chapters 2 through 4, and the second occupies Chapters 5 through 7. Somewhat less roughly, Chapters 2 through 4 set the stage for assessing compatibilist and incompatibilist interpretations of responsibility. They present an account of what we are doing when we hold people morally responsible, and develop an interpretation of what is at issue in the debate between compatibilists and incompatibilists. Chapter 2 offers an account of the reactive emotions of guilt, resentment, and indignation, connecting them with the stance of holding people to expectations. Drawing on this account, Chapter 3 explains what it is to hold someone morally responsible; it argues that the responses of blame and moral sanction characteristic of holding people responsible can best be understood in terms of the reactive emotions. Chapter 4 presents my normative interpretation of the debate about responsibility. The upshot of this discussion is that the conditions of responsibility must be conditions that make it fair to hold someone to moral obligations, in the way that is connected with the reactive emotions.

Determining what those conditions are therefore requires a normative inquiry into our principles of fairness; Chapters 5 through 7 undertake an inquiry of this kind. I begin by considering our ordinary judgments of excuse and exemption from responsibility, in response to such conditions as physical constraint, coercion, behavior control, and insanity. These moral judgments reflect our commitment to principles of fairness, and the most promising strategy for defending incompatibilism is to try to show that the principles thus required to account for our judgments of excuse and exemption identify conditions—such as the availability of alternate possibilities—that are defeated universally if determinism is true. I argue against this "generalization strategy" (as I call it) in Chapters 5 and 6. On the alternative account I offer, the moral principles anchored in our considered judgments of excuse and exemption do not identify any factor that would generally be undermined if determinism is true. What makes it fair to hold an agent to moral obligations is not the availability of alternate possibilities, or any other condition that would involve strong freedom of the will, but rather the possession of the powers of reflective self-control. This conclusion is reinforced by the argument of Chapter 7, which considers other possible strategies for defending incompatibilism, and offers a diagnosis of incompatibilist tendencies in our thinking about responsibility.

The final chapter briefly considers some of the social and personal implications of my broadly Kantian account of moral agency, with special attention to cases of childhood deprivation. Appendix 1 adds some detail to the account of the reactive emotions presented in Chapter 2, while Appendix 2 surveys some recent philosophical debates about freedom and alternate possibilities, to explain why I do not enter directly into those debates in the body of the book.

2

Emotions and Expectations

On P. F. Strawson's view, emotions such as guilt, resentment, and indignation—what Strawson calls the reactive attitudes—provide the key to understanding moral responsibility and its conditions. I intend to develop this idea by working out an account of the stance of *holding* someone responsible, in terms of the reactive emotions. Before this can be done, however, it will first be necessary to get clear about the nature of the reactive emotions. What are the essential features of these emotions? What distinguishes them from other forms of moral and non-moral sentiment, and holds them together as a class? Answering these questions will provide the foundation for the account of responsibility and its conditions that follows.

A venerable approach to the reactive emotions holds that they are distinguished by the moral beliefs that give rise to them. Thus Joseph Butler suggested that deliberate resentment is excited by the belief that an *injury* has been done, where injury is construed as a moral concept, to be distinguished from mere suffering or harm or loss.[1] More recently, John Rawls has maintained that the moral sentiments are emotions whose explanation requires the invocation of a moral concept.[2] In these terms, the reactive attitudes of guilt, resentment, and indignation are set apart by the *kind* of moral concept that figures in their explanation; specifically, explanation of these reactive emotions must invoke the concept of the right, as distinguished from that of the good. The appeal of these suggestions is the connection they postulate between the reactive attitudes and a certain kind of belief. The emotions of resentment, indignation, and guilt all have a propositional content—one feels indignant *about* something, or guilty *for* something one has done. It is

---

1. Joseph Butler, *Fifteen Sermons Preached at the Rolls Chapel,* sermon 8, "Upon Resentment."
2. John Rawls, *A Theory of Justice* (Cambridge, Mass.: Harvard University Press, 1971), sec. 73.

tempting to characterize these contents in moral terms, by holding (for instance) that the reactive emotions must be caused by the belief that an injustice or an injury has been done. But the temptation should be resisted. It amounts to an excessive moralization of the reactive attitudes; for though these attitudes are often—perhaps even standardly— caused by distinctively moral beliefs, they do not have to be so caused. It is notoriously the case that one can feel guilt, for instance, without sincerely believing oneself to have done anything that would amount to a moral injury or an infraction of right.

Reflection on such cases has led some philosophers to sever altogether the connection of reactive emotions with beliefs. But if Butler and Rawls go too far in the direction of moralizing the reactive emotions, this alternative approach deprives us of the resources for acknowledging something that is characteristic of the reactive emotions as a class. For by severing their essential connection with beliefs, the alternative approach deprives the reactive emotions of their propositional content. If it seems plausible that guilt may be experienced in the absence of the belief that one is at fault, it seems equally plausible that a state that lacks a propositional object would not really be a genuine state of guilt at all. We need a way of explaining the distinctive propositional content of the reactive emotions, without characterizing that content in exclusively moral terms. This is particularly important if we are to improve on Strawson's account of responsibility in terms of the reactive emotions: a successful interpretation of what it is to hold someone responsible, that draws on the reactive emotions, must credit those emotions with propositional objects—something Strawson's own account does not clearly manage to do.

My own account of the reactive emotions aims to solve this problem. My main contention is that there is an essential connection between the reactive attitudes and a distinctive form of evaluation, or quasi evaluation, that I refer to as holding a person to an expectation (or demand). This form of evaluation is not conceptually prior to the reactive attitudes, but rather is defined in terms of them: to hold someone to an expectation, I maintain, is to be susceptible to the reactive attitudes in one's relations with the person. If this is right, then the task of characterizing the reactive attitudes must go hand in hand with the task of characterizing this distinctive form of quasi evaluation, for the two can only be understood in terms of each other. Among other things, pursuing the connection between reactive attitudes and expectations should help us to account for the characteristic propositional content of the reactive attitudes, without falling into the trap of overmoralizing them from the start. To be in a state of reactive emotion, one must believe that a person has violated some expectation that one holds the person to; and in terms of this belief, we can give an account of how the reactive emotions have the kind of propositional content that distinguishes them from other emotional states. But it need not be the case that the expectation that gives the content of a reactive emotion is a moral one, or even that it is an expectation one sincerely endorses. (This is why I refer to the attitude of holding a person to an expectation as a form of "quasi evaluation.")

Section 2.1 offers a brief sketch of my approach to the reactive emotions. The approach is then contrasted with that of Strawson and his commentators (section 2.2); in particular, I explain and defend the suggestion that the class of reactive emotions should be construed narrowly, as including principally the emotions of resentment, indignation, and guilt. In section 2.3 I show how my narrower interpretation of the reactive emotions yields an improved way of distinguishing between moral and nonmoral reactive emotions, and between reactive and nonreactive moral emotions. Section 2.4 then focuses on the case of guilt, to explain how reactive emotions can be felt irrationally or inappropriately, without prejudice to their possession of propositional content. This will complete in outline my basic account of the reactive emotions; Appendix 1 adds some detail to the outline, for the sake of those readers with a particular interest in moral psychology.

2.1   The Approach Sketched

To start with, note that there is one way of expecting a thing to happen that does not have any special connection with morality, or with the moral emotions. This is the sense in which to expect something to happen is simply to believe there is a high probability that the expected event will occur. Thus when I hit the appropriate button on the remote control, I expect my television to turn on; as the summer draws to a close, I expect that classes will soon begin; and when I assign the *Prolegomena* to my beginning students, I expect that they will not understand it on their own. Expectations in this sense are often associated with emotions of various kinds. For example, my expectation about the start of classes may be suffused with a feeling anxiety that has its roots in my childhood experiences of school; the failure of my TV to go on as expected when I activate the remote control may provoke a fit of rage and frustration. But it is not in general the case that expectations of this sort—that is, beliefs about the future—are presumptively associated with any particular attitude. I may equally contemplate the expected start of classes with depression, enthusiasm, or with complete indifference, and none of these emotional responses would necessarily be more fitting than the others.

There is, however, a different way of expecting something to occur that is essentially tied to particular emotional responses. This is the sense in which, as we might say, we "hold someone to an expectation," or in which we demand of people that they act as we expect them to. In the case of my students, for instance, I not only expect, in the first sense, that they will not understand the *Prolegomena,* I also hold them to the expectation that they will not lie, cheat, attempt to blackmail me or their fellow students, and so on. In holding them to these various expectations, I often believe that the expectations will be fulfilled. Thus I generally believe that my students will not in fact attempt to blackmail me. But even when a belief of this sort is present, it does not capture what is centrally involved in holding a person to an expectation, or in making a demand of the person. The crucial element, I would suggest, is attitudinal: to hold someone to an expectation is essentially to be susceptible to a certain range of emotions in the case that the expectation is not fulfilled, or to believe that the violation of the expectation would make it appropriate for one to be subject to those emotions. For reasons that will become clear in the course of my discussion, we may refer to this stance of holding someone to an expectation as a "quasi-evaluative" stance.

Emotions that are constitutively linked to expectations, in this sense of holding someone to an expectation, are the reactive attitudes, as I will interpret them. Take the central examples of resentment, moral indignation, and guilt. These are not mere feelings that one might happen to be subject to in any circumstances whatsoever. I may dislike my television set or be frustrated and annoyed when it fails to turn on; but insofar as I do not hold the TV to expectations, I cannot, properly speaking, be said to resent it or to be indignant at it. Resentment, indignation, and guilt are essentially tied to expectations that we hold ourselves and others to; susceptibility to these emotions is what constitutes holding someone to an expectation. This mutual dependence of emotion and expectation distinguishes the reactive attitudes, on the account of them I defend—a class of attitudes that includes a central group of moral emotions, but that also includes some nonmoral emotions as well.

Before we can develop this suggestion, however, a word or two of clarification is in order. So far I have used the terms "expectation" and "demand" in sketching the stance that is constitutively connected with the reactive attitudes. I have chosen these terms because they point at once in two different directions, in a way that is appropriate to the psychological phenomena I wish to call attention to.[3] Thus a demand is both a psychological stance we might adopt toward someone and that which we demand of the person when we adopt the stance. Strictly speaking, however, when I write of "holding someone to a demand or expectation," "demand" and "expectation" are to be taken in the latter sense: that which we demand or expect of the person. They are thus equivalent ways of expressing the notion of a practical *requirement* or *prohibition* in a particular situation of action. So construed, expectations must in principle be capable of being formulated linguistically, though for my purposes it will not be important to settle on a canonical formula for expressing such expectations in words. We might express an expectation by using the concepts of prohibition or requirement explicitly, say as an operator on sentences that describe kinds of action in a particular situation (for instance: "It is prohibited that you should break the promise you made to your sister"). Alternatively, expectations might be expressed by imperatives ("Do not break the promise you made to your sister").

However we choose to express expectations, when so construed there are several further points about them that must be noted. First, it is important that expectations should be capable of being supported by practical reasons. It is not necessary that expectations, to count as such, should either be or be believed to be supported by such reasons; as I will show, it is an important fact about us that we often hold ourselves and others to expectations that are supported by no justification that we may accept. But expectations can be supported by justifications that the agent accepts, and in the favorable cases they are supported in this way, so the possibility of such support needs to be left open. Second, though expectations must be capable of linguistic formulation, it is not required that the agents who hold themselves and others to such expectations should always be in a privileged position to produce such a formulation.

3. The terms will be used interchangeably in the text that follows.

Thus an agent might not be aware that she holds other people to a given demand, and might only come to grasp that demand discursively by inference from patterns in her emotional life (involving, for instance, the kinds of situations that move her to resentment). Finally, we should allow the possibility that expectations may conflict, so that in a given situation there are mutually inconsistent kinds of action that one is required to perform. At least, nothing in the very concept of an expectation, as I construe it, should rule out the possibility of such conflicts.

Something must now be said about the connection between expectations, construed in this way, and the reactive emotions. In characterizing this connection, I have used a disjunctive formulation: to hold someone to an expectation, I suggested, is to be susceptible to a certain range of emotions if the expectation is violated, or to believe that it would be appropriate for one to feel those emotions if the expectation is violated. This disjunction is to be understood nonexclusively. Thus there are three different ways in which one might count as having the attitude of quasi evaluation that I have referred to as "holding someone to an expectation": (1) one simply finds oneself reacting with the emotions of resentment, indignation, or guilt in respect to the violation of a certain set of expectations, and it is part of the explanation of the emotions to which one is thus subject that one believes the expectations in question have been breached; (2) one is not consistently subject to these various emotions oneself on occasions when a given set of expectations has been violated, but one believes that it would be appropriate for one to react to their violation with this range of emotions, and one thinks that what would make these emotional reactions appropriate is the fact that the expectations have been breached; (3) one feels the emotions of resentment, indignation, and guilt on occasions when the expectations have been violated, *and* one believes that these are appropriate emotions for one to feel on such occasions, because the expectations have been breached.

Holding someone to a demand, in any of these ways, can be either a long-term or a short-term condition. One might hold a person to a given demand only long enough to feel momentary resentment toward the person, or one might hold the person to a range of demands over a period of many years. Notice, too, that beliefs figure prominently and variously in my explanation of the stance of holding someone to a demand. There is, first, the belief that someone's violation of a demand would make one of the reactive emotions appropriate. Having such a belief is not necessary to count as holding the person to the demand (compare case 1), but even in the absence of the appropriate reactive emotion, this belief would be sufficient to qualify one as holding the person to the demand (case 2).

Moreover, when one is subject to a state of reactive emotion, the preceding account entails that a different kind of belief will figure in the explanation of the emotion. This is the belief that some demand has been breached. Even if we choose to express demands as imperatives, and hence as lacking truth-conditions, there will still be room for the belief that a demand has been violated. Furthermore, some belief of this kind must be present whenever an agent is in a particular state of reactive emotion, and must contribute to explaining why one is in the state.[4] This explanatory role of beliefs in accounting for particular states of reactive emotion is extremely important, since it will eventually provide the key to understanding the propositional content characteristic of the reactive emotions as a class. For the present, though, it will suffice to make the following observations. The *stance* of holding someone to a demand, as I interpret it, does not have explanatory priority vis-à-vis the reactive emotions: to be subject to the reactive emotions is to take this stance toward a person, and to adopt this stance is in turn to be subject to the reactive emotions. At the same time, the nature of the connection between the reactive emotions and this stance is such that particular *states* of reactive emotion must always be explicable in terms of some belief concerning the violation of a demand. In this way, beliefs about the violation of demands have a kind of priority in accounting for particular states of reactive emotion.

Regarding particular states of reactive emotion, it should be further noted that I have not provided, and do not intend to provide, a complete analysis of what it is to be in such an emotional state. For purposes of discussion, we may assume that each of the reactive emotions is associated with a distinctive syndrome of sensory, behavioral, and linguistic dispositions. The state of guilt, for instance, is associated with characteristic patterns of salience and attention, dispositions to

---

4. By "belief" here, I mean an exclusively cognitive state whose propositional content is directly assessable as true or false. In these terms, a state in which one entertains a proposition one does not fully accept—to which one assigns an extremely low probability, for instance—may be allowed to count as a belief, at least in a degenerate sense. For the suggestion that the content of many emotions can best be understood in terms of beliefs of this degenerate sort, see P. S. Greenspan, *Emotions and Reasons: An Inquiry into Emotional Justification* (New York: Routledge, Chapman and Hall, 1988).

action, expectations regarding the reactions of others, susceptibilities to feel certain sorts of sensation, and so on.[5] Such syndromes may be taken to provide a rough characterization of the various emotional states (and more will be said later in this chapter about some of the syndromes that characterize the particular reactive emotions). But it is not clear that these characterizations can be regarded as complete analyses of the various emotional states, in the sense of providing a specification of sufficient conditions for being in those states. For my purposes, it is not important that we have an analysis in this sense available.

What I do wish to insist on is that there is one characteristic that is essential to the reactive emotions, and that may be taken to distinguish them as a class from other types of attitudes. This is their connection to expectations, the connection I have described in terms of the quasi-evaluative stance of holding someone to an expectation. To pursue this strategy for understanding the reactive attitudes is to define them together with the stance of quasi evaluation. The quasi-evaluative stance of holding someone to an expectation is characterized in terms of a susceptibility to the reactive emotions. And those emotions in their turn are characterized in terms of this evaluative stance, as the emotions one is susceptible to in virtue of holding someone to an expectation. Since neither of these items is taken to be conceptually prior to or independent of the other, the strategy will only be illuminating if they can both be characterized together in ways that differentiate them from other evaluative stances, and that help us to mark important and recognizable distinctions between the reactive attitudes and other kinds of (moral and nonmoral) emotions.

2.2   Narrowing the Class

As I have explained, the expression "reactive attitude" derives from P. F. Strawson, whose paper "Freedom and Resentment" urged the importance of this class of moral sentiments for understanding moral responsibility. Indeed, the strategy I have pursued so far, of linking the reactive attitudes with the notion of an expectation, is suggested by Strawson himself, for Strawson often appears to take for granted the kind of connection between reactive attitudes and expectations that I have been at pains to emphasize. His descriptions of the individual reactive attitudes are frequently presented in terms of the concepts of

5. See, for example, Rawls, *A Theory of Justice*, sec. 73.

expectation and demand,[6] suggesting an endorsement of the idea that such attitudes can be understood in terms of their connection with such concepts. And at one point he writes: "[the] attitudes of disapprobation and indignation are precisely the correlates of the demand in the case where the demand is felt to be disregarded. The making of the demand *is* the proneness to such attitudes."[7] This comes very close to characterizing the form of quasi evaluation that I have referred to as holding someone to an expectation—though Strawson himself does little to explain his suggestive remark.

But if this really is the key to understanding the reactive attitudes, why doesn't it figure more prominently in Strawson's discussion? And why have Strawson's commentators so far failed to appreciate its significance? An answer to these questions is suggested by Jonathan Bennett, whose essay "Accountability" contains the most extensive attempt yet to give a principled definition of the Strawsonian reactive attitudes. Bennett concludes pessimistically that he cannot come up with a satisfactory theoretical account of what makes an attitude reactive.[8] On the way to reaching this conclusion, he considers—and rejects—the suggestion I have endorsed, that the reactive attitudes are distinguished by their essential connection with expectations.[9] Bennett concedes that reactive attitudes may be essentially linked with expectations in this way, but he does not think this link can be used to explain what a reactive attitude is, because the relevant concept of an expectation is not sufficiently independent from the reactive attitudes it is supposed to explain.

It should be evident that I would agree with Bennett here, insofar as he believes that the relevant concept of an expectation is not independent from the concept of a reactive attitude. The relevant notion of an expectation is the notion of holding someone to an expectation, and as I explained this idea, it must be understood as involving a susceptibility to a certain range of emotions—namely, the reactive ones. This means that we cannot hope to provide a *reductive analysis* of the

6. P. F. Strawson, "Freedom and Resentment," as reprinted in Gary Watson, ed., *Free Will* (Oxford: Oxford University Press, 1982), pp. 59–80, at pp. 63, 65, 71–73, 77.

7. Strawson, "Freedom and Resentment," p. 77.

8. Jonathan Bennett, "Accountability," in Zak van Straaten, ed., *Philosophical Subjects: Essays Presented to P. F. Strawson* (Oxford: Clarendon Press, 1980), pp. 14–47, at pp. 38–42.

9. Bennett, "Accountability," pp. 41–42. Actually Bennett here considers only the case of the impersonal and self-reactive attitudes (see sec. 2.3 of this chapter for the distinction), but his remarks, if cogent, would tell equally against the attempt to understand all reactive attitudes in terms of demands. Strawson himself seems to agree with Bennett's objections to construing the notion of a reactive attitude in terms of demands, or the "acknowledgment of a claim"; see his "Reply to Ayer and Bennett," in van Straaten, ed., *Philosophical Subjects*, pp. 260–266, at p. 266.

reactive attitudes in terms of the idea of holding a person to an expectation. It does not follow, however, that the link to expectations is not the distinguishing characteristic of reactive attitudes. Even if we cannot reduce reactive attitudes to the stance of holding someone to an expectation, we may still say that the defining mark of reactive attitudes is their connection to the expectations we hold people to—provided, that is, that the reactive emotions and the stance of quasi evaluation can jointly be characterized in ways that illuminate our psychological and moral concepts.

A different objection that Bennett brings against the proposal is that it does not seem to cover all the cases of reactive attitudes.[10] Bennett follows Strawson, for instance, in considering reciprocal love to be a reactive attitude;[11] and Strawson's own lecture cites a great many other emotions as reactive attitudes that do not seem to have any presumptive relation to expectations at all—for example, gratitude, hurt feelings, and shame. This inclusive interpretation of the reactive attitudes has generally been followed in discussions of Strawson's lecture, which display a tendency to construe the reactive attitudes as any emotions that involve, or point us toward, interpersonal relations.[12] If this is right, then such attitudes as embarrassment, friendly affection, and sympathy would have to be counted as reactive attitudes as well, and yet these emotions do not seem to involve any special connection with expectations that we hold people to, of the sort I have been trying to characterize.

Of course, this would be grounds for objecting to the strategy I have sketched only if one had an independent reason to follow Strawson and his commentators in adopting a more inclusive interpretation of the reactive attitudes. But there is no reason to follow them on this point; on the contrary, clarity is far better served by adopting a narrower interpretation of the reactive attitudes along the lines I have sketched out. What one finds in Strawson and his commentators is a tendency to run together what are better viewed as two very different distinctions: (1) the distinction between reactive attitudes and other attitudes one might take toward persons; and (2) the distinction between (in Strawson's words) "the attitude (or range of attitudes) of involvement

---

10. Bennett, "Accountability," p. 42.

11. Bennett, "Accountability," p. 42; compare Strawson, "Freedom and Resentment," p. 62.

12. See Bennett, "Accountability," sec. 18; he suggests that the distinguishing feature of reactive attitudes is that they "point toward" certain sorts of interpersonal relations. See also Susan Wolf, "The Importance of Free Will," *Mind* 90 (1981), pp. 386–405; Wolf treats the reactive attitudes as emotional reactions one has toward individuals "insofar as one views those individuals as persons" (p. 390), and assumes that the emotional aspects of friendship and love are to be counted among the reactive attitudes (p. 391).

or participation in a human relationship, on the one hand, and what might be called the objective attitude (or range of attitudes) to another human being, on the other."[13] As Strawson understands it, the objective attitude is associated primarily with scientific or scholarly inquiry, therapeutic treatment, or social policy—though it is a stance available, to some extent, to all of us, which we occupy when we wish to manage people rather than to interact with them (or simply as a refuge from "the strains of involvement"[14]). Objectivity of this sort, Strawson suggests, can be emotionally tinged in various ways (for example, through repulsion or pity, or even some kinds of love), but it cannot include the reactive attitudes, which he associates exclusively with "involvement" or "participation" in interpersonal relations. Thus the contrast between reactive and nonreactive attitudes is taken to coincide with the contrast between participation in relationships with people and the objective stance characteristically adopted by scientists or therapists toward their subjects and patients.

In fact, the elision of these two distinctions is crucial to Strawson's original statement and defense of the naturalist idea that the reactive attitudes are practically inevitable for us. As I explained in Chapter 1, Strawson takes it as obvious that the reactive attitudes are natural human phenomena to which persons, as they are constituted, cannot help but be subject. But as Strawson presents it, the force of this idea depends quite crucially on taking the reactive attitudes to be coextensive with the full range of emotions we experience insofar as we are involved in interpersonal relationships. Thus, in introducing the naturalist idea, Strawson writes: "The human commitment to participation in ordinary inter-personal relationships is, I think, too thoroughgoing and deeply rooted for us to take seriously the thought that a general theoretical conviction might so change our world that, in it, there were no longer any such things as inter-personal relationships as we normally understand them; and being involved in inter-personal relationships as we normally understand them precisely is being exposed to the range of reactive attitudes and feelings that is in question."[15] Strictly speaking, what Strawson here holds to be naturally inevitable for humans is involvement in normal interpersonal relationships. This yields the con-

13. Strawson, "Freedom and Resentment," p. 66.

14. Strawson, "Freedom and Resentment," p. 67.

15. Strawson, "Freedom and Resentment," p. 68. Strawson is here talking about what he calls "personal" reactive emotions, not about the distinctively moral reactive emotions as he understands them.

clusion that the reactive attitudes are similarly inevitable only on the further assumption that involvement in interpersonal relationships "precisely is" a liability to the reactive attitudes. But this last idea seems questionable.

One problem is that, if we accept this idea, it becomes extremely difficult to say which emotions should count as reactive, or to explain the incompatibility of the reactive attitudes with objectivity of attitude. Reactive attitudes need to be characterized in a way that brings them into play whenever one enters an interpersonal relationship with someone, and that excludes them from the kind of objective stance taken by therapists or social scientists toward their subjects. But a characterization that satisfies these requirements is elusive. It will not do, for instance, simply to define the reactive attitudes as the emotions one has insofar as one is involved in interpersonal relationships. This puts all of the weight of the account of reactive attitudes (and of their incompatibility with objectivity of attitude) on the notion of interpersonal relationships; but we do not have an independent concept of an interpersonal relationship suitable to play the required role in the account. What is it, for instance, about the relation between therapists and their subjects that is not "interpersonal," or that is "interpersonal" in the wrong way?[16] A related problem is that the inclusive interpretation frustrates the attempt to give any general account of the kinds of propositional objects that the reactive emotions might have in common. The category of reactivity becomes so capacious that there is no illuminating way to say what reactive emotions are reactions *to,* and this exacerbates the difficulty of characterizing these emotions as a class.

These problems suggest very strongly that the category of reactivity does not represent an illuminating way of grouping emotions, so long as the contrast between reactive and nonreactive attitudes is assimilated to the contrast between interpersonal relationships and objectivity. We would do better, I suggest, to adopt the narrower interpretation of reactive attitudes proposed in section 2.1, on which such attitudes are distinguished by their connection with expectations. Construed in this

16. This is essentially Bennett's question, and part of what leads him to despair of adequately characterizing the reactive attitudes and their opposition to objectivity of attitude; see his "Accountability," pp. 34–36. Compare Strawson, "Reply to Ayer and Bennett," pp. 265–266, where it is agreed that we do not have a "strict definition" of the reactive attitudes. Strawson suggests that we do not need a strict definition of the reactive attitudes, so long as our proneness to them can be taken for a natural fact. Even if we do not have a strict definition, however, we need at least a characterization of the reactive attitudes adequate to enable us to formulate and assess the claim that our susceptibility to them is a matter of natural fact.

way, the central cases of reactive attitudes are the emotions of resentment, indignation, and guilt; other proposed candidates, such as sympathy, love, hurt feelings, and shame, are simply not counted as reactive attitudes (or at least not as unambiguous cases of such attitudes). This has the consequence that many of the natural emotions one feels in virtue of entering into variously intimate relationships with people cannot be viewed as reactive attitudes, and so it may no longer be possible to follow Strawson in equating involvement in such relationships with susceptibility to the reactive attitudes. But the narrower construal of reactive attitudes can be taken to support two further and more important claims that Strawson wishes to defend—indeed, it offers a better interpretation and defense of those claims than is possible on Strawson's own, more inclusive account of the reactive attitudes.

The first of these is Strawson's claim that the reactive attitudes are opposed to the objective stance of the scientist or therapist or the executor of social policy. As I have pointed out, when the reactive attitudes are taken to embrace all of the emotions one has in interpersonal relations, it becomes hard to explain why objectivity of stance should be antithetical to reactivity. Indeed, the claim that objectivity and reactivity are opposed seems false according to this interpretation of reactivity—therapists or psychologists, for example, might well feel love or sympathy or hurt feelings in their professional interactions with their patients and human subjects, even if most of them do not ordinarily feel these emotions toward their patients or subjects. Taking the reactive attitudes more narrowly, however, the claim that there is an opposition between reactivity and objectivity becomes both well defined and true. Thus it is part of how we understand the objective stance of scientists or therapists toward their subjects and patients, that such a stance is incompatible with holding the subjects and patients to expectations in the way that is connected with resentment and indignation. A therapist, for instance, might consistently feel certain kinds of love and sympathy for her patients; but if she were to resent her patients, or feel indignant toward them, she would in doing so have ceased relating to them in the objective way that is characteristic of her professional role. Of course, I have not yet explained why the objective stance of scientific investigation or therapy or policy is at odds with reactivity, more narrowly construed, but the claim that there is an opposition between the reactive and objective stances at least appears plausible on this interpretation of it, as a descriptive claim about how the objective stance is understood.[17]

A second important claim of Strawson's is that the reactive attitudes are natural, in that human beings are inevitably subject to them. Now, as has been discussed, Strawson's original argument for this conclusion rests on two struts: first, he makes the (plausible) assumption that interpersonal relationships are inevitable for normal human beings; second, he contends that involvement in interpersonal relationships "precisely is" a susceptibility to the reactive attitudes. But in light of the narrower interpretation of the reactive attitudes that I have urged, this second contention appears false. The reactive attitudes are not coextensive with the emotions one feels toward people with whom one has interpersonal relationships, rather they constitute a particular category of emotion specially distinguished by its constitutive connection with expectations. If this is right, however, then it may not be as difficult as Strawson suggests to picture human life without the reactive attitudes. Even if interpersonal relationships are inevitable for humans, it does not necessarily follow that the reactive attitudes are similarly inevitable; there may be cultures whose members do not have in their repertoire the quasi-evaluative stance of holding people to expectations in the way that is connected with resentment, indignation, and guilt. At any rate, nothing in the very idea of this quasi-evaluative stance rules out the possibility of cultures whose members are not subject to the distinctively reactive emotions.

There is, however, a different way of making out the claim that people are naturally susceptible to the reactive attitudes, at least within the kinds of cultures that make available the quasi-evaluative stance of holding people to expectations. Let us begin by assuming, with Strawson, that involvement in interpersonal relationships is inevitable for normal human beings, and that it involves a susceptibility to a range of emotions and feelings, such as friendship, attachment, concern, sympathy, and love. Call these the natural emotions. Strawson's original argument depends on the idea that the class of natural emotions, in this sense, is coextensive with the class of reactive attitudes; but on the

17. I will not be in a position to explain this phenomenon until the argument in Chapters 5 and 6 is complete. But to anticipate, the moral reactive emotions are only fair responses when directed toward people whom we see as potentially standing in a certain kind of moral relationship with us, one distinguished by the exchange of moral criticism and justification. But this is not the way in which therapists or scientists conceive their professional relations with their subjects.

interpretation of reactivity I have offered, this idea is false, and it is at least conceivable that cultures might exist in which people are subject to the natural emotions without being subject to the reactive attitudes. Suppose, however, that we are dealing with a culture in which the quasi-evaluative stance of holding people to expectations is available. It is plausible to suppose that people in this culture will naturally acquire a susceptibility to the reactive attitudes, because of the *continuities* between such attitudes and the natural emotions. Thus someone who develops ties of friendship with another person will not only be concerned for her friend's welfare; she will also tend to feel indignant when the friend's claims have been violated, and guilty when she has violated such claims herself (assuming the concepts of indignation and guilt to be available in her repertoire). Similarly, a child who loves his parents will typically not only want parental affection and attention, but will also be prone to guilt when he violates the demands his parent makes of him (again, assuming guilt to be available in his culture). As Rawls writes, "the presence of certain natural attachments gives rise to a liability to certain moral emotions once the requisite moral development has taken place."[18]

In this way we can give sense to the claim that the reactive attitudes are emotions that people are naturally susceptible to, without simply conflating the natural and reactive emotions, as Strawson himself seemed to do. It is important to bear in mind, however, that the claim that the reactive attitudes are natural, on this reading of it, does not entail that they are strictly inevitable for human beings, and it is at least conceivable that there might be cultures that lack the peculiar stance toward expectations that is distinctive of the reactive attitudes.

Thus, the narrow interpretation of the reactive attitudes I support offers a plausible (though modified) reading of Strawson's idea that people are naturally susceptible to the reactive attitudes. It also clarifies and sharpens the opposition between objectivity of stance and the reactive emotions, and avoids the conceptual confusion that is caused when the reactive emotions are taken to be coextensive with the emotions one feels in virtue of participating in interpersonal relationships. For these reasons alone, it seems preferable to the inclusive interpretation of reactivity favored by Strawson and his commentators. In the end, however, the case for interpreting the reactive attitudes as

18. Rawls, *A Theory of Justice*, p. 487. For an explanation and development of the idea that there are these continuities between the natural and the moral sentiments, see secs. 70–74.

I have depends on showing that they hang together as a recognizable class of emotions, and that distinguishing this class can help to illuminate our moral and psychological categories. It is to these matters that I now turn.

2.3   Reactive and Nonreactive, Moral and Nonmoral

The reactive attitudes of resentment, indignation, and guilt all seem to have fairly complex propositional objects: one feels resentful or indignant *about* something that somebody has done, or guilty *for* having done something oneself. To account adequately for this aspect of the reactive emotions, we must suppose them to have a cognitive dimension; in particular, it seems that a person subject to a reactive emotion must have some kind of evaluative belief, one that figures in the explanation of the emotional state. Reactive attitudes are also often moral sentiments, in that the evaluative beliefs that give rise to them are often beliefs that some moral transgression has been committed (by oneself or some other party), and yet they are not the only moral sentiments to which people are subject, nor are they exclusively moral sentiments. We need an account of the cognitive dimension in reactive attitudes that will enable us to draw the right kind of line between the moral and the nonmoral reactive attitudes, and between moral reactive attitudes and other kinds of moral sentiment.

The approach I have sketched suggests a straightforward characterization of the cognitive dimension of reactive attitudes. On that approach, reactive attitudes as a class are distinguished by their connection with expectations, so that any particular state of reactive emotion must be explained by the belief that some expectation has been breached. It is the explanatory role of such beliefs about the violation of an expectation that is the defining characteristic of the states of reactive emotion as a class, and that provides them with their distinctive propositional objects; beliefs of this sort will therefore always be present when one is in one of the reactive states. Take indignation: a particular state of indignation will be focused on a specific propositional object; there must be something *about* which one is indignant, if the emotional state one is in is to count as indignation at all. According to the approach I have sketched, this propositional object of indignation can be specified by the belief that some expectation one holds people to has been breached. And what entitles us to suppose that this belief specifies the propositional content of the emotional state is the fact that it explains why one is in the emotional state.

Of course, it is possible to have the belief that an expectation has been violated without being in one of the reactive states, and so such beliefs will not always be sufficient conditions, by themselves, to produce a state of reactive emotion. One might believe that a demand has been violated that one does not hold people to oneself, in the sense I have been trying to characterize, and in this case the belief that the demand has been violated would not give rise to one of the reactive emotional states. How, then, to characterize the difference between the agent for whom beliefs about the violation of prohibitions or requirements suffice to produce states of reactive emotion, and the agent for whom they do not? It is tempting to say that the difference consists in the *stance* of the two agents toward the expectations in question: the first agent adopts a stance toward the expectations, in virtue of which we can say that she holds people to them in a way that the second person does not. This is so far correct, but it should be borne in mind that the relevant stance is not necessarily something distinct from a susceptibility to states of reactive emotion when the expectations in question are breached. For this reason we should not say that the stance—together with an agent's belief that an expectation has been breached—*explains* the agent's state of reactive emotion. Rather, that the agent has the stance *displays* itself in the fact that beliefs about the violation of certain expectations give rise to states of reactive emotion.

If this account of the cognitive element in reactive emotions is right, it suggests a natural way of distinguishing between moral and nonmoral reactive attitudes, as well as a way of distinguishing the moral reactive attitudes from other kinds of moral emotions. I will start with the distinction within the category of reactive attitudes, between the moral and the nonmoral cases. Whether a reactive emotion is or is not a moral one would seem to depend on the kind of belief that gives rise to it, and hence the kind of propositional content that it has. At least on the face of it, there is no reason to suppose that all of the expectations we hold people to are distinctively moral in character, and so we might distinguish between the belief that a moral expectation has been violated and the belief that some nonmoral expectation has been violated. In these terms, a moral reactive emotion (say, resentment) would be one that is explained by a belief of the first type and therefore has a distinctively moral content, while nonmoral resentment would have a content specified by beliefs of the second (nonmoral) type.

This strategy for distinguishing between moral and nonmoral reactive attitudes may usefully be compared with Strawson's way of carving up the reactive attitudes, which also differentiates between moral and nonmoral varieties. Strawson identifies three different kinds of reactive attitudes. What he calls personal reactive attitudes are "the non-detached attitudes and reactions of people directly involved in transactions with each other," where one demands of others a degree of consideration toward oneself; resentment is the primary example here, but Strawson also mentions gratitude, love, forgiveness, and hurt feelings.[19] The distinctively moral reactive attitudes, Strawson seems to think, are not these personal attitudes, but vicarious analogues of them, such as moral indignation or disapprobation, where one holds people to standards of behavior and attitude, not specifically in relation to oneself, but in regard to others.[20] Finally there are self-reactive attitudes, associated with demands made on oneself in one's conduct with others; examples include guilt, remorse, shame, and the sense of obligation.[21]

Taken literally, however—and ignoring for the moment Strawson's inclusive interpretation of reactivity—this approach has some peculiar consequences. It would rule out the possibility of an agent's feeling moral resentment on her own behalf, about the violation of moral expectations by other people in their behavior toward the agent; resentment about being treated unfairly, for instance, would not count as a moral sentiment. More strangely still, Strawson's approach classifies guilt as an exclusively nonmoral sentiment, since it involves the imposition of demands on oneself rather than on other parties.[22] We get a more recognizable division of the reactive attitudes into moral and nonmoral varieties if we follow the suggestion I have made, that what makes a reactive attitude a moral one is not its vicarious quality but the

---

19. Strawson, "Freedom and Resentment," p. 62.

20. Strawson, "Freedom and Resentment," pp. 70–71. Strictly speaking, Strawson says only that the moral reactive emotions must be "capable" of being vicarious; but he does not explain how a nonvicarious emotion might be potentially vicarious. My alternative account of moral reactive emotions suggests a natural unpacking of this idea: a personal emotion may be capable of being vicarious if the demand it rests on is supported by reasons that generalize to cases that do not directly involve the agent subject to the emotion.

21. Strawson, "Freedom and Resentment," pp. 71–72.

22. A similar point is made by Bennett, who suggests that the two basic categories of reactive attitudes are the "principled" and the "nonprincipled" ("Accountability," pp. 45–47). But Bennett thinks that personal reactive attitudes, in Strawson's sense, are a species of nonprincipled cases, whereas I have been suggesting that a personal reactive attitude might still be principled or moral, so long as the expectation on which it rests is a perfectly general one. In his "Reply to Ayer and Bennett," Strawson admits that it was an error "so to use the word 'moral' as to exclude the self-reactive attitudes from its scope" (p. 266). But he, like Bennett, does not seem to acknowledge that personal reactive attitudes might also be moral sentiments, depending on the character of the expectations with which they are connected.

kind of expectation that it is essentially bound up with. The most plausible development of this suggestion would begin by noting that many expectations we hold people to are supported by justifications, which identify reasons for complying with the expectations. Moral expectations can then be defined as expectations that are justifiable in terms of distinctively moral reasons.[23] I will refer to expectations that admit of this kind of moral justification as *obligations*.

I propose that reactive emotions be classified as moral when they are connected with moral obligations in this sense. More precisely, we should count reactive emotions as moral when they are linked to obligations for which the agent is herself able to provide moral justifications; these justifications identify reasons that explain the agent's own efforts to comply with the obligations in question, and they provide moral terms that the agent is prepared to use to justify such compliance on the part of others, whom the agent holds to the obligations.[24] When they are linked with obligations of this kind, it is natural to treat reactive emotions as moral sentiments, since their explanation essentially requires moral beliefs, namely beliefs about the violation of what the agent herself correctly regards as moral obligations. The explanatory role of such moral beliefs gives these emotional states a distinctively moral content. And in fact we commonly do regard resentment, indignation, and guilt to be moral emotions when they are incited by beliefs about the violation of moral obligations.[25]

It is a further consequence of this general approach, however, that not all reactive attitudes need be distinctively moral in this way. Insofar as some of the expectations to which we hold ourselves and others are not moral obligations (that is, expectations supported by moral justifications), the reactive emotions to which they give rise will not have a distinctively moral content. There is nothing peculiar in the supposition that we might resent a breach of etiquette in the behavior of another

23. It is not necessary to opt here for a particular account of what makes reasons moral. For purposes of discussion in this book, however, I shall assume that moral reasons need not be impersonal or "agent-neutral," but may also be "agent-relative" (containing an essential reference to the particular agent who has the reasons). On the distinction between agent-neutral and agent-relative reasons, and the implications of the distinction for issues of objectivity in ethics, see Thomas Nagel, *The View from Nowhere* (New York: Oxford University Press, 1986), chaps. 8–9.

24. The moral obligations in question would thus be ones that the agent *accepts* (to anticipate a distinction I explain in the following section).

25. Many of the demands we hold people to are supported by both moral and nonmoral reasons. In these cases we might say that the emotions caused by the violation of the demands are moral *insofar as* the reasons that support those demands are moral.

person toward us,[26] or that we might feel guilty about our failure to measure up to expectations that we have taken over from our parents or our church, but that we do not consider to be supported by any justifications at all. In both cases, however, it is required that there be some belief about the breach of an expectation that figures in the explanation of the reactive emotion. In this way we can begin to move away from the excessive moralization of the reactive attitudes, without denying them the kind of propositional content that sets them apart from other emotional states.

It remains to say something about the distinction between moral reactive attitudes and other types of moral sentiment. Here again it would seem that the beliefs that give rise to the emotions of various kinds may provide the key. Thus moral reactive attitudes are explained by the belief that some moral obligation has been violated. But this is not the only kind of moral belief that we entertain. Consider the various modalities of moral value, such as the values of kindness or consideration or benevolence or even justice. Such values often coincide with our moral obligations. Just as we demand, for example, that people keep their promises, or help others in extreme distress, so may we value acts of fidelity and benevolence, regarding them as good and admirable. But moral values can also diverge from moral obligations, construed as strict prohibitions and requirements. For instance, we may think that a certain sort of character is especially virtuous, even though we do not, strictly speaking, demand of people that they exhibit a character of that sort; or we might think that a particular action displays a degree of beneficence or consideration that goes well beyond what we actually demand of each other in our normal interactions. In all of these cases—the cases in which moral values coincide with our moral obligations, and the cases in which they exceed those obligations—there are often characteristic moral sentiments that are caused by evaluative moral beliefs. In addition to feeling guilt about my failure to act in accordance with the demands to which I hold myself, I may feel moral shame because I lack the moral excellences that I aspire to. And I may feel gratitude toward someone whose actions toward me are unusually beneficent, or admire someone whose character is virtuous to an exemplary degree. Thus we may distinguish moral reactive emotions from other moral sentiments in terms of the kinds of moral beliefs that give rise to the moral

26. Some such breaches of etiquette will be resented, because they violate a distinctively moral obligation of respect or consideration. But I am imagining a case in which resentment is occasioned solely by the belief that a requirement of etiquette has been violated, not by a distinct moral belief.

sentiments, and that fix the content of those sentiments: the reactive attitudes are explained exclusively by beliefs about the violation of moral obligations (construed as strict prohibitions or requirements), whereas other moral sentiments are explained by beliefs about the various modalities of moral value.[27]

In the previous section I suggested that it is at least conceivable that there might be cultures whose members do not have the stance of holding people to expectations in their repertoire. The distinction just drawn between moral reactive attitudes and other kinds of moral emotions may help to flesh out this suggestion. The nonreactive moral emotions, I have suggested, are connected with beliefs about the various modalities of moral value. A shared set of such values might conceivably have sufficient structure to constitute an ethical system for regulating social interactions within a culture, and yet the members of that culture might not be subject to the distinctively reactive emotions at all. Perhaps they respond to their own failure to live up to their values with shame rather than guilt, and hold others who similarly fall short of such standards in contempt or derision, rather than resenting them or feeling indignation; a susceptibility to these nonreactive emotions might be sufficient to guide their conduct and to provide a framework for some kind of common ethical discourse.

It has frequently been claimed that there are "shame cultures" of this kind, whose members lack the characteristic emotional resources of guilt and the other reactive attitudes. Whether such claims are true is not a question that needs to be decided here. For my purposes it is sufficient to note the following points. First, there seems to be nothing in the very idea of the reactive emotions that rules out the possibility of shame cultures. The distinctive features of resentment, indignation, and guilt do not seem to be given along with the bare facts of human social life, and so one can see how there might be human communities whose members are not subject to these emotions.[28] Second, a shame

---

27. Compare Rawls, *A Theory of Justice*, p. 484: "In general, guilt, resentment, and indignation invoke the concept of right, whereas shame, contempt, and derision appeal to the concept of goodness."

28. The claim that there are, in fact, cultures without the reactive emotions presupposes that such emotions cannot be understood in exclusively biological terms, but that they are instead somehow culturally constituted. For a summary discussion of endogenous (biological) and exogenous (cultural) accounts of emotions, see Paul Heelas, "Emotions across Cultures: Objectivity and Cultural Divergence," in S. C. Brown, ed., *Objectivity and Cultural Divergence, Philosophy* (supp.) 17 (1984), pp. 21–42. The idea that reactive emotions are culturally constituted presupposes that

culture would not necessarily be one in which there are no recognizable ethical norms, construed as norms that make social cooperation possible; nor would it be the case that the members of such a culture would not internalize these norms, in the sense of having incentives for compliance with the norms whose effectiveness is potentially independent of externally administered sanctions and rewards. On the contrary, the plausibility of the claim that there are shame cultures seems to me to rest crucially on the assumption that conformity with ethical norms can be sustained by emotional resources that do not include the distinctively reactive emotions—that conformity can be sustained by the internal sanctions of shame and anger, for instance, rather than those of guilt and indignation.[29] This assumption may be empirically ungrounded, but there seems to be no reason to reject it on conceptual grounds alone. This is what I meant in saying that nothing in the very idea of the reactive emotions rules out the possibility of shame cultures.

But even if it should turn out that there are in fact no pure shame cultures, we should still distinguish between the different ways in which emotions contribute to sustaining social cooperation. What I have called the reactive emotions differ from such emotions as shame and anger in their presumptive connection with the kind of prohibitions or requirements that I have referred to as moral obligations. These emotions help to define what Bernard Williams has called "the morality system," to mark a contrast between a conception of the moral and its demands that is especially prominent in modern, Christianized cultures and other

---

susceptibility to, say, guilt requires the ability to make attributions of guilt; but it does not presuppose the stronger and less plausible claim that one can only be in a state of guilt if one believes of oneself that one is in such a state at the time. Allan Gibbard seems to slide between these two claims when discussing what he calls "attributional" accounts of emotion in his book *Wise Choices, Apt Feelings: A Theory of Normative Judgment* (Cambridge, Mass.: Harvard University Press, 1990), pp. 141–150. (The less plausible claim has been advocated by Stanley Schachter, in *Emotion, Obesity, and Crime* [New York: Academic Press, 1971]. For a criticism of Schachter's interpretation of his experimental results, see Robert M. Gordon, *The Structure of Emotions: Investigations in Cognitive Philosophy* [Cambridge: Cambridge University Press, 1987], chap. 5.)

29. The distinction between shame and guilt cultures does not necessarily carry with it the implication that shame cultures are psychologically and morally primitive, by comparison with guilt cultures. Indeed, shame-based moralities have recently been defended as superior to systems centered around the reactive emotions: see Bernard Williams, *Shame and Necessity* (Berkeley: University of California Press, 1993), chap. 4; and, in a similar vein, Annette C. Baier, "Moralism and Cruelty: Reflections on Hume and Kant," *Ethics* 103 (1993), pp. 436–457. I take issue with some of Williams's and Baier's criticisms of guilt-based moralities in the chapters to follow; but they are surely correct to challenge the complacent "progressivism" that characterized many earlier discussions of the distinction between guilt and shame cultures.

aspects or forms of ethical life.[30] Though I do not share Williams's evident hostility toward the morality system so construed, I agree that it represents a distinctive interpretation of ethical prohibitions and requirements, and in the next chapter I shall argue that the special connection it postulates between moral obligations and the reactive emotions is the key to understanding what it is to hold someone morally *responsible*. First, however, it will be necessary to say more about the stance of holding someone to an expectation, in terms of which the reactive attitudes have so far been defined.

2.4   Irrational Guilt

It is notoriously the case that one can feel guilt without believing that one has really done anything wrong. We might express this by saying that one can feel guilt without believing that one has violated any demands that one *accepts*. But if guilt is a reactive attitude, and if I am right in suggesting that reactive attitudes are connected with demands that we hold people to, then the stance of holding someone to a demand must be distinct from that of accepting the demand. How is this distinction to be made out?

To value an end, most would agree, is not simply to be motivated to pursue it. To be motivated to pursue an end is simply to have some desire that prompts one to pursue the end or that is strong enough to lead one to do so. To value this end, by contrast, it is not enough simply to be subject to desires to pursue it; a susceptibility to desires of this sort may be a necessary condition of valuing an end, but it is not by itself sufficient.[31] To value an end, it is a further requirement that one approves of pursuing the end when one engages in reflection about how it would be good to lead one's life; one must also see some reason for pursuing the end that could enter into one's own practical deliberation, and that could be cited in discourse with other people to explain and justify why one has pursued the end (or why one is inclined to do so). Happily, it is often the case that one's motivations completely coincide with one's values, in this sense. But it is a permanent hazard of human agency that values and motivations may come apart,

30. See Bernard Williams, *Ethics and the Limits of Philosophy* (Cambridge, Mass.: Harvard University Press, 1985), chap. 10.

31. Of course, the desires to which one is subject need not be so strong as to carry one all the way to action—that would rule out the possibility of acting against one's better judgment.

so that one is motivated to pursue ends that one does not value at all (or that one does not value as strongly as one is motivated to pursue them).[32]

A similar distinction can be drawn with respect to expectations or demands, which we might mark (following Allan Gibbard) in terms of a distinction between "internalizing a demand" and "accepting a demand."[33] To internalize a demand, in Gibbard's sense, is basically to have some consistent motivation to act in conformity with the demand. Using the term "norm" in place of the terms "demand" and "expectation" that I have favored, Gibbard writes: "where norm N prescribes a certain behavioral pattern B, an organism *internalizes N* if and only if it has a motivational tendency . . . to act on pattern B."[34] Internalizing a demand can thus be thought of as a special case of motivation more generally, where the actions one is motivated to engage in have sufficient structure to fall under the linguistic expression of a demand; but insofar as bare motivation does not necessarily commit one to valuing what one is motivated to pursue, internalizing a demand is not an evaluative state. Accepting a demand, by contrast, is an evaluative state. It involves more than just having a motivational tendency to engage in actions that conform with the demand (though internalization, in this sense, is a necessary condition of accepting the demand[35]). It involves a further tendency to adduce reasons that support the demand, reasons that weigh with one for purposes of practical deliberation, and that one is prepared to call on to justify one's behavior and perhaps to address criticisms and recommendations to others.[36] Since accepting a demand, in this sense, involves some motivational tendency to comply with the demand, all cases of acceptance of a demand will also be cases of internalization of the demand. But the converse does not hold, and it is possible to internalize a demand without actually accepting it, insofar as the demand does not play a role in one's practical reasoning and delibera-

---

32. For an influential statement and development of the distinction between motivations and values, see Gary Watson, "Free Agency," as reprinted in Watson, ed., *Free Will*, pp. 96–110.

33. Gibbard, *Wise Choices, Apt Feelings*, chap. 4.

34. Gibbard, *Wise Choices, Apt Feelings*, p. 71.

35. Again, it is not required that the motivations to which one is subject carry one all the way to action, only that one has some motivational tendency to conform with the demands one accepts.

36. Compare Gibbard, *Wise Choices, Apt Feelings*, p. 75. I depart here from Gibbard in offering a characterization of accepting a demand that is not specially intended to be naturalistic, and that places correspondingly greater emphasis than Gibbard does on the role of demands in practical reasoning and deliberation. For a case in which the demands one accepts for practical deliberation would not necessarily be deployed in criticism of the actions of others, see the discussion of personal moralities or moralities of supererogation, in Appendix 1.

tion, and one is not disposed to avow the demand in the context of public normative discussion.[37]

I will take this distinction between internalizing and accepting demands as given. What I now want to ask is how the stance of holding someone to a demand relates to this distinction. Holding someone to a demand, it will be recalled, is characterized in terms of the reactive emotions, as a tendency to feel those emotions in cases where the demand has been violated, or to believe that it would be appropriate to feel the reactive emotions in those cases. So characterized, it seems clear that holding someone to a demand can and often does coincide with acceptance of the demand, in the sense distinguished above. Thus the very same demands that one is motivated to comply with, and that one accepts in practical deliberation and in normative discussion, may prompt guilt when one violates them oneself, and resentment and indignation when they are violated by others.

Indeed, if one accepts a demand, and one is in a culture that makes available the reactive emotions of guilt, resentment, and indignation, one might count as holding oneself and others to the demand even if one does not have a reliable disposition to feel the reactive emotions in all the cases in which the demands in question are violated. To count as holding someone to a demand, it is enough that one believes that the reactive emotions would be *appropriate* in case the person should violate the demand, even if one does not actually feel those emotions oneself (recall the disjunctive formula discussed in section 2.1). For example, one might accept a demand prohibiting dishonesty and yet have trouble working up any resentment in a case where a charming acquaintance (a new lover, say) has lied to one; nevertheless one would probably still believe that it would be appropriate if one felt resentment toward the acquaintance because of the violation of the demand. In this case, I want to say, one both accepts the demand and holds one's acquaintance to the demand, even though one is not actually subject to the reactive emotions one believes to be appropriate, for one believes that the acquaintance's violation of the demand would make it appropriate for one to feel resentment in the case. The coincidence of acceptance of a demand and holding someone to the demand is clearer still in cases where one is directly subject to the reactive emotions when

37. Gibbard refers to this as "being in the grip" of a norm, and cites Stanley Milgram's famous experiments on obedience to authority as illustrating the phenomenon; see *Wise Choices, Apt Feelings,* pp. 58–61.

the demands one accepts have been violated. But while the demands to which one holds oneself and others are often demands that one accepts, this is not the case all of the time. Focusing on the reactive emotion of guilt, I will argue that the stance of holding someone to a demand is sui generis; it cannot be assimilated either to the stance of internalizing a demand or to that of accepting a demand.

Take, first, the narrower category of accepting a demand. It seems clear that one can hold oneself to a demand that one does not accept, in the sense just distinguished. Thus people who have had a strongly Catholic upbringing often continue to feel pangs of guilt about recreational sex well into adulthood, even when they do not themselves take a general prohibition on recreational sex to be justified, and so reject such a prohibition both for purposes of their own practical deliberation and for purposes of normative discussion with others. These people are not apt to believe that the guilt they feel is an appropriate response to their sexual activities, because they do not accept the Catholic demands as a basis for practical deliberation and public justification; but insofar as they are subject to guilt all the same, they will count as holding themselves to those demands. Again, people sometimes feel guilty simply for harboring aggressive thoughts or desires, without having done anything to translate these mental states into action. And yet someone who is subject to such guilt feelings might at the same time reject demands that proscribe mere thoughts or desires, in contexts of practical deliberation and public criticism, finding such demands superstitious or puritanical. In such cases, we apparently find people holding themselves to demands that they do not accept.

Conversely—though for my purposes perhaps less importantly—it seems possible that someone might accept a demand without holding herself or other people to it, in the sense that I have been trying to characterize. Consider, for example, the (hypothetical) shame culture I described in the previous section, whose members do not have the reactive attitudes in their emotional repertoire. People in such a culture might well accept demands proscribing or requiring certain forms of behavior, both as a basis for practical deliberation and as providing terms for public normative discussion. Yet insofar as the reactive attitudes are not available to the members of the culture, the acceptance of such demands would not involve any special susceptibility to guilt if they should violate the demands themselves, or even a belief that guilt would be appropriate in those cases; and so we could not describe these people as holding themselves to the demands that they accept.[38]

Thus, accepting a demand is neither a necessary nor a sufficient condition for holding oneself to the demand. But if acceptance is not sufficient for holding oneself to a demand, then the latter stance cannot be assimilated to the stance of internalizing a demand, either, for as acceptance and internalization have been characterized, all cases of acceptance involve internalization of a demand. This is just to say that one might have a tendency to behave in conformity with a given demand without having any susceptibility to guilt when one violates the demand, and without believing that guilt would be appropriate in that case. For example, one might have assimilated cultural demands governing conversational distance between people, in that one consistently behaves in accordance with the demands, adjusting one's distance from conversational partners automatically as the demands prescribe (by stepping backward or forward, as necessary).[39] And yet the occasional violation of the demand by the person who thus internalizes it might produce, at best, discomfort without any tendency to guilt, or without even the belief that guilt would be an appropriate emotion to feel. Here, then, is internalization of a demand without holding oneself to the demand.

There may, however, be a residual sense in which all cases of holding oneself to a demand involve the internalization of the demand. Guilt, after all, has an unpleasant phenomenology. Assuming that one ordinarily wishes to avoid unpleasant experiences, a susceptibility to guilt for the violation of a demand will involve some disposition to be motivated to comply with the demand (as a strategy for avoiding the pangs of conscience)—though, of course, the motivations in question might rarely (if ever) move one all the way to action. Notice, however, that in this case the agent would not appear to have a *direct* behavioral disposition to act on the demand; the immediate object of the agent's motivations is the avoidance of the unpleasant sensation of guilt, and

38. This presupposes, plausibly enough, that the members of a shame culture might have the linguistic resources to express demands, construed as prohibitions or requirements. What is ruled out is the idea that the moral emotions that sustain social cooperation within such a culture should be caused specifically by beliefs about the violation of such demands. (Perhaps the members of the culture think of whatever demands they accept as derivative from an ideal conception of the good life, so that the offenses that occasion shame and anger are seen essentially as departures from that ideal, and not merely as violations of a demand.)

39. The example is from Gibbard, *Wise Choices, Apt Feelings*, pp. 69–70, though I use it to illustrate a point that he does not himself make.

compliance with the demand is seen only as a means for attaining this end. (Therapy might be a different, and better, means.) This is why I said that it is only in a residual sense true that holding oneself to a demand always involves the internalization of the demand.

The preceding remarks strongly support the conclusion that holding someone to a demand is a sui generis stance, which cannot be assimilated either to the evaluative stance of accepting a demand or to the behavioral stance of internalizing the demand. Even if the three stances often overlap, our psychological concepts allow us to imagine and to describe cases in which they come apart from one another—at least that is what I have tried to show. But if one grants that holding someone to a demand is a sui generis stance, it seems a straightforward matter to explain how one might come to feel the reactive emotion of guilt without believing that guilt is an appropriate emotion to be subject to in the circumstances. Situations of this sort occur when one holds oneself to a demand that one does not accept; the possibility of such situations is already acknowledged in saying that the quasi-evaluative stance of holding someone to a demand is a sui generis condition.

This is, to be sure, a peculiar kind of situation. After all, for any given person at any given time, there are going to be arbitrarily many demands that the person will have violated that the person does not accept (construing demands, again, as practical prohibitions or requirements). What distinguishes these demands from the rejected demands whose violation does provoke guilt? It is tempting to think that there must be some further evaluative belief present if the violation of a demand is to give rise to guilt: for instance, the belief that because one has violated the demand, one has disfigured or harmed oneself in some way.[40] Certainly, on many occasions of guilt, evaluative beliefs of this sort are going to be present, but it seems strained to insist that such beliefs must be present in all cases of guilt. If one feels guilty for violating a demand that one really does not accept, one need not sincerely believe that one has harmed or disfigured oneself by violating the demand. The lapsed Catholics referred to earlier, for instance, need not believe that the recreational sex that makes them feel guilty in any way harms them— indeed, they may have rejected demands prohibiting recreational sex partly because they do not believe that sexual activity necessarily harms those who engage in it.

---

40. See Gabriele Taylor, *Pride, Shame, and Guilt: Emotions of Self-Assessment* (Oxford: Clarendon Press, 1985), p. 103, for this suggestion.

Still, those in the grip of Catholic guilt are apt to feel "as if" they had disfigured themselves by violating the sexual demands they were brought up to respect. Their guilt will prompt them to entertain evaluative thoughts of disfigurement that they need not accept, but that they tend to find natural. A proneness to evaluative thoughts that one does not necessarily endorse thus seems to be part of the stance of holding oneself (and others) to demands.[41] If this is right, then inappropriate guilt will involve a complex structure of rifts in the self. First, insofar as one is prompted to think of oneself in terms of disfigurement, there will be a rift between the self that has been disfigured and the self that committed the guilty act—the rift, we might say, that constitutes the disfigurement. And second, insofar as one does not really endorse these evaluative thoughts about disfigurement, there will be a rift between the perspective of the emotional state of guilt and that of one's sincere evaluative beliefs. It is because holding oneself to a demand in this way disposes one to entertain negative evaluative thoughts one does not necessarily endorse that I earlier referred to the stance as "quasi-evaluative." It is an emotional relation to a demand that is in some ways like an evaluative attitude, insofar as violation of the demand prompts one to think of oneself (or others) in evaluative terms; yet it does not require that one be fully committed to evaluative thoughts, either in practical deliberation or as a basis for public discussion. These peculiar features of the stance are apparent in cases where one holds oneself to a demand that one does not accept.

It may be helpful to compare this treatment of irrational guilt with the two traditional strategies for understanding the reactive emotions mentioned at the start of this chapter. First there is the approach of Butler and Rawls, which defines the reactive attitudes as emotions that are distinctively caused by moral beliefs concerning injury (understood as a specially moral concept) or concerning a violation of standards of moral right. Now, the preceding section already suggests one important reason for objecting to this approach. It seems to overmoralize the reactive attitudes, insofar as it does not allow for reactive emotions that are prompted by violations of nonmoral demands. A further and related problem is posed by the case of inappropriate guilt. Very often when one feels guilt inappropriately, what makes the guilt seem inappropriate is precisely the fact that one does not believe oneself to have done anything morally wrong at all; there are no moral obligations one

---

41. These thoughts would count as beliefs only in the degenerate sense alluded to in sec. 2.1.

accepts that one believes oneself to have violated. If this is correct, however, then genuine guilt cannot always be explained by distinctively moral beliefs, as Butler and Rawls propose.

Rawls himself is perfectly aware of this consequence of his position, suggesting that when one feels guilt inappropriately, one is not really subject to "proper guilt feelings," but only to "residue guilt feelings," which resemble in certain respects the sensations one experiences when one is properly guilty.[42] Now of course there is one sense in which everyone could agree that the person who feels guilt inappropriately is not subject to proper guilt. This is the sense in which "improper guilt" just means guilt that one takes to be inappropriate. But Rawls's general approach to the reactive attitudes—to identify them as emotions whose explanation requires the moral concept of right—commits him to a stronger position: namely, that people who feel guilt that they believe is inappropriate are not genuinely subject to guilt at all. In support of this strong claim, Rawls notes that when one is subject to guilt feelings that one believes to be inappropriate, one is not disposed to apologize to anybody for what one has done, or to make amends, or to try to modify one's behavior in the future, and so forth—where these are parts of the complex psychological and behavioral syndrome that constitutes the state of proper guilt in the first place. There is an important insight here, insofar as the behavioral dispositions of guilt that one believes to be justified are very different from those of guilt that one believes to be inappropriate. But to suppose that one cannot count as being genuinely subject to the emotion of guilt unless one has the former dispositions seems to go too far in the direction of defining the emotional state in terms of its behavioral manifestations under one set of conditions. The fact is that we frequently ascribe guilt to people who do not believe that they have really done anything morally wrong; moreover, the kinds of neurosis and anguish often associated with guilt in such

42. Rawls, *A Theory of Justice*, pp. 481–482. It should perhaps be emphasized that Rawls's primary concern is with the case of a well-ordered society. He is trying to characterize the kinds of moral emotion that the members of a well-ordered society will be subject to; he is not giving an account of irrational emotions, or of the pathologies to which the moral sentiments can lead. Still, the claims made about guilt and the other moral sentiments in a well-ordered society should not be so formulated as to exclude the possibility of the irrational and pathological cases. When those claims are suitably modified along the lines I have proposed, much of what Rawls says about the development of the moral sentiments in the members of a well-ordered society can shed light on how the irrational and pathological cases emerge. For instance, it seems clear that many of those cases can be traced back to events that occur in a child's life in the stage Rawls calls the "morality of authority" (sec. 70), where parental authority is used to enforce compliance with demands that the child later comes to reject.

cases presuppose that there is something one feels guilty about, some propositional object of one's emotional state. We can only do justice to this aspect of irrational guilt if we give up the claim that genuine guilt requires the belief that one has violated precepts of right, and acknowledge that the behavioral and psychological consequences of (proper or genuine) guilt will vary, depending on whether the demands whose violation prompts the guilt are or are not demands that one accepts.[43]

The other traditional strategy is followed by Gibbard, who sets himself against what he calls "judgmentalist" accounts of the reactive emotions. A judgmentalist account, as Gibbard describes it, holds that the reactive emotions are to be identified, in whole or in part, with cognitive judgments.[44] Gibbard is particularly worried about accounts that identify the reactive attitudes with moral evaluations—saying, for instance, that guilt involves a judgment that one is at fault or that one has done something wrong. He is concerned about such accounts because he himself wishes to understand moral evaluations of wrongness and blameworthiness in terms of the reactive emotions (holding, for instance, that to think an act morally blameworthy "is to accept norms that prescribe, in such a situation, guilt on the part of the agent and resentment on the part of others"[45]). This approach can only avoid circularity if we have an independent grip on the reactive emotions, so that we can characterize them without presupposing the category of moral judgment that is to be defined in terms of them. Against the judgmentalist accounts that he rejects, Gibbard repeatedly complains that they cannot allow for inappropriate guilt and resentment,[46] and he sketches alternative accounts of the reactive emotions that do not necessarily attribute to the subject of the emotions any particular beliefs about the commission of moral wrongs or even the violation of de-

43. This is not to deny the possibility of experiencing the kinaesthetic sensations involved in guilt without the belief about the violation of expectations that genuine guilt requires, on my account. Perhaps we are sometimes subject to such "residue guilt feelings" (see the discussion of survivor guilt and vicarious guilt in Appendix 1, for some possible examples). My present point is only that we cannot plausibly account for all cases of irrational guilt in these terms.

44. Gibbard, *Wise Choices, Apt Feelings*, pp. 129–132. Though I have not strictly identified the reactive emotional states with beliefs, the essential role I have attributed to a certain class of beliefs in explaining the reactive emotions may be equivalent to what other philosophers have meant in identifying emotions with beliefs; see, for example, the notion of "identificatory belief" introduced by Taylor, in *Pride, Shame, and Guilt*.

45. Gibbard, *Wise Choices, Apt Feelings*, p. 47.

46. Gibbard, *Wise Choices, Apt Feelings*, pp. 130, 147, 148–149.

mands.[47] The details of these accounts are not of concern here. The general strategy, however, is to treat resentment or anger as an adaptive syndrome continuous with animal emotions, to be identified by its characteristic causes and by the forms of expression and behavior to which it characteristically gives rise, and to treat guilt as a refinement of more basic biological adaptations in specific cultural circumstances (namely, those in which the concept of guilt is available), such that one can only be in a state of guilt if one believes of oneself that one is in that state.

We should agree with Gibbard, I think, in rejecting judgmentalist accounts that treat reactive emotions as incorporating moral judgments, and we should reject them in part for the reason that Gibbard gives. As was seen in the discussion of Rawls, accounts of this sort do not allow us to ascribe those emotions to people who find the emotions uncalled for from the perspective of moral demands that they accept.[48] But in seeking an alternative to this kind of judgmentalist account, Gibbard goes to the opposite extreme, denying altogether the role of beliefs in explaining the reactive attitudes. The inadequacy of this move is most clearly apparent in the adaptive-syndrome account of anger and resentment that Gibbard sketches: this account runs the two emotions together by assimilating them to the behaviorally identified syndromes of animals (such as the anger of a dog, identified by the kinds of events that typically cause it and by the barking and aggressive behavior it typically gives rise to[49]). Even if an account of this sort could yield an adequate understanding of anger in persons,[50] it omits something essential to the content of resentment as we understand it, which seems distinctively to be a response to violations by others of the demands we hold them to in their conduct toward us. A similar point applies to Gibbard's version of the attributional approach to guilt. As Gibbard develops it, this approach concedes that subjects of guilt must have a

---

47. Gibbard, *Wise Choices, Apt Feelings,* pp. 135–150.

48. We should also reject accounts of this type for the reason given in sec. 2.3: they excessively moralize the reactive attitudes from the start, ruling out the possibility of guilt or resentment about the violation of nonmoral demands that one accepts.

49. Gibbard, *Wise Choices, Apt Feelings,* pp. 132–135, 145.

50. See Gordon, *The Structure of Emotions,* pp. 71–73, for some doubts about an adaptive-syndrome analysis of human fear: the state of fear that the syndrome picks out, and that is common to animals and humans, cannot be the basis of human fear more generally, both because human fear has a complex intentionality that the biological state of fear lacks, and because the causes and motivational effects of human fear range far more widely than those that define the adaptive syndrome. Similar remarks apply, I believe, to the case of anger.

certain sort of belief—namely, the belief that they are in a state of guilt.[51] But it misses the definitive role of beliefs about the violation of demands in giving rise to states of guilt. Only if I believe (at least subconsciously) that there is *some* such demand that I have failed to abide by can I be said to be in a state of guilt at all. For beliefs of this sort are what give guilt and the other reactive emotions their characteristic propositional content.[52]

To summarize, I have suggested that the quasi-evaluative stance of holding someone to a demand is a sui generis condition, unlike either the fully evaluative stance of accepting a demand or the behavioral stance of internalizing a demand. Distinguishing between these various stances completes my basic characterization of holding someone to a demand, and of the reactive attitudes in terms of which that stance was defined. In doing so, it also helps us to understand how one may be subject to states of reactive emotion inappropriately. I have argued that the connection between the reactive emotions and demands enables us to account for guilt that an agent believes to be (morally) inappropriate—by contrast to Rawls's approach. But it does this without falling into the trap that Gibbard gets caught in, of assimilating the reactive emotions too closely to other emotional and adaptive states, and hence depriving them of their distinctive propositional objects. With this understanding of the reactive emotions in place, I am now in a position to explore some of the more positive contributions that those emotions make to moral life, by locating their role in our practice of holding people morally responsible.

51. Gibbard, *Wise Choices, Apt Feelings*, p. 148.

52. Gibbard has other grounds for rejecting the approach to the reactive attitudes that I have been advocating. His norm-expressivistic account of moral judgments takes our most fundamental moral norms to be norms for the appropriateness of guilt and resentment (*Wise Choices, Apt Feelings*, pp. 40–48). My approach to guilt and resentment, by contrast, requires that we have independent (moral and nonmoral) norms proscribing and requiring certain actions directly. If this is right, then our most fundamental moral norms cannot be norms for guilt and resentment, because those reactive emotions themselves presuppose antecedent (moral) norms for action. There is not the space here to discuss this issue further. But if (as I suppose) the approach to the reactive attitudes I have sketched is independently plausible, it raises a basic doubt about Gibbard's account of moral judgments and moral norms.

3

Responsibility

❧

The question of what we are doing when we hold people responsible
has not been adequately treated in discussions of freedom and responsibility. A common assumption is that moral responsibility can be
understood primarily in terms of moral blame and sanction, so that to
hold people morally responsible is to be prepared to blame or sanction
them for their moral offenses, where the sanctions tend, at the limit,
toward punishment. This is all right, so far as it goes, but philosophers
have not yet given us a satisfactory interpretation of the stance that issues
in these forms of treatment. As I explain in section 3.1, the stance of
holding people responsible cannot be reduced to a behavioral disposition, because moral blame has an essential attitudinal dimension. An
interpretation of what it is to hold people morally responsible should
account for this attitudinal aspect of blame, explaining its distinctively
backward-looking focus and its conventional connection with sanctioning behavior.

I take up these problems in section 3.2, developing an approach to
moral responsibility that builds on the account of the reactive emotions
defended in the preceding chapter. According to that account, the
reactive emotions of resentment, indignation, and guilt are distinguished
by their connection with expectations (construed as prohibitions or
requirements); so that to hold someone to such an expectation is to be
susceptible to the reactive emotions in the case that the expectation is
breached, or to believe that the reactive emotions would be appropriate
in that case. To hold a person morally responsible, I now want to argue,
is to hold the person to moral expectations that one accepts. This
approach correctly treats holding people responsible as a basic stance
that we take toward them, that cannot be reduced to a behavioral
disposition to sanction them for what they do. Furthermore, it connects
the practice of holding people morally responsible with the notions of

moral obligation, moral right, and moral wrong, which form the nexus of concepts in which responsibility would seem to belong. At the same time, the interpretation I offer suggests an appealing explanation of how moral blame and the various sanctioning responses hang together as a class: to blame someone is to be subject to one of the reactive emotions in terms of which the stance of holding people responsible is essentially defined, and these emotions are *expressed* by the sanctioning behavior to which the stance of holding people responsible inclines us. This point is developed in section 3.3, which considers the question of how judgments of moral responsibility may be understood to go beyond mere descriptions of what an agent has done, and explains how we may hold someone responsible for a moral wrong without actually being subject to an episode of reactive emotion.

3.1   Responsibility, Blame, and Moral Sanction

To hold someone morally responsible is to view the person as the potential target of a special kind of moral appraisal. People who are *morally* responsible are not seen merely as acting in ways that happen to be good or bad; they are not just causally responsible for certain welcome or unwelcome happenings, the way a clogged drain might be said to be responsible for the unfortunate overflowing of a basin. Rather, the actions of morally responsible people are thought to reflect specially on them as agents, opening them to a kind of moral appraisal that does more than record a causal connection between them and the consequences of their actions. As Susan Wolf has suggested, assessing people as morally responsible has a quality of "depth," going beyond mere description of the moral character of what they do, or of their causal role in bringing their actions about.[1] An account of what it is to hold people responsible should start by characterizing this quality of depth, so as to locate more precisely the distinctive aspect of the phenomenon that is to be explained.

Note, to begin with, that moral responsibility is not the only kind of responsibility that could be described as "deep." Consider the mature artist's responsibility for a striking and successful work of art. In praising or admiring such a work, we do not just think of it as a successful production that happens to have been causally related to the artist who produced it. Rather, our praise and admiration reflect a kind of credit

---

1. Susan Wolf, *Freedom within Reason* (New York: Oxford University Press, 1990), p. 41.

on its creator, opening the artist to direct assessment in virtue of the qualities reflected in the work. We can say that the artist is responsible for the work of art in a way we cannot say that a very young child is responsible for her finger paintings, even if the latter should turn out to be lovely in their way.[2] To view people as responsible in this sense is to see them as autonomous agents who are reflective about their lives, who have a set of values or commitments sufficiently structured to constitute what we might call a "conception of the good," and who aim to advance that conception in their action. When they succeed in realizing this aim, autonomous agents can be thought of as being specially responsible for their actions, insofar as those actions disclose the agents' deepest values and commitments—the values and commitments that help to define the agents' "real self." Assessments of people as responsible, in this sense of being autonomously self-revealing in their actions, clearly go beyond mere descriptions of causal responsibility, and so may be said to have a quality of depth. Much of the recent philosophical discussion of freedom and responsibility has focused on identifying the conditions that agents have to satisfy to be open to deep assessments of this kind.[3]

But this sort of deep responsibility for one's actions—I will call it the condition of autonomy—should not be confused with moral responsibility.[4] This may be seen quite clearly if we return to the example of the mature artist. Supposing the artist to satisfy the condition of autonomy, our esteem for her works will reflect directly on the artist, who is therefore open to evaluative appraisal in virtue of what she creates. But this kind of direct appraisal does not seem especially moral in its quality; nor would we ordinarily say that the artist is *morally* responsible for the works of art that she produces. To hold people morally responsible for their actions is to see them as open to a kind of deep appraisal

2. The comparison is Wolf's: see *Freedom within Reason,* pp. 7–8.

3. The classic discussions include Harry Frankfurt, "Freedom of the Will and the Concept of a Person," as reprinted in his *The Importance of What We Care About: Philosophical Essays* (Cambridge: Cambridge University Press, 1988), pp. 11–25; Wright Neely, "Freedom and Desire," *Philosophical Review* 83 (1974), pp. 32–54; and Gary Watson, "Free Agency," as reprinted in Watson, ed., *Free Will* (Oxford: Oxford University Press, 1982), pp. 96–110. For more recent discussions, see Paul Benson, "Freedom and Value," *Journal of Philosophy* 84 (1987), pp. 465–486; John Christman, "Autonomy and Personal History," *Canadian Journal of Philosophy* 21 (1991), pp. 1–24; Gerald Dworkin, *The Theory and Practice of Autonomy* (Cambridge: Cambridge University Press, 1988); and Michael Slote, "Understanding Free Will," as reprinted in John Martin Fischer, ed., *Moral Responsibility* (Ithaca, N.Y.: Cornell University Press, 1986), pp. 124–139.

4. On the distinction between these different kinds of deep responsibility, I am indebted to Gary Watson's unpublished paper "Two Features of Responsibility."

different from that involved in treating people as autonomous, a kind of appraisal that is presumptively moral in its quality and force. An account of what it is to hold people responsible must locate and explain this special kind of appraisal.

People who are morally responsible may be made to answer for their actions, in the sense that their actions render them liable to certain kinds of distinctively moral responses.[5] These responses include most saliently the response of moral blame, which is called for when the responsible agent has done something morally wrong, but they extend beyond simple blame to include a range of sanctioning responses as well, such as avoidance, reproach, scolding, denunciation, remonstration, and (at the limit) punishment.[6] Moral blame and moral sanction may thus be thought of as the special kinds of appraisal to which morally responsible agents are open, and the hallmark of holding people responsible will be a tendency to respond to them with these forms of appraisal. Thus, though the actions of an autonomous agent disclose directly that agent's values and commitments, our assessments of those actions do not necessarily have the special force of moral blame and sanction—we may condemn the pianist's latest performance as empty and unintelligent, for example, in a way that reflects discredit on the pianist, without blaming the pianist morally. To understand what we are doing when we hold people morally responsible, we must clarify the nature of moral blame and moral sanction. What is the point of these forms of response? How do they go beyond mere description of what an agent has done? What holds these responses together as a class?

There is a standard approach to moral responsibility that provides a systematic answer to these questions. This approach, which might be called the economy of threats account, interprets moral blame and moral sanction exclusively in terms of their deterrent effects.[7] These

5. See the discussion of "moral liability responsibility" in H. L. A. Hart, "Postscript: Responsibility and Retribution," in his *Punishment and Responsibility: Essays in the Philosophy of Law* (Oxford: Clarendon Press, 1968), pp. 210–237, at pp. 225–227.

6. I say "at the limit" here, because—outside our roles as parents and schoolteachers—it is rarely the case that we ourselves undertake literally to punish those whom we blame. In serious enough cases, however, we do tolerate and consider justified the punishment of offenders by the state. Note also that in the reflexive instance, in which we hold ourselves responsible, the sanctioning responses will take slightly different forms, including confession of wrongdoing, self-reproach, acceptance of the criticism of others, efforts to compensate for harms done and to make amends, and (in some cases) penance.

7. I borrow the expression "economy of threats" from H. L. A. Hart, "Legal Responsibility and Excuses," as reprinted in Hart, *Punishment and Responsibility,* pp. 28–53, at pp. 43–44. The classic application of the approach to the case of moral responsibility—dating originally from

forms of moral treatment are construed as part of an economy of threats designed to influence people—the person directly blamed or sanctioned, as well as others in that person's milieu—to avoid undesirable actions. Appealing as it does to our forward-looking concern to influence peoples' behavior for the better, a kind of generalized beneficence, the economy of threats approach has a recognizably utilitarian character. In fact, it can be seen as an application to the case of moral responsibility of a familiar, utilitarian approach to punishment in the law. Construed as an interpretation of our actual practice of holding people morally responsible, however—and not as an allegedly enlightened replacement for our existing practices—utilitarian accounts of this sort encounter familiar objections. Without wishing to rehearse all of these problems in detail, I would like to note three ways in which the economy of threats approach fails to account convincingly for the point and unity of moral blame and moral sanctions; this should help to stake out the territory that an account of holding responsible must cover, and also to clarify the constraints that an adequate account must satisfy.

In distinguishing moral responsibility from autonomy, I have isolated moral blame and moral sanction as the kinds of responses distinctive of holding people responsible. It is a strength of the economy of threats approach that it offers an interpretation of these moral responses; but the interpretation seems to go astray from the start by treating blame and moral sanction too behavioristically. Blame is taken to go beyond mere description of what an agent has done by being linked to special kinds of behavior, the exemplary case of which is punishment.[8] This move is crucial to the strategy, because it is only insofar as responsibility is linked to behavior that it can influence people as part of a system of threats. But it puts the cart before the horse. In saying this I do not

---

1930—is found in Moritz Schlick, *Problems of Ethics,* trans. David Rynam (New York: Dover Publications, 1962), chap. 7; variations of the strategy may be found in P. H. Nowell-Smith, "Freewill and Moral Responsibility," *Mind* 57 (1948), pp. 45–61, and J. J. C. Smart, "Freewill, Praise, and Blame," *Mind* 70 (1961), pp. 291–306. For a more recent version, see Daniel C. Dennett, *Elbow Room: The Varieties of Free Will Worth Wanting* (Cambridge, Mass.: MIT Press, 1984), chap. 7. Of course the strategy has deeper roots in empiricist ethics—it is already evident, for instance, in Hobbes's and Hume's remarks about praise and blame. For a brief critical discussion of the strategy, see Jonathan Bennett's remarks about the "Schlickian rationale" in "Accountability," in Zak van Straaten, ed., *Philosophical Subjects: Essays Presented to P. F. Strawson* (Oxford: Clarendon Press, 1980), pp. 14–47, at pp. 19–21.

8. Both Schlick and Dennett take punishment to be our exemplary response to people whom we hold responsible, and develop their versions of the economy of threats strategy mainly by reference to the case of punishment: see Schlick, *Problems of Ethics,* pp. 151–154, and Dennett, *Elbow Room,* p. 158.

mean to deny that we often act in ways that express blame toward people whom we hold morally responsible. Of course we do: this is what I was earlier referring to when I suggested that responsibility involves a disposition to moral sanctions, which are, after all, forms of behavior. The mistake is to treat holding people responsible exclusively as a disposition to sanctioning behavior, for this leaves out the underlying *attitudinal* aspect of moral blame. Though blame often and naturally finds expression in sanctioning behavior, it is not necessarily so expressed—thus I can blame a person "privately" without expressing my response to anyone at all, much less sanctioning the person whom I blame (who may anyway be outside my sphere of causal influence). While the economy of threats approach offers a possible explanation of moral sanctions, it does not seem to account for the more basic attitude of moral blame. And without an account of moral blame, the approach cannot capture our familiar practice of holding people responsible; for what unifies the various kinds of moral sanction is the fact that they express the underlying attitude of moral blame.

Against this it might be objected that the economy of threats approach can acknowledge that holding people responsible is more than a bare behavioral disposition. The point of sanctioning behavior, according to this approach, is deterrence; but behavior that aims at deterrence expresses an underlying attitude, namely the forward-looking attitude of generalized beneficence, refined into a concern for the maximization of expected utility. The proponent of the economy of threats approach might suggest that this is the attitude that underlies and unifies the sanctioning responses to which we subject those whom we hold responsible, so that the stance of holding someone responsible is not treated as a bare behavioral disposition.

Here, however, a second problem arises, for the attitude of forward-looking beneficent concern is not the right kind of attitude to account for our actual practice of holding people responsible. The attitudinal aspect of blame is backward-looking and focused on the individual agent who has done something morally wrong; insofar as sanctioning behavior expresses the attitude of blame, it too looks back to the commission of a moral wrong, and is directed at the individual agent who is morally at fault. But forward-looking beneficent concern does not have this kind of focus. It is not directed exclusively toward the individual agent who has done something morally wrong, but takes account of anyone else who is susceptible to being influenced by our responses—thus moral sanctions are not meant to deter only the agent at fault from future wrongdoing, but to serve as an example that will deter other agents as well, on the economy of threats approach. Even to the extent that beneficent concern is focused on the individual wrongdoer, it looks (as it were) in the wrong direction, aiming to improve the agent in the future rather than to respond directly to the past deed. This aspect of the economy of threats approach makes it notoriously vulnerable to the complaint that it cannot draw the right kind of line between those who are responsible and those who are not, since forward-looking beneficent concerns might in some circumstances give us reason to sanction people we know to be innocent of past wrongdoing. But the present objection is different, and more fundamental. Even if beneficent concern led us to sanction only people who are blameworthy in fact, the attitude expressed by such sanctions is not the attitude expressed by our actual moral responses to wrongdoing. To this extent the economy of threats account fails to explain the quality and force of moral blame.

The first two problems I have identified are vividly brought to light when one considers what is involved in the reflexive case, in which we hold ourselves responsible. Having done something I believe to have been wrong, I may blame myself for my action, but to blame myself in this way is not necessarily to *express* my blame at all, to myself or anyone else; still less does it mean I necessarily engage in sanctioning behavior toward myself—hair shirts need not be deployed. Furthermore, when I do express my blame (acknowledging my guilt to the person I have wronged, say), what I am expressing needs to be understood in terms of the prior attitude of self-directed blame, which cannot be treated simply as a refinement of beneficent concern. In neglecting this point, the economy of threats account of the reflexive case has an almost comically external aspect. Holding oneself responsible is treated as an attempt to raise in oneself motives or emotions, such as guilt and remorse, that will decrease the likelihood that one will perform actions of the sort one blames oneself for in the future.[9] Now, it is important to acknowledge that people are characteristically subject to these sorts of emotions when they blame themselves for something they have done. But even if we suppose that guilt and remorse have the self-deterrent effect that the account attributes to them, we cannot explain

9. See Schlick, *Problems of Ethics*, p. 156: "To blame oneself means just to apply motives of improvement to oneself, which is usually the task of the educator." Compare Dennett, *Elbow Room*, pp. 166–167.

how people come to have those emotions in terms of their deterrent effects alone. One has those motives and emotions just because one blames oneself, or holds oneself responsible for something one has done; if one's sole interest were the forward-looking concern to influence one's future behavior, it seems very unlikely that one would succeed in raising the motives or emotions that are characteristic of this reflexive stance.

A third and final difficulty for the economy of threats strategy is that it seems unable to explain the persistence of incompatibilist elements in our thinking about moral responsibility. There is a fairly deep temptation to suppose that moral responsibility requires freedom of will in the strong sense (the sort of freedom, that is, that would be defeated by determinism). Students, for instance, are quite easily led to the conclusion that it would not be justifiable to hold people morally responsible for what they do if determinism were true—this is surely part of what makes freedom of the will an especially gripping philosophical problem for many people. The seductiveness of incompatibilism, as one might refer to this phenomenon, may well have its basis in conceptual confusion, but if so, the confusions in question lie fairly deep in our thinking about moral responsibility, and it is important that an account of what we are doing when we hold people responsible should be able to explain how these confusions might have arisen. On this point the economy of threats strategy seems deficient. If, as it maintains, holding people responsible is a disposition to blame and sanction them in ways that will influence their behavior, it is very hard to see why there should be any deep or persistent temptation to think about moral responsibility in incompatibilist terms. It is *obvious* that the effectiveness of blame and moral sanction, as part of an economy of threats, in no way depends on the supposition that people have freedom of the will in the strong sense. This is precisely what has led compatibilists to embrace the economy of threats approach to responsibility, despite its deficiencies— it is the compatibilist strategy par excellence. But in making deterministic worlds so obviously safe for responsibility, the strategy deprives itself of the resources for explaining the attraction of alternative, incompatibilist views. One might say that the economy of threats approach renders compatibilism *so* plausible that it cannot be correct as an account of what we are actually doing when we hold people morally responsible.

A sophisticated utilitarian might respond to these arguments by granting that the attitudinal aspect of blame cannot be explained simply as a refinement of generalized beneficence. Conceding this point, it could still be maintained that there are good utilitarian reasons for our continuing to hold people responsible, reasons that might lead us (for example) to educate our children in ways that encourage their natural tendency to adopt this stance. It is surely plausible to suppose that our susceptibility to moral blame, and to the forms of sanctioning behavior that express this attitude, does contribute usefully to the economy of threats, helping to deter people from undesirable actions. To take this line, however, would be to abandon the goal of explaining what we are doing when we hold people morally responsible. Instead of trying to account for that stance, the utilitarian would retreat to the position of taking the stance to be part of the natural repertoire of human responses (at least within certain cultural formations), arguing that it is simply a stance that we should welcome and try to encourage, from the standpoint of utilitarian assessment, because of its beneficial consequences. This means that if we wish to understand the stance of holding people responsible—what are the direct aims of moral blame and moral sanction, how they go beyond mere description of what an agent has done, and what holds these responses together as a class—we will have to look elsewhere.

But where else are we to look? Part of the appeal of the economy of threats approach is that the alternatives to it have been thought to be freighted with metaphysical or moral presuppositions that are objectionable on their surface. It has been suggested, for example, that our ordinary practices of blame and moral sanction are metaphysically loaded, insofar as they commit us directly to the belief that those who are blamed or sanctioned have strong freedom of will.[10] Morally, blame and sanction can easily seem to be part of a primitive retributivist streak in human nature, reflecting the cruel and discredited thought that it would be an intrinsically good thing if those who have done wrong should suffer harm.[11] But if our ordinary practices are taken to have these objectionable metaphysical and moral commitments, perhaps our primary philosophical task with respect to them is not to account for those practices as they are, but rather to work out an acceptable replacement for them. In this spirit, the economy of threats account might be recommended as describing an alternative to our existing

10. See Smart, "Freewill, Praise, and Blame," pp. 303–306; compare A. J. Ayer, "Free-will and Rationality," in van Straaten, ed., *Philosophical Subjects*, pp. 1–13, at pp. 11–13.

11. Thus Schlick suggests that the only alternative to the economy of threats approach would be to endorse a retributivist account of punishment: see *Problems of Ethics*, p. 152.

practice of holding people responsible, one that subserves the still-useful functions of that practice without its objectionable metaphysical and moral baggage.[12]

But this line of thought tendentiously begs the question of what we are doing in holding people morally responsible. Metaphysically, it might turn out that our practice of moral responsibility commits us to seeing people as free in the strong sense—after all, this is what is at issue in the debate between compatibilists and incompatibilists, and it would be premature to presume to decide that debate before it has even been entered into. It would prejudge the debate in a different way, however, if one built into the stance of holding people responsible the belief that the targets of that stance have strong freedom of will. To do so would overintellectualize our practices, making incompatibilism virtually an analytic consequence of what we are doing when we hold people morally responsible, whereas we actually tend to adopt this stance without entertaining any clear ideas about whether those at whom the stance is directed have strong freedom of will. (We typically think of those we hold responsible as being free, while having only a vague conception of how this freedom is to be understood.) Morally, too, I think we should be careful not to take for granted an overtly retributivist understanding of what we are doing when we hold people responsible.[13] It certainly seems that I could blame someone for a wrong, and even engage in sanctioning behavior toward that person (avoidance and censure, say), without believing it to be an intrinsically good thing that the person should suffer harm. While our practice of holding people responsible may tolerate a retributivist interpretation, it would be a mistake to suppose that such an interpretation is necessarily imbedded in the self-understanding of ordinary participants in the practice.[14]

Even if we succeed in avoiding this last mistake, however, there

---

12. This is how Smart sees the matter, in "Freewill, Praise, and Blame"; he recommends that we give up our metaphysically loaded notions of praise and blame in favor of assessments that "grade" people for their moral qualities without presuming to "judge" them, noting that such grading assessments could continue to contribute to the economy of threats.

13. For purposes of discussion I shall construe retributivism rather narrowly, as the view that it is intrinsically good that wrongdoers should suffer harm, and that we therefore have a positive moral obligation to inflict such harms on them.

14. It seems to me that Ulrich Pothast commits this mistake; he builds into his account of the stance of holding people responsible not only the responses of blame and sanction, but also (more strikingly) the belief that people held to blame have "personally earned" the harmful consequences that may redound to them as a result of their wrongdoing: see his *Die Unzulänglichkeit der Freiheitsbeweise: Zu einigen Lehrstücken aus der neueren Geschichte von Philosophie und Recht* (Frankfurt am Main: Suhrkamp Verlag, 1987), pp. 26, 375–379. Perhaps we think it fitting or just that those

remain subtler and more troubling grounds for moral concern about the practice of holding people responsible. The hallmarks of the practice, I have suggested, are the responses of blame and moral sanction; these are the forms of "deep" assessment that people are open to, insofar as we view them as morally responsible. It is striking, though, that the responses of blame and sanction are negative and punitive in character. Of course, there are positive responses to which holding people responsible occasionally disposes us as well: we praise people, for instance, who are outstandingly good and virtuous. But praise does not seem to have the central, defining role that blame and moral sanction occupy in our practice of assigning moral responsibility.[15] Given the punitive and potentially harmful aspect of these responses, the suspicion arises that there is something intrinsically cruel about the practice of holding people responsible that makes it morally suspect. Even if a retributivist interpretation is not built into the self-understanding of participants in the practice, such an interpretation could be the best way to make sense of the strikingly negative responses characteristic of the practice, so that we are driven, on reflection, to see blame and moral sanction as the expression of cruelty and blind vengeance. In that case it might seem morally desirable to replace the existing practice with a less cruel and vengeful alternative, such as the alternative that the economy of threats account describes.[16]

This seems to me a real danger. To avoid it, we will need an account of the stance of holding people responsible that satisfies a further constraint. Not only should such an account explain the point and unity of the blaming and sanctioning responses distinctive of holding people responsible; the account provided should also yield a way of understanding these responses that does not make them out to be merely cruel or vengeful. Of course, it is possible that this constraint cannot be

---

who have acted wrongly should be subject to blame and moral sanctions (considered as such); but this is not to say that it would be intrinsically good for wrongdoers to suffer harm, and still less that they have "personally" earned such harms (whatever that may mean).

15. This is not to rule out the very possibility of a system of social reactions organized primarily around the positive responses of praise and reward rather than blame and sanction; such a system might even be superior to our present practice, in some respects. Before we can address such questions, however, we need to understand our existing practice, and the hallmarks of that practice are the negative responses of blame and sanction.

16. Compare Annette C. Baier, "Moralism and Cruelty: Hume and Kant," *Ethics* 103 (1993), pp. 436–457. Baier develops the cruelty objection by way of a critique of Kant's morality of guilt, but her objection, if sound, should apply equally to what I have been calling the practice of moral responsibility. (Baier's own preferred alternative is not specifically the economy of threats interpretation of responsibility, but a kind of shame morality, which she finds in Hume.)

satisfied, because our practice of holding people morally responsible *is* essentially cruel and vengeful. We would then rightly be tempted to conclude: so much the worse for moral responsibility. Before this pessimistic conclusion is endorsed, however, one should take the time to look at what we are doing when we hold people responsible, to see whether the practice admits of a different and more charitable interpretation.

3.2   Responsibility and the Reactive Emotions

In the preceding chapter I argued that the reactive emotions of resentment, guilt, and indignation should be understood in terms of the quasi-evaluative stance of holding people to expectations. I now want to suggest that this stance provides the key to understanding what we are doing when we hold people morally responsible.

Holding someone to an expectation has been characterized in terms of the reactive emotions: to hold someone to an expectation is to be susceptible to the reactive emotions, or to believe that it would be appropriate for one to feel the reactive emotions, in the case that the expectation is violated. Now it would seem that when we hold people morally responsible we are similarly susceptible to the reactive emotions, if those held responsible breach our expectations, and that we believe it would be appropriate for us to feel the reactive emotions in those cases. This suggests that moral responsibility might be analyzed in terms of the quasi-evaluative stance of holding people to expectations. To hold a person responsible, we might suppose, is simply to hold the person to expectations in the way that is connected with the reactive emotions.

This is a promising suggestion. The reactive emotions of indignation, resentment, and guilt seem to be natural candidates for the attitudinal component of moral blame, and with this component in place, one could understand the various moral sanctions to be unified by their common function of expressing the reactive emotions. But as formulated so far, this account cannot be correct, for two reasons. First, when we hold people morally responsible, we are interested in whether their behavior does or does not comply with distinctively moral requirements. But it is possible to hold people to expectations that are not supported by specially moral justifications; in these cases, then, the stance of holding someone to an expectation would seem to range more widely than the stance of holding someone morally responsible. A second and more important possibility of divergence between the two stances is presented by cases of irrational guilt and resentment. As explained in Chapter 2, such cases should be understood as cases where one holds oneself or others to expectations that one does not fully accept, for purposes of practical deliberation and normative discussion. But if we do not accept a given set of expectations, I do not think that we would hold ourselves or others morally responsible for the failure to comply with them. A person who feels irrational guilt, for instance about the violation of a parental prohibition on going to the movies, is not apt to blame herself for the action that prompts the guilt, but to view the guilt as a symptom to be treated and cured. Moral responsibility seems to be tied to distinctively moral expectations, which are supported by reasons that we ourselves accept as a basis for practical deliberation and normative criticism and discussion.

This suggests the following revision of the initial account: to hold someone morally responsible is to hold the person to moral expectations that one accepts. The set of moral expectations that one both accepts and holds people to is basically the class of what I earlier called *moral obligations*. Restricting the set of expectations to moral obligations that the agent accepts focuses the analysis correctly on the range of cases in which moral responsibility would seem to come into play. To see this, recall that the notion of an expectation, as introduced in Chapter 2, was meant to capture the idea of a *prohibition* or *requirement*. Hence the moral obligations that one accepts, and that one holds oneself and others to, mark out a class of distinctively moral prohibitions or requirements. This class of moral prohibitions and requirements that one both accepts and holds people to constitutes a special sphere within our ethical concepts. It is the sphere of moral rightness or wrongness—a sphere that is narrower than the sphere of morality as a whole, but broader than the sphere of justice and injustice. The sphere is narrower than the sphere of morality as a whole, because there are moral considerations that confer value on actions and character traits without being strictly matters of moral obligation, right, or wrong. For instance, a person who is superlatively beneficent will act in ways that go beyond our moral expectations but that are still morally valuable; this is the sphere of the supererogatory. At the same time, the sphere of moral right and wrong encompasses more than considerations of justice and injustice alone, since there are things that it would be morally wrong to do, such as causing others unnecessary suffering, that may not strictly violate requirements of justice. The term "obligation," as I have introduced it, captures the set of moral requirements of right that an agent accepts.[17]

The account I am developing thus situates our practice of holding people morally responsible within a distinctive nexus of moral concepts, namely those of moral obligation, moral right, and moral wrong. This seems to be the context in which moral responsibility properly belongs, for judgments of responsibility, with their characteristic connection to moral blame and moral sanction, would appear to come into play primarily in cases where people have violated the moral obligations we hold them to. The special connection between moral obligation and moral responsibility and blame has been remarked by G. E. M. Anscombe and Bernard Williams, both of whom trace the strict notion of moral obligation to theological ideas that no longer have a secure place within contemporary moral life.[18] Anscombe contends that the notion of moral obligation is only intelligible within the context of a divine law conception of ethics, which we do not now accept, and Williams suggests that the notion of obligation is the central normative concept of "the morality system," which he takes to be a simplifying and aggressive interpretation of our ethical ideas under pressure of recognizably Christian concerns.

But even if Anscombe and Williams are correct in thinking that the notion of moral obligation was originally part of a distinctively theological conception of ethics, it does not follow that it is only intelligible within the context of religious ideas. Whether it is or is not depends on whether we can find an interpretation of moral obligation, right, and wrong—and, I should add, the associated ideas of moral responsibility, blame, and sanction—that relates them to a secular understanding of human nature and practical reason (a project begun, though hardly completed, by the moral philosophers of the modern period, from Hobbes through Kant). So the genealogical association of moral responsibility with theological assumptions does not necessarily call into ques-

17. In using "obligation" to refer to all the requirements of right, I depart from some other conventions that have been adopted. Rawls, for instance, restricts the term to requirements on individuals that derive from voluntary acts whereby those individuals benefit from a just institution or practice; see John Rawls, *A Theory of Justice* (Cambridge, Mass.: Harvard University Press, 1971), sec. 18. By contrast, "obligation" as I shall use it ranges over all the requirements of right on individuals, including what Rawls calls natural duties, as well as obligations in his sense.

18. G. E. M. Anscombe, "Modern Moral Philosophy," as reprinted in *Ethics, Religion and Politics*, vol. 3 of *The Collected Philosophical Papers of G. E. M. Anscombe* (Oxford: Basil Blackwell, 1981), pp. 26–42; Bernard Williams, *Ethics and the Limits of Philosophy* (Cambridge, Mass.: Harvard University Press, 1985), especially chap. 10.

tion the modern practice of moral responsibility. If the genealogical proposal is correct, however, it implies that the members of societies that never had the relevant theological ideas could not, strictly speaking, be said to hold each other morally responsible. This seems peculiar, since it is natural to think of such people (the Athenian contemporaries of Plato and Aristotle, for example) as having had available to them the responses of blame and moral sanction.[19] What are we to make of this thought?

The genealogical suggestion seems to me to go together with the idea, broached in the preceding chapter, that there might be shame cultures whose members do not have the reactive emotions in their repertoire. The moral reactive emotions will only be available where the moral notions of obligation, right, and wrong are in place, and if Anscombe and Williams are correct, those ideas are historically and culturally local, linked to theological outlooks that are far from universal. But to suppose that there are cultures without the reactive emotions is not to suppose that the members of those cultures are altogether lacking in moral emotions. On the contrary, the idea of cultures without the reactive emotions seems plausible only on the assumption that other moral emotions are available in such cultures, such as shame and anger, and that these emotions are capable of providing internal sanctions sufficient to motivate general compliance with a system of ethical norms. But if the members of a shame culture are susceptible to motivating emotions of this sort, we can understand how something analogous to our practice of moral responsibility might emerge in such a culture. The analogous practice, like ours, would involve the responses of blame and moral sanction, but these responses would be understood in terms of the different moral emotions that facilitate social cooperation within the shame culture: blame would involve the emotions of shame and anger, rather than the reactive emotions of resentment, indignation, and guilt, and moral sanctions would serve to express these nonreactive emotions.[20] This approach postulates a generic stance of holding people morally responsible that is defined in terms of what-

19. Aristotle's famous discussion of the voluntary, for instance, seems to presuppose a form of moral assessment that is "deep," in that it goes beyond mere evaluative description of what an agent has done; see *The Nicomachean Ethics,* bk. 3, chaps. 1 and 5.

20. Bernard Williams has defended the idea that the ancient Greeks had a sophisticated conception of moral responsibility—analogous to distinctively modern conceptions, and in many ways superior to such conceptions—even without such reactive emotions as guilt; see his *Shame and Necessity* (Berkeley: University of California Press, 1993), especially chap. 3.

ever moral sentiments prevail within a given culture, and so is available even where the theological ideas identified by Anscombe and Williams may not have left their traces. *Our* practice of holding people morally responsible, centered as it is around the notions of moral obligation, right, and wrong, would then be distinguished by its connection to a specific subset of moral sentiments, namely the reactive emotions of resentment, indignation, and guilt.[21] In this way, we preserve the privileged connection between our practice of holding people responsible and the notions of obligation, right, and wrong, while allowing that cultures without these moral ideas could have analogous patterns of response to moral offenses.

What is immediately striking about this approach is the role it ascribes to the moral emotions. The approach says that we hold people morally responsible for complying with moral obligations only if we *hold them to* those obligations. Since holding people to an expectation is in turn understood in terms of its connection with the reactive emotions, the strategy essentially links moral responsibility to the moral reactive emotions. Specifically, one may say that the basic stance of holding someone morally responsible involves a susceptibility to the reactive emotions if the person breaches moral obligations that we accept, or the belief that it would be appropriate for us to feel those emotions if the person should violate those obligations.[22] Because of the central role this account ascribes to the reactive emotions, I will refer to it as the reactive account of moral responsibility.

By connecting moral responsibility to the reactive emotions in this way, the reactive account promises to improve on the economy of threats approach criticized in the preceding section. It treats the stance of holding people responsible essentially in terms of attitudinal conditions, and so avoids the behavioristic danger of associating responsibility

21. I should emphasize that I have not taken a stand on the genealogical hypotheses of Anscombe and Williams, or on the related idea that there are shame cultures that lack the reactive emotions of resentment, indignation, and guilt. My aim has rather been to explore the implications of these proposals for the account of moral responsibility I have been developing. If the proposals should turn out to be incorrect, then what I have called the "generic" stance of holding people morally responsible would include only the familiar modern form of responsibility connected with the reactive emotions.

22. Of course, *which* reactive emotions would be appropriate depends on who has violated the obligations, and how the act that violates the obligations is related to the subject of the emotions. Guilt is appropriate to one's own violations, indignation to violations by others, and resentment to others' failure to comply with moral obligations in their relations with oneself. I shall henceforth take these qualifications as understood when I refer either to the susceptibility to reactive emotions or to the belief that those emotions would be appropriate.

too exclusively with moral sanctions. To hold myself responsible for a moral wrong, for example, it is sufficient that I should feel guilt about my violation of a moral obligation that I accept, or at least believe that that violation would make it fitting for me to feel guilt; these conditions could of course be satisfied without my expressing my guilt to myself or anyone else, and certainly without my sanctioning myself. Furthermore, the reactive emotions seem to have the right kind of content to capture the attitudinal dimension of moral blame. On the account of them I have offered, resentment, indignation, and guilt are backward-looking emotions, responses to the actions of a particular agent (or agents); they are essentially *about* such actions, in a way that exactly captures the backward-looking focus of moral blame. In addition, the actions to which the reactive emotions are responses are violations of expectations we accept, and this correctly connects blame with the moral notions of obligation, right, and wrong.

Once blame is understood in terms of the reactive emotions, however, we also have a natural and appealing explanation to hand of what unifies the sanctioning responses to which the stance of holding people responsible disposes us (such as avoidance, censure, denunciation, reproach, and scolding). These can all plausibly be understood as forms of behavior that serve to express the reactive emotions to which we are subject when we blame people for their moral failings. Finally, in contrast to the economy of threats approach, the reactive account appears to make some allowance for the seductiveness of incompatibilism; at any rate, it is not obvious that the reactive emotions, and the sanctioning behavior that expresses those emotions, do not in some way require that their targets should have strong freedom of will.

For all of these reasons, the reactive account seems a promising interpretation of the stance of holding people morally responsible. But does it satisfy the further constraint I introduced at the end of section 3.1? Does the account yield a way of understanding the practice of holding people responsible as something other than an expression of cruelty and vengeance? It is difficult to answer this question without knowing what cruelty and vengeance consist in, and I do not have a general account of these things to offer; but to start with, it should be noted that not all actions that aim to inflict harm are necessarily cruel— if, for example, I deliberately harm someone who has attacked me, as a strategy of self-defense, what I have done is not cruel. What matters is the goal that the infliction of harm is designed to achieve. Thus we might take as a paradigm of cruelty behavior that aims to inflict suffering (physical or psychic) as a way of subordinating the sufferer to one's will.[23] The worry will then be that the blame and sanctioning responses characteristic of holding people responsible are responses that of their nature approximate to this paradigm, so that they are *essentially* cruel and vengeful.

No doubt many things have been done in the name of blame and moral sanction that are cruel and vengeful in this way—the history of punishment in the law provides a host of familiar and sobering examples.[24] But the issue is whether approximation to the paradigm of cruelty is essential to the practice of holding people responsible, and the reactive account suggests that it is not. Granted, blame and moral sanction often cause suffering for the person at whom they are directed. But it need not be the case that they aim to cause suffering, as part of a strategy of subordinating the sufferer to one's will. What is essential to the harmful moral sanctions, on the reactive account, is their function of expressing the emotions of resentment, indignation, and guilt; this is the real point of such responses as avoidance, denunciation, reproach, censure, and the like, and what holds them together as a class. Sanctioning behavior belongs to the syndrome of responses to which the reactive emotions dispose those who are subject to them, because the connection with reactive emotions is part of the conventional meaning of such behavior.[25] We learn the concepts of indignation, resentment, and guilt in part by learning to see their connection to sanctioning behavior, and the adequate expression of those emotions often requires such behavior. Insofar as it plays this expressive role, however, sanctioning behavior would not seem to be essentially cruel or vengeful, for the expressive role does not require the deliberate infliction of suffering as a means to the domination of another; it is one thing to inflict harm with the aim of subordinating a person to one's will, and quite another to inflict

23. Compare Judith N. Shklar's definition of cruelty, in *Ordinary Vices* (Cambridge, Mass.: Harvard University Press, 1984), p. 8: "the willful inflicting of physical pain *on a weaker being* in order to cause anguish and fear" (my italics). The mistaken restriction of cruelty to cases involving physical pain is corrected by Shklar on p. 37 of *Ordinary Vices,* where she acknowledges a species of moral cruelty that involves deliberate humiliation without physical pain. The references to the weakness and humiliation of the victim of cruelty capture the element of subordination and domination made central in my paradigm of cruelty.

24. Consider also Nietzsche's bad conscience and Freud's unconscious sense of guilt, discussed in Appendix 1. These are cases where guilt has a sado-masochistic aspect, being experienced as part of a strategy for inflicting torment on oneself.

25. Perhaps this is what P. F. Strawson means when he writes that a preparedness to acquiesce in the infliction of suffering is "all of a piece" with the reactive emotions; see "Freedom and Resentment," as reprinted in Watson, ed., *Free Will,* pp. 59–80, at p. 77.

harm with the aim of expressing a moral emotion to which one is subject.

Of course, if the emotions expressed by sanctioning behavior were themselves emotions of blind hatred or anger, involving a desire to inflict harm on their object as an end in itself, the expressive function of that behavior might not rescue it from the charge of cruelty. But the reactive emotions expressed by moral sanctions are not of this kind. Rather, they are focused emotional responses to the violation of moral obligations that we accept. In expressing these emotions, then, we are not just venting feelings of anger and hatred, in the service of an antecedent desire to inflict harm for its own sake; we are demonstrating our commitment to certain moral standards, as regulative of social life. Once this point is grasped, blame and moral sanction can be seen to have a positive, perhaps irreplaceable contribution to make to the constitution and maintenance of moral communities: by giving voice to the reactive emotions, these responses help to articulate, and thereby to affirm and deepen, our commitment to a set of common moral obligations.[26]

The reactive account thus reveals that holding people responsible need not be wedded to attitudes of cruelty and vengeance. But it continues to tie this stance to emotions that are negative and disapproving, and this raises different questions. For instance, it seems that we hold people morally responsible not only for actions that violate moral obligations we accept, but also for the morally worthy actions they perform. There is a difference between doing something that inadvertently helps another person and deliberately aiming to help another person, and part of the difference seems to be that in the latter case, but not the former, we credit the agent for the good deed in a way that implies responsibility for it. Can this positive conception of moral responsibility be captured within the framework of the reactive account?

To answer this question, it will be useful to articulate a hitherto

---

26. See Joel Feinberg, "The Expressive Function of Punishment," as reprinted in his *Doing and Deserving: Essays in the Theory of Responsibility* (Princeton, N.J.: Princeton University Press, 1970), pp. 95–118, for similar remarks about the different practice of punishment in the law. Of course, legal punishment incurs a higher justificatory burden than the stance of holding people morally responsible, since the harms to which it exposes people are far graver and more systematic—there is a great difference between imprisonment and reproach. Expressive considerations help us to understand the nature of punishment, and perhaps to rebut the suggestion that the institution of punishment is essentially cruel, but they do not by themselves suffice to *justify* hard treatment of criminal offenders.

implicit equivocation in the notion of holding a person to a moral obligation (which one accepts). That stance, as presented so far, would seem to admit of a dispositional and an occurrent interpretation. On the occurrent interpretation, to hold a person to a moral obligation is either to be subject to an episode of reactive emotion because the person has breached some moral obligation that we accept, or to believe that the violation would make it appropriate for one to be subject to such a reactive emotion. Obviously we cannot hope to understand responsibility for morally worthy acts in terms of this occurrent notion alone, because the person held responsible for a worthy action has not violated any moral obligation we accept, and is not believed to have done so. The occurrent reading yields an interpretation of holding a person responsible for some particular moral wrong; it tells us what it is to regard a person as having done something *blameworthy*.[27] But to regard someone as blameworthy for an action is miles away from the idea of responsibility for a morally worthy or admirable performance.

Consider, then, the dispositional reading of holding someone to an obligation. According to this construal, to hold a person to a moral obligation is to be *susceptible* to reactive emotions in the case that the person breaches the obligation, or to believe the person to be the *sort* of person whose violation of moral obligations would make it appropriate to be subject to a reactive emotion. This reading of the notion yields an interpretation not of regarding someone as blameworthy for a particular act, but of regarding someone as a morally *accountable* agent. To hold a person to moral obligations one accepts, in this dispositional sense, is to view the person as the sort of agent whose violation of moral obligations one accepts would render reactive emotions appropriate.[28] But clearly one can view people as morally accountable in this way— adopting toward them the dispositional stance of holding them to obligations one accepts—even on occasions when they have done things that satisfy or exceed our moral obligations. This suggests the

27. It is important to bear in mind that what is at issue is *moral* responsibility for a wrong. Of course I might hold someone *legally* responsible for an act without either being subject to resentment and indignation or thinking such emotions would be appropriate (by bringing charges against the person in court, for instance). This shows that we can hold people legally responsible without holding them morally responsible.

28. Note that holding someone accountable, on this interpretation, is always relative to some set of moral obligations. A given agent is not held accountable *simpliciter,* but with respect to a specified set of moral expectations one accepts. It is accordingly possible to hold a person only *selectively* accountable—accountable with respect to some obligations one accepts, but not others. This possibility will eventually become significant when I take up the topic of "exemptions" in Chapter 6.

following account of responsibility for morally worthy actions: to hold a person morally responsible for such an action is (1) to hold the person to moral obligations one accepts, in the dispositional sense, and so to view the person as a morally accountable agent; and (2) to believe the person has done something that meets or exceeds the moral obligations one accepts.

Proceeding in this way, one in effect treats asymmetrically the cases of responsibility for morally worthy and unworthy actions. When we hold a person responsible for an unworthy act, we are subject to a negative reactive emotion because we believe the person to have violated a moral obligation we accept, or we believe that such an emotion would be rendered appropriate by the violation. By contrast, in the case of responsibility for worthy acts, we do not suppose there to be any particular positive sentiment that we are or ought to be subject to. We suppose only that the agent held responsible has done something that meets or exceeds the moral obligations we accept, and that at the time of action she was the sort of person we hold to such obligations, in the way that is dispositionally connected with the negative reactive emotions. This asymmetry in the accounts of the negative and positive cases seems to me to mirror our practice of holding people morally responsible, with its special connection to the negative responses of blame and moral sanction. Holding a person responsible for an unworthy action, or regarding the person as blameworthy because of the action, goes beyond believing the person to have done something morally unworthy in that it is linked with a range of disapproving emotions that hang together as a class (as I argued in the previous chapter). To hold a person responsible for a worthy action, on the other hand, does not seem presumptively connected to any positive emotions in particular. Of course when people exceed our moral demands in ways that benefit us (for instance, by suffering great inconvenience to do us a good turn), we are often subject to feelings of gratitude.[29] But gratitude is not called for in all cases where actions exceed the moral obligations we accept: consider the category of supererogatory acts that do not benefit us in any way. More generally, we hold people responsible for morally worthy acts that do not *exceed* the moral obligations we accept, but that merely comply with those obligations—acts such as keeping promises, telling the truth, not harming others, and so forth. In these cases it is

---

29. It has been pointed out to me that gratitude is sometimes also appropriate in cases where no action that is morally exceptional has been performed—one might feel grateful toward a secretary who has served one dutifully for many years. What one feels grateful for, in a case of this sort, is loyalty or dependability or service over time (which might itself be exceptional).

especially clear that responsibility for worthy acts need not be connected with any distinctive sentiments.[30]

Even if this point about the morally worthy cases is granted, however, it might still be thought that the reactive account associates responsibility too closely with negative and potentially punitive emotions. Isn't it possible to hold people morally responsible without being subject to any malicious sentiments toward them when they violate the moral obligations we accept? Gandhi and King have been suggested as interesting cases in this connection, as persons who demanded conformity with important moral principles but forswore malicious or punitive responses toward those who had flouted such principles in the past.[31] Their example seems to tell against the claim that the stance of holding people responsible should be understood in terms of the susceptibility to such emotions as guilt, resentment, and indignation. As I have defined them, these emotions are negative attitudes, in that they are forms of disapproval and include a disposition to sanctioning behavior that serves (I have suggested) to express the emotions when they are felt. But Gandhi and King apparently avoided disapproval and the sanctioning behavior that expresses it, while continuing to hold their opponents accountable for the moral wrongs they committed. Can this be understood as a refinement of the stance of holding people morally responsible, consistent with the reactive account of it that I have proposed?

I think it can, if we see the attitude of Gandhi and King toward moral transgressors as one of forgiveness and love. To forgive someone, in the spirit of love, is a complicated stance. It presupposes that one views the person to be forgiven as having done something that would make resentment or indignation a fitting response—one cannot rightly forgive a person for having done something that would not have rendered one of these reactive emotions appropriate in the first place

---

30. I have tried to account for *moral* responsibility for dutiful actions. But there is another kind of "deep" responsibility that one may have for such actions, that which I referred to in sec. 3.1 as autonomy. Thus an agent might be responsible for dutiful actions not just in the sense of being a morally accountable agent who complies with moral obligations, but also in the sense that those actions disclose her own values and commitments (her acceptance of the obligations with which she complies, for instance). It may be that this notion of autonomy yields a more interesting conception of responsibility for positive performances than the notion of moral responsibility.

31. See Lawrence Stern, "Freedom, Blame, and Moral Community," *Journal of Philosophy* 71 (1974), pp. 72–84; also Gary Watson, "Responsibility and the Limits of Evil: Variations on a Strawsonian Theme," in Ferdinand Schoeman, ed., *Responsibility, Character, and the Emotions: New Essays in Moral Psychology* (Cambridge: Cambridge University Press, 1987), pp. 256–286, at pp. 285–286.

(as with the actions of an infant). Rather, in forgiving people we express our acknowledgment that they have done something that would warrant resentment and blame, but we *renounce* the responses that we thus acknowledge to be appropriate.[32] If this is correct, however, then forgiveness turns out to be a way of holding people morally responsible, according to the reactive account of responsibility. For on that account, it is sufficient for holding a person morally responsible that one believes that the person's violation of moral obligations would make it appropriate for one to be subject to the reactive emotions.

Ordinarily, forgiveness is a reaction to an acknowledgment of fault on the part of the person who is to be forgiven.[33] Where Gandhi and King seem to go well beyond ordinary responses, in the spirit of love, is in their adopting the stance of forgiveness *presumptively* toward people who have violated moral obligations, independently of whether those at fault have acknowledged wrongdoing. For my purposes here, however, the important point is that this attitude is compatible with their continuing to hold people morally responsible, insofar as it includes the belief that violations of moral obligations they accept would render the reactive emotions appropriate. Of course, it would be possible for a moral reformer to try to abandon even this belief—for all I have said, this may well have been the aspiration of the historical Gandhi and King, at least some of the time. On the reactive account, one would have to say about such reformers that they are no longer in the game of holding people morally responsible at all. But this does not seem an implausible line to take. On the contrary, without the belief that violations of moral obligations one accepts would at least render the reactive emotions appropriate, the reformer's stance toward other moral agents would no longer have any connection with the kinds of deep assessment that distinguish moral responsibility. This point will be explained and defended in the section that follows.

---

32. Renunciation is a complicated intentional stance: in renouncing the reactive emotions, we *deliberately* undertake to rid ourselves of those emotions, or refuse to behave in the ways that ordinarily express them, while recognizing that the conditions that would make the emotions appropriate are nevertheless present. For more detailed discussions of this double aspect of forgiveness, see Aurel Kolnai, "Forgiveness," as reprinted in *Ethics, Value, and Reality: Selected Papers of Aurel Kolnai* (Indianapolis: Hackett Publishing Co., 1978), pp. 211–224, and Jean Hampton, "Forgiveness, Resentment and Hatred," in Jeffrie G. Murphy and Jean Hampton, *Forgiveness and Mercy* (Cambridge: Cambridge University Press, 1988), pp. 35–87.

33. See Strawson, "Freedom and Resentment," p. 63, where this is built into the notion of forgiveness. Compare Jeffrie G. Murphy, "Forgiveness and Resentment," in Murphy and Hampton, *Forgiveness and Mercy*, pp. 14–34, especially pp. 24–29.

3.3   The Reactive Account and Moral Judgment

The reactive approach, as presented so far, is a recognizable development of the account of responsibility found in Strawson's "Freedom and Resentment." Strawson there writes: "Only by attending to this range of attitudes [the reactive attitudes] can we recover from the facts as we know them a sense of what we mean, i.e. of *all* we mean, when, speaking the language of morals, we speak of desert, responsibility, guilt, condemnation, and justice."[34] Picking up on this idea, Gary Watson has taken Strawson to be making the "radical claim" that the reactive attitudes "are *constitutive* of moral responsibility; to regard oneself or another as responsible just is the proneness to react to them in these kinds of ways under certain conditions."[35]

Construed along these lines, Strawson's own approach appears to have a markedly noncognitivist character. Holding people morally responsible is understood not in terms of beliefs about the people who are held morally responsible, but in terms of the emotions one feels toward them. This apparent noncognitivism of Strawson's approach can make it seem vulnerable to the defects of other forms of noncognitivism in ethics. For example, T. M. Scanlon has criticized the Strawsonian approach to responsibility for failing to get at what is essential to moral judgment.[36] Scanlon evidently detects an emotivist undercurrent in Strawson's discussion, a tendency to emphasize too exclusively the fact that our practices of responsibility, blame, and sanction serve to express our emotions. Scanlon agrees that expressing attitudes is one of the things we characteristically do in making moral judgments—as is attempting to influence other peoples' behavior, as part of an economy of threats. But he does not think that this expressive function is the *essential* feature of moral judgment (any more than the function of influencing others' behavior is), since it is quite possible to endorse a moral judgment without feeling or expressing any attitude in particular.

Now it may or may not be the case that Strawson's own account of moral responsibility goes along with a general emotivism about moral judgment; but this does not seem to be a fair complaint to bring against the version of the approach that I have sketched above. The reactive

---

34. Strawson, "Freedom and Resentment," p. 78.

35. Watson, "Responsibility and the Limits of Evil," p. 257.

36. T. M. Scanlon, "The Significance of Choice," in Sterling M. McMurrin, ed., *The Tanner Lectures on Human Values*, vol. 8 (Salt Lake City: University of Utah Press, 1988), pp. 149–216, at pp. 165–166, 169–170.

approach to responsibility I have offered is not committed to the emotivist view that all moral judgments are expressive of reactive emotions. It makes no claim whatsoever about the general meaning or force of moral judgments, but says, at most, that judgments of moral *blame* are to be understood as involving the expression of reactive attitudes. Furthermore, the claim that judgments of blame essentially involve the expression of emotions does not entail that such judgments are *exclusively* expressive; and so even with respect to this more narrow class of judgments, the reactive account should not be confused with emotivist or otherwise noncognitivist accounts. On the reactive account, holding people responsible involves a susceptibility to a range of reactive emotions, so that to blame a person is to be subject to one of these reactive emotions, because of what the person has done. The special force of *judgments* of moral blame can then be understood as consisting in the expression of these reactive attitudes.[37]

Far from being implausible, this more modest claim seems to me to capture an essential dimension of blame, which is neglected by other conventional interpretations of responsibility (such as the economy of threats strategy discussed in section 3.1). As I have explained, blame is a form of deep moral assessment that goes beyond mere evaluative description of what an agent has done. Furthermore, the way in which blame goes beyond mere description cannot be understood behavioristically; it includes an attitudinal aspect, where the attitudes in question have a distinctive content and focus. It is this attitudinal aspect of blame that is accounted for by the reactive emotions. Those emotions are essentially backward-looking, being responses to particular violations of moral obligation, and in this respect they capture exactly the attitude characteristic of blame. Thus, I think it would indeed be strange to suppose that one might blame another person without feeling an attitude of indignation or resentment toward the person, or that one might blame oneself without feeling guilt; attempts to communicate blame generally do function, at least in part, to give expression to such attitudes.

Even if it is granted, however, that judgments of blame are essentially (if not exclusively) expressive of reactive emotions, one might still be

---

37. Thus the account I have offered does not attempt to explain the "special force" of all moral judgments, but only, at most, of those judgments by means of which we blame people. Compare Scanlon, "The Significance of Choice," p. 169, where it is apparently assumed that an expressivist account of the special force of praise and blame would be part of an expressivist account of the special force of moral judgment generally.

in doubt as to whether responsibility can be understood more generally in terms of the susceptibility to such emotions. It is possible, after all, to think that someone has failed to meet the moral obligations we endorse, and to hold the person responsible for the failure—in the terms proposed above, to regard the person as having done something *blame-worthy*—without feeling any particular emotion toward the person. Doesn't this confirm Scanlon's more basic point that the susceptibility to emotions is not the essential feature in terms of which we are to understand responsibility? In considering this objection, it is important to recall what is involved in holding someone to an expectation. When I introduced this notion in Chapter 2, I explained it in terms of a disjunction: for an agent to hold someone to an expectation is for the agent to be susceptible to the reactive emotions in cases where that expectation is breached, *or* for the agent to believe that such emotions would be appropriate ones for him to feel in those cases, and for him to believe that they would then be appropriate because expectations have been breached. It is this second disjunct that now needs to be emphasized. According to the reactive approach, to hold someone morally responsible is to hold the person to moral obligations that one accepts. This notion of holding a person to a moral obligation is in turn understood by reference to a certain range of emotions; but it is not required that we actually feel the relevant emotion in all the cases in which it would be appropriate to do so. All that is required is that we believe that it would be appropriate for us to feel the emotion in those cases, and that what would make it appropriate is the fact that some moral obligation has been breached.[38]

For example, you may believe that an especially charming colleague who has cheated and lied to you has done something morally wrong, insofar as he has violated a moral obligation not to cheat or lie for personal advantage, and yet you may have trouble working up any resentment or indignation about his case. In a situation of this sort it would perhaps be strange to say that you blame the colleague for what he has done. But you might, all the same, continue to hold him morally responsible—to regard him as having done something blameworthy—and that is allowed by the reactive account as I have presented it.[39] On

38. Note that holding a person responsible does not involve the belief that the reactive emotions are *required* by the person's violation of moral obligations, or that one *ought* to be subject to them, but only the weaker belief that it would be *appropriate* or *warranted* for one to feel such emotions in response to the violation of those obligations.

39. Compare Scanlon, "The Significance of Choice," pp. 165–166, on believing a friend's action blameworthy without feeling moral indignation or disapprobation.

the reactive account, blame requires that you actually are subject to a reactive emotion, but an emotional response of this sort is not necessarily required for you to hold your colleague morally blameworthy. It suffices for you to believe that indignation or resentment would be fitting responses on your part, and that they would be fitting because the colleague has done something morally wrong. This seems to correspond to our ordinary judgments of moral responsibility quite exactly. Thus if you know that a moral obligation you accept has been breached, and there are no exonerating circumstances that you are aware of, and you *still* do not believe that the moral response of indignation or resentment would at least be appropriate on your part, then it seems doubtful that you really do hold the colleague morally responsible for his actions or regard him as having done something blameworthy in this case. Of course you might continue to treat the colleague *as if* he were morally responsible, and engage in sanctioning behavior (for educational or deterrent purposes, say); but for reasons sketched in section 3.1 this is not the same as actually holding the colleague morally responsible for what he has done.

In developing the reactive approach in this way, I am in effect exploiting the close connection between reactive emotions and expectations that I was at pains to emphasize in Chapter 2, for this connection is among the things that distinguish the account from cruder noncognitivist theories. Blame is construed essentially in terms of emotions, but the emotions in question are not arbitrary feelings of disapprobation and dislike; rather, they have propositional contents that are fixed by their connection to moral obligations that we accept. Moreover the nature of this connection with moral obligations is such that the reactive emotions are made appropriate by certain kinds of beliefs, about the violation of the moral obligations we hold people to. This connection is what gives the reactive emotions the backward-looking content and focus that is characteristic of the attitude of blame. But it also explains how we can continue to regard a person as having done something blameworthy even when we do not feel the emotions that would be appropriate responses to the person's behavior: namely, by persisting in the belief that such emotions would be warranted on our part, despite the fact that we happen not to feel them, and that they would be warranted in virtue of the fact that a moral obligation we accept has been violated. Because of this connection between reactive emotions and moral obligations, it seems misleading to refer to the reactive approach to responsibility, as I have developed it, as a distinctively noncognitivist strategy. The approach explicates moral responsibility in terms of our susceptibility to a range of emotions, but these emotions, in their turn, have an essential cognitive aspect that is given by their connection with moral obligations.[40]

This raises a question: if it is not really necessary to be subject to reactive emotions for one's stance to count as holding someone morally responsible, why bring in such emotions at all? Could we not understand moral responsibility just as well in terms (say) of the acceptance of moral obligations, and beliefs that such obligations have been violated? On such an account, we might say that to hold someone morally responsible is to be willing to blame the person for violating moral precepts that we ourselves accept for purposes of practical reasoning, deliberation, and public normative discussion, where blame, in turn, simply expresses the belief that those precepts have been breached. But I take it that an account along these lines would not capture what is distinctive about the stance of holding people morally responsible. Blame would be rendered superficial on this account, reduced to a way of describing what an agent has done, and perhaps registering a causal connection between the agent and the action so described. True moral blame, by contrast, is a form of deep assessment, reflecting an attitude toward the agent who has acted wrongly that finds its natural expression in sanctioning behavior (avoidance, denunciation, reproach, censure, and the like). The reactive emotions are needed to explain this attitudinal aspect of true moral blame, and to account for its natural connection with sanctioning behavior. And if the reactive emotions are needed to understand the phenomenon of moral blame, they will be equally necessary to make sense of blame*worthiness*. Thus one can hold a person blameworthy without actually being subject to an episode of reactive emotion; but, as I have argued, blameworthiness does require the belief that some reactive emotion would be appropriate. Without at least this degree of connection with the reactive emotions, we lose the idea that judgments of blameworthiness are forms of deep assessment, and with it the idea that they are ways of holding a person morally responsible.[41]

40. My remarks in this paragraph make clear the degree to which my understanding of the reactive attitudes differs from Bennett's. He writes of "the non-propositional nature of blaming, praising etc. in Strawson's account: feelings are made central, and are not tied systematically to any propositions about their objects" ("Accountability," p. 24). On my account, by contrast, the connection between reactive attitudes and obligations can only be understood if we suppose that those attitudes are systematically tied to propositions about their objects.

41. It follows from this that creatures to whom the reactive emotions were completely unfamiliar would not be capable of holding people morally responsible. This seems in line with ordinary thinking about responsibility. Thus, insofar as Mr. Spock (of *Star Trek* fame) was not susceptible

It is worth dwelling on this point a while longer, for a proper understanding of it is crucial if one is to appreciate the advantages of the reactive approach. How else might one try to explain moral responsibility for particular actions, and the related judgments of blame and blameworthiness? Scanlon has defended an alternative account that makes no special reference to reactive emotions.[42] He agrees that judgments of moral responsibility have a force that goes beyond "mere description" of people's actions, but he contends that this special force cannot be accounted for in terms of what the moral judge is doing in making the judgment (such as expressing a reactive emotion). Instead Scanlon makes the intriguing suggestion that the origin of the special force of judgments of responsibility should be located in the content of those judgments—in "what is claimed about the person judged."[43]

Scanlon explains the content of such judgments in terms of a contractualist moral theory. According to this theory, the basic moral obligations are derived from those principles that could not reasonably be rejected by people seeking unforced general agreement on a common set of principles. "What is essential," he argues, "is that a judgment of moral blame asserts that the way in which an agent decided what to do was not in accord with standards which that agent either accepts or should accept insofar as he or she is concerned to justify his or her actions to others on grounds that they could not reasonably reject. This is description, but given that most people care about the justifiability of their actions to others, it is not *mere* description."[44]

Taken literally, this passage suggests that judgments of blame differ from mere descriptions of an action in that they describe the action as lacking a property—namely, accord with principles that could not reasonably be rejected as a basis for contractualist agreement—that people generally want their actions to possess. But as I noted earlier, and as Scanlon himself agrees, this alone does not distinguish moral blame from many other kinds of description (for instance, descriptions of people as handsome or clever), and so it does not seem to capture what is special about moral responsibility. The further element, he

---

to human emotions, he was depicted as being not quite able to make sense of such human responses as blame, and as not subject to such responses himself. (The question of whether Mr. Spock was completely incapable of such responses is complicated by the fact that he was of partially human ancestry, so that reactive emotions were perhaps not as utterly alien to him as he himself often made out.)

42. Scanlon, "The Significance of Choice," lecture 1, sec. 6 (pp. 167–172).
43. Scanlon, "The Significance of Choice," p. 169.
44. Scanlon, "The Significance of Choice," p. 170.

suggests, is to be found in the connection of moral blame with reasons and justifications. To blame *s,* or to judge *s* morally responsible for what *s* has done, is at least potentially a way of requesting an explanation or justification from *s*.[45] Blame is thus set apart from other forms of unwelcome description by its suitability to serve in a system of public codeliberation; it "differs from mere unwelcome description because it calls for a particular kind of response, such as justification, explanation, and admission of fault."[46] This connection of blame with reasons and justifications points toward the distinctive conditions of responsibility: blame can only be an appropriate response when it is directed at features of a person—such as intentions, actions, or decisions (in contrast to, say, appearance or intelligence)—that are open to assessment in terms of reasons and justifications.

This complicated proposal can be broken down into a plausible claim about the conditions of responsibility and a more dubious suggestion about the special force of judgments of blame. The plausible claim is that blame is an appropriate response only when it is directed at features of a person that are open to assessment in terms of reasons. What is not plausible is the suggestion that the connection with this kind of assessment sets blame apart from other forms of unwelcome description, accounting for its special force. Note, for instance, that beliefs are like intentions in their being explicable by reference to reasons, and hence are appropriate targets of assessment in terms of reasons. Thus we criticize peoples' political and aesthetic and scientific opinions if they do not seem to us to be well justified. Being concerned with justification in terms of reasons, such criticism could in principle influence the reflections of the person whose opinions are being criticized; it is thus suited for interpersonal exchange in a way that sets it apart from unwelcome description of a person's appearance or native talents. But criticism of a person's opinions in terms of reasons is normally very different from moral blame for a person's actions and decisions. Indeed it is different precisely in that it lacks the distinctive force of judgments of moral blame and moral blameworthiness, the connection to attitudes that gives those judgments their special "depth."[47] It is one thing to

45. What follows is an interpretation of Scanlon's difficult remarks on pp. 170–172 of "The Significance of Choice."

46. Scanlon, "The Significance of Choice," p. 171; for the reference to codeliberation, see p. 167.

47. This is not to deny that there are differences in, say, the content and nature of moral and nonmoral justifications. But such differences do not alone account for the special force or opprobrium that seems to attach to moral criticism and blame.

criticize a philosopher's views about causation and quite another thing to blame the philosopher for supporting racist or sexist hiring practices; the difference seems to consist in the fact that moral blame has a quality of opprobrium that is lacking in criticism of beliefs or opinions. Hence we cannot hope to account for this special force solely in terms of the connection of moral blame and responsibility with justification.

There is, in any case, something peculiar in the very idea that we might account for the special force of moral blame in terms of its concern with justification. Doing so leads Scanlon to trace the special force to the *conditions* that make blame appropriate; in particular, he looks to the fact that moral blame is appropriately directed only at aspects of persons that are susceptible to being influenced by reasons. But if, as Scanlon seems to agree, judgments of moral blame and moral responsibility have a force that goes beyond "mere description," it is obscure how one could hope to explain this in terms of the conditions that make such judgments appropriate. To try to do so is to look in the wrong place for the *force* of judgments of blame and responsibility. The right place would seem to be not in the conditions that make moral blame appropriate, but in the condition of the judge who assigns blame and endorses judgments of responsibility.

A similar point may be made about the account of holding people responsible that Thomas Nagel has offered.[48] Like Scanlon, Nagel agrees that judgments of moral responsibility go beyond mere description of actions or the character of the agents who perform them. But he attempts to account for this further element not in terms of the susceptibility of actions to the influence of reasons, but by suggesting that we vicariously take up the standpoint of those whom we hold morally responsible. Thus when we hold a person responsible, "the result is not merely a description of his character, but a vicarious occupation of his point of view and evaluation of his action from within it."[49] On this account, ascriptions of moral responsibility are essentially projections of the first-person standpoint of agency onto the person who is held responsible. We try to occupy the perspective of the agent who is held responsible, and to assess that agent's decision and intention in light of the options that were available.

But this seems dubious when taken literally as an account of what it is to hold a person morally responsible. The fact is that we often blame

---

48. Thomas Nagel, *The View from Nowhere* (New York: Oxford University Press, 1986), pp. 120–124.

49. Nagel, *The View from Nowhere*, p. 121.

people for their actions without even *trying* to occupy vicariously their standpoint at the time that they performed the action for which they are held responsible. Indeed, the effort at vicarious occupation of the agent's standpoint often works to undermine blame and judgments of responsibility by prompting us to sympathize with the agent rather than to stand in judgment over her. Nagel has gone wrong, in my view, in confusing an interesting suggestion about the conditions of moral responsibility for an account of what we are doing in holding people responsible. The interesting idea is that it is only appropriate to hold a person responsible for a given action if it would be possible for us to occupy vicariously that person's standpoint, at the time that she performed the action. This is a plausible suggestion, because there is something strange about the idea that we might hold a creature responsible when we could not imagine what it would be like to occupy that creature's point of view (though more needs to be said about why this is so strange). But the idea loses its plausibility when it is made into an account of how judgments of responsibility go beyond description of actions and their agents.[50]

In contrast to Nagel and Scanlon, I have sought to explain moral responsibility in terms of the reactive emotions. To summarize the main ideas, I started with the suggestion that holding people responsible is a form of deep assessment that goes beyond mere description of what an agent has done, insofar as it involves a liability to the responses of blame and moral sanction. I further suggested that the way in which these responses go beyond mere description cannot be understood behavioristically, since the responses have an attitudinal dimension. The role played by the reactive emotions in my account is to capture this attitudinal dimension. The reactive emotions have the backward-looking focus characteristic of the attitude of blame, and their connection with moral expectations one accepts properly situates blame in the nexus of moral obligation, right, and wrong; at the same time, it is a conventional function of morally sanctioning behavior to express these reactive emotions, and in these terms one may account for the unity of

50. Nagel sees the problem of free will as an instance of the general tension between the subjective and objective perspectives on the world. Hence the basic problem arises in attempting to reconcile the first-person standpoint of agency with the detached conception of an agent as part of the objective world. Moral responsibility is considered problematic insofar as it involves the projection of the first-person standpoint onto the agent who is held responsible; see *The View from Nowhere*, chap. 7. The implausible account of moral responsibility that results seems to me to illustrate the strains that can emerge when one tries to fit all philosophical problems into a single, overarching framework.

the responses to which one is disposed when holding people responsible. My account does not, however, strictly require that one actually be subject to an episode of reactive emotion to hold someone responsible for a moral wrong. Though blame does involve an episode of reactive emotion, one can judge someone blameworthy for a moral wrong without feeling such an emotion, so long as one believes that the person's commission of a moral wrong would make a reactive emotion appropriate.

What becomes of the special force or depth of judgments of moral responsibility in such cases? One can say, I think, that judgments of blameworthiness go beyond mere description of the person who is held responsible, insofar as they express the judge's belief that the person has acted in a way that would warrant one of the reactive emotions. Their special force, on this reading, is really a special aspect of their content; in particular, it is traced to their *reflexive* content, their expression of the belief that it would be appropriate for the judge to be subject to a reactive emotion because of what the person held responsible has done. It is unclear how else one could account satisfactorily for judgments of moral blameworthiness if, like Scanlon, one both agrees that these judgments have a special force and denies that the force can be traced to something that the judge is necessarily doing in endorsing them.

4

Methodological Interlude

❧❧

My argument to this point has provided an interpretation of the reactive emotions and a story about what we are doing when we hold people morally responsible. What I am ultimately interested in, however, are the conditions of responsibility—what it is to *be* a morally responsible agent. How should one approach this question? How, more specifically, might the reactive account of holding people responsible help us to get clear about what the conditions of responsibility are?

Incompatibilists claim that freedom of the will in the strong sense— the kind of freedom that determinism would undermine—is a condition of responsibility. To fix terms for understanding this claim, recall the distinction sketched in the last chapter, between holding a person accountable and regarding a person as having done something blameworthy. In correspondence to this distinction, one can distinguish between two different conditions of responsibility. Accountability conditions (or "A-conditions," for short) are facts about a given agent that make that agent morally accountable, whereas blameworthiness conditions (or "B-conditions") render the agent responsible for some specific moral wrong.[1] In these terms, the incompatibilist can be seen as arguing that strong freedom of will is either an A-condition or a B-condition of responsibility (or perhaps that strong freedom is both an A-condition and a B-condition), while the compatibilist maintains that such freedom is required neither for accountability nor for blameworthiness.

Before this dispute can be resolved, it will help to step back and try to clarify what the dispute is about. In the following section of this chapter, section 4.1, I identify two ways of interpreting the debate about

---

1. Presumably an agent is only going to be blameworthy for a particular action if the agent is accountable in general. If this is right, then any A-condition could also be viewed as a B-condition. For my purposes, though, B-conditions may be construed as those conditions that must be present, *beyond* the A-conditions, to render a given agent blameworthy for a specific action.

responsibility that ought to be avoided, if possible. What I call meta-physical interpretations, on the one hand, postulate facts about respon-sibility that are completely prior to and independent of our practice of holding people responsible; but these interpretations seem unpromising, since it is hard to make sense of the idea of a prior and independent realm of facts about moral responsibility. Extreme pragmatist interpre-tations, on the other hand, abandon the idea that there is any fact of the matter about what it is to be responsible; but this calls into question the basic assumption that there is an issue about which the parties to the dispute might be either correct or incorrect. To make sense of the debate, we need an interpretation of the facts about responsibility that makes them dependent—in the right way—on our practice of holding people responsible. I propose such an interpretation in section 4.1, arguing that the debate should be seen as essentially a normative debate, about the conditions that render it appropriate to hold a person morally responsible.

But what normative standards might be appealed to, to decide when it is appropriate to adopt the stance of holding someone responsible? I suggest that the question should be seen as turning essentially on our *moral* norms. Incompatibilists typically contend that it would be unfair to hold people responsible if they lack strong freedom of the will, whereas compatibilists deny this; to settle the issue, it is necessary to take a step into normative moral theory, determining the content of the principles of fairness to which we are committed, to see what those principles imply about the fairness of holding people morally responsi-ble. I develop this idea in sections 4.2 through 4.4. Among other things, I try to show that two of Strawson's most influential arguments against incompatibilism prove misconceived, once the debate is understood in the normative terms that I propose; and I explore the possible applica-tion of alternative methods of substantive moral reflection to the debate. By the end of the chapter, with the normative interpretation securely in place, I will be in a position to draw on the account of holding people responsible defended in the preceding chapter, to determine what it is to be a morally responsible agent.

4.1   Understanding the Debate

This section is written in a spirit of gentle polemicism. I invite the reader to think about the question that divides compatibilists and in-compatibilists in a certain way, by sketching out a rough interpretation of that question. My hope is that the sketch here presented will have some immediate appeal, but the real test of the approach will have to await its development in the following sections and its application in subsequent chapters. Only then can it be judged whether the interpretation allows us to represent perspicuously the claims of the traditional parties to the debate, and to assess those claims in a way that is illuminating and fair.

To begin, note that we have available various and competing pictures of what it is to be a morally responsible agent. This can be illustrated by considering the apparent truism that moral responsibility involves a kind of control over one's action. One way of developing this idea would construe control essentially by reference to the range of alternatives with which agents are presented in particular situations. To be in control of one's actions, on this account, is to have the causal power to determine which of these various alternatives is realized, so that when responsible agents act, it is always true that they had alternatives available, that they could have done otherwise. Developing the idea of control in this way yields a picture of responsibility as consisting in a kind of freedom of choice. This picture in turn invites an incompatibilist understanding of responsibility, as requiring strong freedom of will, since determinism can plausibly be said to deprive us of the alternate possibilities in terms of which responsibility is essentially understood.[2]

But this is not the only way in which the idea of control might be pictured. We get a quite different result when we construe control not in terms of freedom of choice, but rather as a kind of normative competence or power. The sorts of competence that seem most relevant to responsibility include the power to grasp and apply moral reasons, and to regulate one's behavior by the light of such reasons. These are the sorts of abilities we take people to acquire in the course of moral education, and their possession is a salient characteristic of normal, morally responsible adults. To have control over one's actions, according to this picture, is to perform those actions intentionally, while possessing the relevant sorts of normative competence: the general ability to grasp moral requirements and to govern one's conduct by the light of them. But if the first picture I sketched seemed congenial to an incompatibilist conclusion, this second picture suggests that moral responsibility may be compatible with determinism. For determinism, though it might deprive us of genuine alternatives, would not neces-

2. Of course, the issues here are much more complicated than I can represent them as being in this brief sketch. A particularly controversial question is whether the availability of alternate possibilities really would require the falsity of determinism; I address this question briefly in Appendix 2.

sarily deprive us of the forms of normative competence that the second picture makes central to moral responsibility.[3]

These two pictures of moral responsibility thus suggest different answers to the question of whether responsibility is compatible with determinism. At the same time, they both appear to be appealing ways of understanding what it is to be a morally responsible agent; each of the two pictures can be refined into a philosophical account of moral responsibility that has some foothold in our prephilosophical convictions (in ordinary ideas about control, for instance).[4] To decide what are the conditions of responsibility, then, we will need to choose between these alternative pictures of responsibility, and perhaps to choose among others as well.[5] For to opt for a given account of the conditions of responsibility will in effect be to favor one picture of moral responsibility over the others that are available, and that also have some apparent appeal. How should we understand this choice?

A natural suggestion is that we should favor the picture that is true, or that captures the facts about what it is to be morally responsible. This seems plausible enough, as far as it goes, but we need to look more closely at how the facts in this area are to be conceived.[6] One possibility would be to interpret these facts as conceptually independent from our practice of holding people responsible. On this interpretation, which might be called the metaphysical interpretation of the question, we would suppose that there is a fact of the matter about responsibility "in itself," a fact about what it is to be *genuinely* or *really* responsible, and that this fact is prior to and independent of our practice of treating people as morally responsible agents. That practice would then be in good order to the extent it succeeds in tracking or meshing with the

3. Compare Susan Wolf's account of the "reason view," in *Freedom within Reason* (New York: Oxford University Press, 1990), chap. 4. Like the claims made about the first picture, my assertions about the compatibilist implications of the second conception obviously need further defense. I attempt to develop a compatibilist interpretation of this position in Chapters 5 through 7.

4. This is not to say that both pictures are necessarily fully coherent. For example, doubts have often been raised about the coherence of the first, incompatibilist account that I sketched, on the grounds that the alternate possibilities it takes to be genuine conditions of choice at the same time render such choices arbitrary, thereby defeating responsibility for what we do. See, for example, R. E. Hobart, "Free Will as Involving Determinism and Inconceivable without It," as reprinted in Bernard Berofsky, ed., *Free Will and Determinism* (New York: Harper and Row, 1966), pp. 63–95. For a more recent statement of the point, see Galen Strawson, *Freedom and Belief* (Oxford: Clarendon Press, 1986), chap. 2.

5. Another common picture is that of responsible agents as uncaused initiators of their actions, the complete sources of what they do.

6. In what follows, I generally speak of "facts" rather than "truths," though most of the points I make could be expressed equally with either term.

prior and independent facts about moral responsibility. As to the choice between competing pictures of responsibility, the metaphysical inter-pretation suggests that we should prefer the picture that provides the best articulation of the independent facts concerning responsibility, capturing what it is to be a genuinely responsible agent.

But the metaphysical interpretation strikes me as most unpromising. The trouble stems from the postulation of a prior and independent realm of "moral responsibility facts," to which our practice of holding people responsible should answer. It is not merely that this metaphysical assumption seems to lead inevitably to a kind of radical skepticism; for the sake of argument I am willing to grant that we might be system-atically and irremediably mistaken about what it is to be morally re-sponsible. My worry is more basic, if perhaps also less articulate. It is that I cannot see how to make sense of the idea of a prior and independent realm of moral responsiblity facts. As the preceding chapter made clear, the practice of holding people responsible is characterized by a highly structured set of emotions and actions, namely the reactive emotions and the blaming and sanctioning behavior that expresses them. But it seems incredible to suppose that there is a prior and independent realm of facts about responsibility to which such emotions and actions should have to answer. This is not to deny that we want our practice of holding people responsible to answer to the facts, including facts about what it is to be morally responsible (if there are such). It is rather to question whether we really have an application for the picture of a realm of moral responsibility facts, inhering in the fabric of the world completely independently of our activities and interests in holding people responsible. Admittedly I have not myself shown that this pic-ture could not have an application. I think the burden is on someone who wishes to interpret the issue in these metaphysical terms to defend and develop the supposition that there is a prior and independent realm of facts about responsibility—something I, for one, cannot see how to do.

An extreme response to this concern would be to give up entirely the idea that there are facts about what it is to be morally responsible. Proceeding in this way, we might suppose that neither of the competing pictures of responsibility is either correct or incorrect. Instead, each picture might be thought to capture a strand in our thinking about responsibility, where neither strand can be said to represent the fact of the matter about what it is to be morally responsible. But this approach has the unhappy consequence that both parties to the conventional dispute about responsibility must be mistaken, insofar as both assume that there is a correct answer to the question of whether responsibility requires strong freedom of the will. Abandoning this common assumption, it would still be open to us to choose between the competing pictures of responsibility; but any choice we made would be completely underdetermined by the facts, and so it would have to be grounded exclusively in our practical interests and desires.[7] This radical pragmatism, as we might call it, undermines the debate about responsibility just as effectively as the metaphysical interpretation. Whereas the latter is wedded to the dubious image of a prior and independent realm of facts about moral responsibility, the pragmatist alternative prevents the debate from ever getting off the ground, rejecting from the start the assumption that there is a real issue concerning which picture of responsibility is correct. We ought to embrace this pessimistic conclusion only as a last resort, after we have exhausted other attempts to make sense of the issue.

To see what alternatives might be available, I wish to return to the initial suggestion that there is a fact of the matter about what it is to be responsible, to try to develop the suggestion in a way that avoids the burdens of the metaphysical interpretation. The difficulty with that interpretation lies in the assumption that the facts about responsibility are completely prior to and independent of our practice of holding people responsible. So to avoid the pitfalls of the metaphysical interpretation, we must interpret the relevant facts as somehow dependent on our practices of holding people responsible. The problem is to find a way to do this that will allow us to represent the concerns of all parties to the traditional debate.

One possible interpretation would take the facts about responsibility to be fixed by our dispositions to hold people responsible in favorable circumstances, in accordance with the following biconditional:

(D) S is morally responsible (for action x) if and only if we are disposed, under favorable conditions,[8] to hold s morally responsible (for action x).

This dispositional schema (D) allows us to say that there are facts about moral responsibility, without postulating the complete independence of

---

7. For this way of proceeding, see Ted Honderich, *The Consequences of Determinism,* vol. 2 of *A Theory of Determinism* (Oxford: Clarendon Press, 1986), chaps. 1 and 2.

8. This clause makes room for the possibility of error in our judgments about responsibility. Of course, different ways of filling out the favorable conditions clause would yield widely divergent applications of the dispositional strategy, some of which might be more promising than others.

those facts from our practice of holding people responsible. It specifies truth-conditions for claims about moral responsibility in terms of our dispositions to hold people responsible, and in these terms, we can take the facts about moral responsibility to be fixed by the conditions that engage our dispositions to hold people morally responsible. Thus we see that a nonmetaphysical interpretation of the question need not be committed either to the noncognitivist position that claims about moral responsibility lack truth-conditions, or to the eliminativist position that there are no facts about moral responsibility. These theoretical virtues have led some philosophers to favor similarly dispositional accounts of such concepts as color and value.[9]

Whatever the prospects for dispositional accounts in these other areas, however, I do not think that schema (*D*) provides the best framework for approaching questions about the conditions of responsibility. The main reason for this is that it does not allow us to formulate perspicuously the incompatibilist position. To see this, note that if determinism is true, and incompatibilism correct, then nobody ever is or was morally responsible for what they do. And yet for all that, we might still be disposed to hold people morally responsible. One might put this by saying that the incompatibilist is making a *normative* claim—the claim, namely, that it would be *inappropriate* or *incorrect* to hold people responsible if determinism is true.[10] This is quite different from saying that we would be disposed not to hold people responsible if determinism is true.[11] The incompatibilist maintains that whatever might be the case concerning our dispositions to hold people morally responsible, determinism would make it inappropriate or incorrect to acquiesce in that

9. For differing assessments of the prospects of this approach in the case of value, see the contributions by Mark Johnston, David Lewis, and Michael Smith to the symposium on "Dispositional Theories of Value," *The Aristotelian Society* supp. vol. 63 (1989), pp. 89–174.

10. I use the term "normative" to signal a concern with reasons or justifications, even if explicit norms or rules are not immediately in the offing.

11. Of course, any dispositional approach will rely on normative notions to specify what I have referred to as the "favorable" conditions of response. Furthermore, it would be possible to specify these favorable conditions so that the resulting analysis would be normative in just the way required to capture what is at issue in the debate about responsibility. If, for instance, the dispositional analysis says that the favorable conditions are conditions of *ideal rationality*, then what the analysis is interested in is not really whether we are disposed to respond in a specified way in given circumstances, but whether it would be rational or appropriate to do so; see Michael Smith, "Dispositional Theories of Value," for this way of filling out a dispositional analysis of value. An analogous understanding of the favorable conditions clause in schema (*D*) might yield an interpretation of the debate about responsibility only notationally different from the one I will develop. My proposal remains more perspicuous, however, in bringing normative questions explicitly into the foreground.

practice, giving us a reason to refrain from holding people responsible that applies across the board.

This suggests a different way of making out the dependence of facts about responsibility on our practice of holding people responsible, which we might refer to as the normative interpretation. The normative interpretation offers the following schema for understanding the conditions that make a person responsible:

(N) S is morally responsible (for action x) if and only if it would be appropriate to hold s morally responsible (for action x).

Unlike (D), this schema construes the conditions of responsibility in explicitly normative terms. What makes something a condition of responsibility, according to (N), is not the fact that it would engage our dispositions to hold people responsible, but that it would make it appropriate to hold people responsible. At the same time, (N) borrows some of the virtues that have made dispositional approaches attractive in other areas of philosophy. It specifies truth-conditions for claims about moral responsibility, and it thereby enables us to avoid the noncognitivist position that such claims lack truth-conditions. It also suggests a way to avoid the eliminativist position that there are no facts of the matter about whether people are morally responsible for what they do: such facts can be interpreted as facts about whether it would be appropriate to hold people morally responsible.[12]

We have, then, a schema for understanding how there could be facts about moral responsibility that depend in some way on our practice of holding people responsible. If there are such facts, we can at least render intelligible the debate between compatibilists and incompatibilists, as a debate about a genuine issue. Parties to this debate favor different pictures of responsibility. Since there are facts about what it is to be responsible, we can make sense of the idea—presupposed by both parties—that the competing pictures are open to assessment as correct or incorrect (something we could not do according to the radical

---

12. Speaking more precisely, there are two kinds of facts about responsibility allowed for by this approach: (1) facts about the obtaining of the specific conditions—such as the kind of normative competence mentioned earlier, or strong freedom of will—that make it appropriate to hold a person responsible, and (2) the fact that conditions of this sort make it appropriate to hold a person responsible. Facts of the first type may not, strictly speaking, depend on our practice of holding people responsible, but the second fact does depend on that practice, insofar as it is specified essentially in terms of it. It is by reference to the second fact that the debate between compatibilists and incompatibilists is to be resolved.

pragmatist interpretation); but this is achieved without postulating a prior and independent realm of moral responsibility facts. Instead, the facts by reference to which the debate is to be decided are specified in terms of our practice of holding people responsible: they are facts about whether it would be appropriate to adopt toward people the stance of holding them responsible, if determinism is true.

So far, however, this is only an abstract outline of an approach to moral responsibility. According to schema (N), an agent will be responsible if it would be appropriate to hold that agent responsible. This suggests that deciding between the competing pictures of responsibility will require that we undertake a certain sort of normative inquiry. Specifically, we must investigate just what the conditions are that make it appropriate to hold people morally responsible, to try to discover whether those conditions include freedom of the will in the strong sense. This investigation, in turn, can only go forward if two prior questions are settled. First, we need to know what it is to hold someone morally responsible, what is involved in taking up this stance. Second, we need to specify the norms by reference to which the appropriateness of that stance is to be gauged. We already have an answer to the first of these questions in hand, as the reactive account defended in the preceding chapter tells us what it is to take up the stance of holding someone morally responsible. But we do not yet know how to proceed in assessing the appropriateness or correctness of that stance; that is the issue I now address.

The terms "appropriate" and "correct" are bland and noncommittal terms of generalized appraisal. To render the normative interpretation more determinate, it will be necessary to specify particular substantive norms by reference to which the question of the appropriateness of holding people responsible might be answered. Very roughly, one may distinguish between two broad classes of substantive norms: theoretical norms, which subserve our interests in the fidelity of our beliefs with facts or truths, and in the explanation of such facts and truths; and practical norms, which subserve our divers practical commitments (to moral justifiability, strategic effectiveness, or politeness, for instance). It seems clear that the kind of inquiry determined by the normative approach could not appeal solely to theoretical norms to determine the conditions that make it appropriate to hold people responsible. To do so would be to assess our practice of holding people responsible in terms of its fidelity to the facts about whether people are morally responsible. But on the normative approach, the facts about whether people are morally responsible are not yet available to be appealed to at this stage in the inquiry. Those facts are fixed by the answer to the question of when it is appropriate to hold people responsible, and so they cannot be invoked to decide that very question.[13]

According to the reactive account I have defended, to hold people responsible is essentially to adopt a stance in which one is susceptible to the reactive emotions when the obligations one accepts are breached, or one believes that the violation of those obligations would render the reactive emotions appropriate. This stance does not necessarily give rise to determinate forms of behavior—as we have seen, it is not merely a behavioral disposition; nevertheless the stance is naturally associated with certain kinds of behavior, namely those that serve to give expression to the reactive emotions. In particular, the stance involves a disposition to engage in a variety of sanctioning activities, whereby people who are held to blame are shunned, chastised, reproached, or scolded. But this behavioral side of the stance of holding people responsible opens the stance to assessment in light of our practical norms. I have already shown in the preceding chapter that this is the case, where I considered the complaint that the harmful consequences of the practice of holding people responsible render that practice essentially cruel. This complaint took the form of an appeal to norms prohibiting cruelty, criticizing the practice of holding people responsible in light of those norms; and though I rejected the details of the complaint, it illustrates how the behavioral dimension of the stance of holding people responsible makes it possible to bring practical norms to bear in assessing that stance.

But which practical norms might be at issue? Should we look to moral norms, or rather to norms of strategic effectiveness or even of etiquette? Though all of these practical norms might potentially be brought to bear, I believe the conventional debate between compatibilists and incompatibilists is centrally a debate about our *moral* norms and what they commit us to concerning the conditions of responsibility. Thus, though they are seldom self-conscious about the fact, incompati-

13. This is not to say that theoretical norms can have no bearing at all on the assessment of our practice of holding people morally responsible. Recall that on the reactive account defended in the preceding chapter, to hold someone responsible for a particular wrong is (in part) to believe that the person violated a moral obligation one accepts. Insofar as the stance incorporates this belief, one condition that can make it inappropriate to adopt the stance will be the falsity of the belief—the failure of the belief to conform with the facts about whether the agent held responsible really did violate a moral obligation one accepts. See sec. 5.2 for further discussion of this point.

bilists often appeal to our distinctively moral interest in *fairness,* suggesting that it would be unfair to hold people responsible if determinism is true.[14] For instance, many of us are tempted, in reflective moments, to think that it would somehow be unfair to treat people as morally responsible if they are deprived of alternate possibilities for action. A common incompatibilist strategy is to elaborate this thought, arguing that determinism would make it unfair ever to hold people morally responsible, because it would deprive us universally of alternate possibilities for action. But if this is the form that incompatibilist arguments take, then compatibilists need to mount a similarly moral kind of inquiry. Specifically, they need to show that our moral norms of fairness do not commit us to any condition of responsibility that would be universally defeated if determinism is true—that, for instance, it can be fair to hold people responsible even if they do not have alternate possibilities for action.

Of course, it would be possible to bring other practical norms to bear in assessing the stance of holding people responsible. Such norms might even support a verdict at odds with the conclusion that is grounded in moral considerations of fairness. For instance, it might turn out that there are good strategic reasons to hold responsible a class of people whom it would clearly be unfair to treat in that way—perhaps such treatment would materially advance our interests in security, or happiness, or the eventual attainment of a more egalitarian social world.[15] About such a case, we would surely not say that it is indeterminate whether the people in question are responsible agents, but that there are strategic reasons for treating as responsible a class of people who are not responsible in fact. This shows that moral norms of fairness have a privileged position in determining what it is to be a responsible agent: they set the standards of appropriateness in terms of which schema (N) is to be interpreted.[16] One must therefore focus on the issue of fairness,

14. Claims of this sort are often made, though seldom developed very far. For some of the more extended discussions of the point, see Jonathan Glover, *Responsibility* (London: Routledge and Kegan Paul, 1970), pp. 70–73; Morton White, *Foundations of Historical Knowledge* (New York: Harper and Row, 1965), chap. 7; and Morton White, *The Question of Free Will: A Holistic View* (Princeton, N.J.: Princeton University Press, 1993).

15. For an example of an argument along these lines—to the effect that there are strategic reasons to hold men responsible for their sexist behavior, even though their ignorance of its culpability might make such treatment unfair—see Cheshire Calhoun, "Responsibility and Reproach," *Ethics* 99 (1989), pp. 389–406. (Calhoun seems to agree that the ignorant men in question would not really be responsible for their sexist behavior, strictly speaking.)

16. Compare H. L. A. Hart's discussion of "moral liability responsibility," in "Postscript: Responsibility and Retribution," in his *Punishment and Responsibility: Essays in the Philosophy of Law* (Oxford: Clarendon Press, 1968), pp. 210–237, at pp. 225–227. Hart says that people are respon-

to see what are the conditions under which it would be fair to adopt toward people the stance of holding them responsible.

Some incompatibilists will perhaps resist this way of characterizing the debate. They will maintain that, though fairness is part of what is at stake in the debate about responsibility, it cannot be the whole story; distinct from the question of the fairness of our practice of holding people responsible, there is the further issue of whether it is true that people are morally responsible agents.[17] Moreover, this truth will only be secured if there actually obtains an objective fact in the world, prior to and independent of our practices, which our judgments of moral responsibility track and reflect: the fact, namely, that responsible agents have strong freedom of will. But nothing I have said so far rules out the possibility that responsibility requires strong freedom of will; nor have I denied that there is an objective fact of the matter, prior to and independent of our moral practices, about whether people have freedom of will in the strong sense. My concern in this section has been to understand a different class of facts, about moral responsibility. I have claimed that we make best sense of these facts by interpreting them nonmetaphysically, taking them to be bound up with our practice of holding people responsible. And we do this in a way that most sympathetically captures the traditional incompatibilist's concerns, I have suggested, by focusing on the question of whether determinism would render it unfair to hold people responsible for what they do. If incompatibilists wish to maintain that judgments of responsibility should track prior and independent facts about strong freedom of will, they will need to establish the normative significance of such facts by showing that it is only fair to hold people responsible when those facts obtain.

4.2 Strawson's Arguments

The discussion in the preceding section suggests that compatibilist and incompatibilist alike are engaged in a normative inquiry internal to our moral practices. By this I mean that they should both be seen as bringing distinctively moral norms of fairness to bear in assessment of our distinctively moral practice of holding people responsible. Interpreting the

---

sible, in the moral liability sense, just insofar as they *deserve* blame, suggesting the view that moral norms of fairness (construed as desert) will have a privileged connection with moral responsibility for what one does.

17. This reply was suggested to me by an anonymous reader of an early draft of this book, who pointed out that most philosophers attracted to incompatibilism are equally attracted to some version of realism.

debate in this way enables us to make sense of it as a debate about a genuine issue, while at the same time doing justice to the moral content of the intuitions that have traditionally been invoked by many participants in the debate. In this section I wish to refine this interpretation of the debate, by considering in light of it some of P. F. Strawson's influential arguments about freedom of the will.

Strawson's "Freedom and Resentment" contains the seeds for at least three different kinds of argument against incompatibilism. First, there are hints of what I have just called internal arguments, appealing to an account of what we are doing in holding people responsible to show that determinism would not make it morally inappropriate to treat people in that way. Specifically, Strawson suggests that the demands bound up with our reactive emotions are demands that others display toward us certain qualities of will, and he contends that determinism would have no bearing on the issue of whether or not such demands are satisfied. In addition to this internal argument, however, Strawson runs two quite different lines of defense against incompatibilist worries. One of these—I shall call it the naturalist argument—builds on the idea considered in section 2.2, that the reactive emotions are natural sentiments, given to us inevitably as conditions of our social life. A further, pragmatic argument (as I shall call it) turns on the claim that our lives would be immeasurably impoverished if we were to give up the reactive emotions. Strawson's own presentation conveys the impression that these two lines of argument effectively undermine the incompatibilist challenge independently of the success or failure of his internal arguments; his naturalist and pragmatic arguments have accordingly been taken by many to be Strawson's most important contributions to the debate about freedom of the will. I wish to challenge this conclusion, drawing on the normative interpretation I have offered to show that the naturalist and pragmatic arguments are not independently effective, and that a successful answer to incompatibilist worries must directly engage the issue of fairness.

Strawson's naturalist argument rests on an appeal to the inevitability of the reactive emotions. In a recent statement of the argument he writes: "We are naturally social beings; and given with our natural commitment to social existence is a natural commitment to [the] whole web or structure of human personal and moral attitudes, feelings, and judgments . . . Our natural disposition to such attitudes and judgments is naturally secured against arguments suggesting that they are in principle unwarranted or unjustified just as our natural disposition to belief in the existence of body is naturally secured against arguments suggesting that it is in principle uncertain."[18] The crucial premise of this argument is the claim that the reactive attitudes are inevitable, given that we are essentially social creatures; but considerations I adduced in Chapter 2 have already called this premise into question. There I showed that the reactive emotions are most plausibly construed as a distinctive subset of the emotions to which we are subject in virtue of our participation in interpersonal relations, and that when this point is grasped it is no longer obvious that the reactive emotions are simply inevitable for us. For my present purposes, however, this objection may be put to the side. I now want to suggest that even if it is true that a susceptibility to reactive emotions is inevitably given with human social life, this does not obviate a direct engagement with the incompatibilist's concerns about fairness.

To see this, it will be helpful to distinguish between two different ways in which an inquiry into the conditions of responsibility might be construed. In accordance with the normative interpretation presented earlier, such an inquiry investigates the conditions that make it appropriate to hold people morally responsible. One way to construe such an inquiry—call it the external interpretation—is as a search for conditions that would justify our adopting toward people the stance of holding them responsible in the first place. That is, we assume that the whole practice of holding people morally responsible is in the balance, and look for considerations that would give us a positive reason to buy into the practice. Furthermore, according to the external interpretation, we assume that a consideration would count as a reason for buying into the practice only if it could move someone to do so who is not already committed to holding people morally responsible; the reasons cited should in this way be external to the practice that is to be justified. Finally, if it should turn out that a positive justification that meets these constraints cannot be provided, then the conclusion to be drawn is that the practice of holding people morally responsible is unwarranted, irrational, or unreasonable, and that it should if possible be given up.

Strawson often seems to construe incompatibilism as an external, skeptical challenge to our whole practice of holding people morally responsible, roughly along these lines.[19] But if we interpret incompati-

---

18. P. F. Strawson, *Skepticism and Naturalism: Some Varieties* (New York: Columbia University Press, 1985), p. 39; compare his "Freedom and Resentment," as reprinted in Gary Watson, ed., *Free Will* (Oxford: Oxford University Press, 1982), pp. 59–80, at p. 68.

19. This is an impression conveyed particularly strongly by the presentation in Strawson's *Skepticism and Naturalism,* chap. 2. In "Freedom and Resentment," his position seems to me more complicated, containing the intimations of "internal" arguments to which I have adverted.

bilism as the possible result of such an external inquiry, then it becomes clear why Strawson might have thought that the naturalist argument is an independently effective answer to incompatibilist concerns. On this interpretation, both incompatibilists and compatibilists are searching for conditions that might provide us with a positive justification for accepting the whole practice of holding people morally responsible; the incompatibilist then claims that freedom of the will, in the strong sense, is the only condition that could provide such a positive justification, while the compatibilist seeks such a justification in conditions that are compatible with the truth of determinism. But if this is how we construe the debate between compatibilist and incompatibilist, then an appeal to the inevitability of holding people morally responsible would be an effective way of bypassing the whole debate. If we are indeed inevitably entangled in the practice of holding people morally responsible, we do not need an external justification for buying into that practice; the lack of such a justification would not leave our participation in the practice unjustified, unwarranted, or unreasonable, but only beyond the reach of reasons and justifications. Incompatibilist worries would, after all, be idle.

As I have shown, however, the external interpretation is not the most plausible way of reconstructing the debate about the conditions of responsibility. The alternative I have defended treats the inquiry as internal to the practice of holding people responsible. On this internal interpretation, we do not start out assuming that the practice hangs in the balance, nor are we looking for a positive justification for buying into that practice to begin with. Rather, we take it as a given that we hold people morally responsible—as the result of normal development in cultures that make the reactive emotions available—and we investigate the conditions that make it appropriate to adopt this stance, where the standards of "appropriateness" appealed to are themselves moral standards. Thus, as I said earlier, the incompatibilist maintains that it would be inappropriate to hold people responsible, unless they have freedom of the will in the strong sense, because it would be *unfair* to adopt this stance toward people who lack strong freedom of the will. In this way, freedom of the will is seen not as providing a positive justification for entering into the practice of holding people responsible in the first place, but as a condition, internal to morality, for the fairness of holding people responsible in individual cases.

Of course, if the incompatibilist is right about this, and if determinism is true, then it will turn out that a condition for the fairness of holding individuals morally responsible is never satisfied. Would it follow from this that the whole practice of holding people morally responsible is irrational, unwarranted, or unreasonable? Perhaps—but not because we were initially seeking an external, rational justification for the practice, but because ordinary moral scrutiny reveals the practice to be unjustified, so that there is a moral objection to be lodged against a distinctively moral activity. Moreover, this conclusion would remain disconcerting even if, as Strawson maintains, we have no choice but to adopt the stance of holding people morally accountable. In that event we would find ourselves necessarily committed to a moral stance that cannot satisfy our own standards of moral justifiability—a kind of practical dilemma. Granted, the discovery of this predicament might not make any difference in practice, if Strawson's naturalist argument is sound. But to insist that the inquiry that might lead to this discovery should be avoided, just because it is idle in this way, would be a form of anti-intellectualism. Being caught up in the practice of holding people morally responsible, and also committed to moral norms of fairness, we might well be led to the conclusion that the practice is essentially unfair, and this conclusion would remain an important and troubling one, even if it would not lead us to cease holding people responsible.[20]

Consider next Strawson's pragmatic argument against incompatibilism. This argument is presented as an answer to the question of "what it would be *rational* to do if determinism were true."[21] Strictly speaking, Strawson believes that this question is not a well-formulated one, because the naturalist considerations just discussed do not so much as allow the question to come up. But he suggests that, "if we could imagine what we cannot have, *viz.* a choice in this matter, then we could choose rationally only in the light of an assessment of the gains or losses to human life, its enrichment or impoverishment; and the truth or falsity of determinism would not bear on the rationality of *this* choice."[22] The suggestion here is that the only way we can interpret

20. Here one can see the importance of construing the dependence of facts about responsibility on our practices in normative rather than dispositional terms. If I had construed this dependence in terms of schema (*D*) rather than schema (*N*), there would have been no room for the practical dilemma I have described to arise. From Strawson's naturalist argument, it follows that we are disposed to hold people responsible regardless of whether determinism would make it unfair to do so; but according to schema (*D*), this by itself would settle the question of whether people are in fact morally responsible.

21. Strawson, "Freedom and Resentment," p. 70.

22. Strawson, "Freedom and Resentment," p. 70; see also pp. 74–75.

the question of whether it would be rational to continue to hold people responsible is as a practical question, about "the gains and losses to human life." Once the question is put in this way, however, it becomes apparent that the answer to it will in no way depend on the truth or falsity of determinism, for the issue of whether determinism is true or false is completely irrelevant to the question of whether holding people morally responsible does or does not enrich human life. What settles this latter question, according to Strawson's view, is the involvement of the reactive emotions in the practice of holding people responsible. Given the connection between responsibility and the reactive emotions, and given that the reactive emotions are inevitably connected with our involvement in interpersonal relations, it follows that to stop holding people morally responsible would be to sacrifice all interpersonal relations in favor of a strict objectivity of attitude. That would obviously be a grave impoverishment of human life.[23]

This pragmatic argument for compatibilism seems to put the debate about responsibility and determinism in an entirely new light. If the argument is sound, it undermines at a stroke the incompatibilist's claim that the truth of determinism would make it inappropriate to go on holding people morally responsible.[24] According to the pragmatic argument, the interpretation that we must give to questions about the rationality of holding people responsible does not leave any room for the incompatibilist claim that the truth of determinism would make it inappropriate to hold people responsible. But why does Strawson suppose that the only possible reasons that might be cited for or against our practice of holding people morally responsible are pragmatic reasons, concerning the gains and losses of the practice for human life? What motivates this crucial assumption?

Once again, it appears that Strawson has temporarily succumbed to the temptation to interpret the debate between compatibilists and in-

23. Actually Strawson does not draw this conclusion explicitly in "Freedom and Resentment," but it seems implicit in the article. The conclusion is explicitly drawn and endorsed by Jonathan Bennett in "Accountability," in Zak van Straaten, ed., *Philosophical Subjects: Essays Presented to P. F. Strawson* (Oxford: Clarendon Press, 1980), pp. 14–47, at pp. 29–30. Note that the argument, as I have reconstructed it, takes for granted that the forms of interpersonal relation we value are possible only for beings who are subject to reactive emotions. On the narrow interpretation of the reactive emotions I have defended, it is not obvious that this assumption is correct—an important qualification that I shall ignore for purposes of this discussion.

24. Presumably this is what moves Bennett to write that "the greatest single achievement of 'Freedom and Resentment' . . . is its showing how the question 'Ought we to retain praise, blame, etc.?' could be a fundamentally practical one rather than having a strict dependence on a troublesome theoretical question." See Bennett, "Accountability," p. 30.

compatibilists as taking place at a level *external* to our actual moral practices. That is, when he presents the pragmatic argument, he seems to assume that the whole practice of holding people morally responsible hangs in the balance, and that we are seeking reasons for retaining or abandoning the practice that are independent of morality. Viewing the question in this way, it becomes intelligible why Strawson should suppose that the only reasons that could conceivably be cited are pragmatic reasons, concerning the gains and losses of the practice to human life. What other considerations might bear on the decision to retain or abandon the practice of holding people morally responsible, if the terms of the question do not permit us to appeal to explicitly moral reasons? What other interests might be at stake?

Both moral norms and pragmatic norms are practical norms, relating to our practical interests in moral and nonmoral ends. Besides appealing to such practical norms as these, the only remaining alternative would seem to be to appeal to theoretical norms, of the sort that subserve our interests in grasping and explaining facts or truths. Thus one might suppose that the question of whether it would be appropriate to hold people morally responsible should be settled by an appeal to our theoretical interest in the truth, so that it will be appropriate to hold people responsible just in the case that it is *true* that they are morally responsible agents, and inappropriate just in the case that it is *false* that they are such agents. This theoretical approach to the question, however, is not available to Strawson. His discussion is premised on the assumption that we cannot settle the issue about whether to hold people responsible by appealing to facts about whether people are responsible in themselves, prior to and independent of our practices. As I suggested in the previous section, there are good reasons to follow Strawson in this assumption— reasons that led me to reject what I there referred to as metaphysical interpretations of the issue that divides compatibilists and incompatibilists. Hence the adoption of a standpoint external to our moral practices does seem to leave us only the alternative of appealing to pragmatic norms to settle the question of whether it would be appropriate to take up the practice of holding people responsible.

But the external interpretation of the issue between compatibilists and incompatibilists is not the only interpretation available. As I have argued, we do better to see the issue as arising internally to our moral practices. It seems integral to those practices that we have a fundamental commitment to *fairness*. This provides us with moral terms for deciding whether it would be appropriate to hold people responsible in particular cases. The central question that divides compatibilists and incompatibilists, in these terms, is whether it would or would not be fair to hold people responsible if determinism is true. Responding to this question, the incompatibilist says that the fairness of holding people responsible depends crucially on a particular fact about the people held responsible, namely whether they have freedom of the will in the strong sense. The incompatibilist contends that, in the absence of such strong freedom of the will, it would not be appropriate to hold a person morally responsible, because under those circumstances it would not be fair to hold the person morally responsible. Once this is made clear, however, one can see that Strawson's pragmatic argument simply changes the question. That argument rests on the idea that the practice of holding people responsible enriches human life, because of its connection with the reactive emotions. But even if this is true, it does not show that it would not be unfair to hold people morally responsible in the absence of strong freedom of the will, and this is all the incompatibilist maintains. To rebut this position, Strawson must show not only that the practice of holding people responsible enriches human life, but also that questions about the rationality of our practices can only be taken as pragmatic questions. As I have shown, however, this latter claim cannot be sustained. It depends on taking questions about the rationality of our practices to have the force of requests for an external justification of those practices, and this is not the only way they can be interpreted.

Thus the pragmatic argument, like the naturalist argument, does not by itself provide a successful strategy for bypassing incompatibilist concerns. Even if we grant Strawson the empirical assumptions on which the argument rests, it will establish at most that the practice of holding people morally responsible enriches human life; to that extent it would give us a reason for retaining the practice, regardless of whether determinism is true. But this conclusion leaves open the possibility that the truth of determinism would give us other reasons, of a moral nature, for not holding people morally responsible. In particular, it might still be the case that the truth of determinism would make it unfair to hold people morally responsible, by depriving those we hold responsible of freedom of will in the strong sense. In that case rationality would seem to pull us in two different directions at once: pragmatic considerations, concerning the gains and losses of our activities for human life, would give us reason to retain the practice of holding people morally responsible regardless of whether determinism is true, but moral considerations of fairness would give us reason not to hold people responsible if determinism should be true.[25] This would be a dilemma of rationality (distinct from, though compatible with, the practical dilemma discussed earlier in this section).[26] But if the traditional incompatibilist arguments lead to a dilemma of this sort, that is reason enough to take them to be a source of concern. We need to find a way of addressing the incompatibilists' arguments on their own terms.[27]

4.3 Fairness

To this point my conclusions are largely in accord with one of Strawson's own leading themes, summarized effectively in the following quotation: "Inside the general structure or web of human attitudes and feelings . . . there is endless room for modification, redirection, criticism, and justification. But questions of justification are internal to the structure or relate to modifications internal to it. The existence of the general framework of attitudes itself . . . neither calls for, nor permits, an external 'rational' justification."[28] Where I differ from him is in thinking that the lack of scope for external rational justification of our practice of holding people morally responsible does not independently suffice to block incompatibilist concerns. The incompatibilist should be seen as saying not that strong freedom of the will would provide us with an external rational justification for holding people responsible, but that our own standards of moral justification commit us to the view

25. Presented with this dilemma, I think we would say that there are good pragmatic reasons to continue holding people responsible even though nobody is really a responsible agent in fact. As I suggested in the preceding section, it seems that moral norms of fairness have a privileged role when it comes to determining the facts about responsibility—what it is to *be* a morally responsible agent—in accordance with schema (N).

26. Compare David Wiggins, "Towards a Reasonable Libertarianism," in Ted Honderich, ed., *Essays on Freedom of Action* (London: Routledge and Kegan Paul, 1973), pp. 33–61, at p. 56: "What Strawson's lecture brings out is the character of the dilemma with which the problem of determinism confronts us—one set of considerations making an attitude rational, the other set undermining that attitude—and the complex conceptual constitution of the notion of rationality which figures in the argument." (This interesting sentence is curiously omitted from the revised version of "Towards a Reasonable Libertarianism" that appears in Wiggins's *Needs, Values, Truth: Essays in the Philosophy of Value,* 2nd ed. [Oxford: Basil Blackwell, 1991], pp. 269–302.)

27. For further discussion of Strawson's arguments, see Galen Strawson, *Freedom and Belief,* chap. 5, and Ulrich Pothast, *Die Unzulänglichkeit der Freiheitsbeweise: Zu einigen Lehrstücken aus der neueren Geschichte von Philosophie und Recht* (Frankfurt am Main: Suhrkamp Verlag, 1987), pp. 162–171. Both authors agree that the naturalist and pragmatic arguments do not suffice to undermine incompatibilist concerns, though they adduce rather different considerations in support of this conclusion from the ones I have advanced.

28. Strawson, "Freedom and Resentment," p. 78; compare Strawson, *Skepticism and Naturalism,* p. 41.

that such freedom is a condition of moral responsibility. It is a consequence of this, perhaps, that internal criticism of our moral practices
may not be restricted to what could accurately be described as the
"modification" or "redirection" of our given moral sentiments and
attitudes. If incompatibilism is correct, and if determinism should be
true, then it would turn out that our practice of holding people morally
responsible is radically defective, to a degree that mere modification and
redirection might not be able to repair. But there is nothing in the
nature of internal moral criticism to rule out a result of this kind.

To proceed beyond this point, it will help to look more closely at
the idea of fairness, and to try to get clearer about the role that this idea
plays in the debate between compatibilists and incompatibilists. To
begin, what exactly does it mean to say that the interest in fairness is
internal to morality? In the most basic terms, this means simply that the
interest in fairness is itself a moral interest, so that having such an interest
is one of the things that distinguish those who participate in the
activities constitutive of moral life. But moral interests are of various
kinds, reflecting a plurality in our moral concepts. In particular, one
should distinguish the following two possibilities. Considerations of
fairness might have the status of basic moral values, so that the moral
interest in fairness should be seen as a concern to promote something
that is recognizably a moral species of the *good*. Alternatively, considerations of fairness might fall under the category of the *right,* in which
case the interest in fairness should be seen as the kind of attitude that
corresponds to what I have called moral obligations. Both of these
possibilities yield an interpretation of incompatibilism as a form of
internal criticism of our moral practices, since they both treat the
interest in fairness to which the incompatibilist appeals as a distinctively
moral interest. The general account of the debate that I have been
urging could thus be sustained without choosing between the two
possibilities.

But there is some independent reason to suppose that the considerations of fairness on which the incompatibilist relies have the force of
obligations, rather than appeals to a species of moral value. On the
internal interpretation, the incompatibilist position is meant to be based
on the kinds of moral reason that are invoked in moral practice, to
support particular normative conclusions. So, for instance, the incompatibilist might say that it would be unfair to hold people responsible,
if determinism is true, in just the way that it would be unfair to blame
a person for an action that resulted from physical constraint, or to hold

infants or the insane fully accountable. But in cases of this sort, it seems, considerations of fairness have the force of obligations. To blame a person for bodily movements that result from her being pushed, or to hold an infant or an insane person accountable—these seem not merely bad or undesirable, from the moral point of view, but wrong. This suggests that considerations of fairness, as they enter into the incompatibilist argument, should be seen as generating obligations and not merely identifying modalities of moral value.

When fairness is construed as a source of obligations, however, the incompatibilist position turns out to have a markedly reflexive character. The incompatibilist is engaged in an examination of the conditions in which it would be appropriate to hold people morally responsible. But on the interpretation of fairness just broached, the incompatibilist conducts this investigation by appealing to the content of the very standards to which we hold people when we hold them responsible. Proceeding in this way, the incompatibilist supposes that the stance of holding people morally responsible is open to assessment in terms of the content of the obligations to which that stance itself commits us. Consider the following questions. What makes it an interest of ours that people should act fairly? Why do considerations of fairness provide terms for normative assessment that we care about, or take seriously? On the present interpretation, the answer would be that we are committed to principles of fairness just in the sense that we take considerations of fairness to generate moral obligations, to which we hold ourselves and others. In appealing to fairness to evaluate the stance of holding people morally responsible, then, the incompatibilist assesses the stance by appealing to standards that we are committed to only insofar as we take up that very stance. Responsibility is asked to satisfy its own standards, one might say.

Once its reflexive character is made clear, however, it may seem that incompatibilism, so interpreted, undermines itself. Thus, suppose that the incompatibilist is correct to think that it would violate an obligation of fairness to hold people morally responsible, if determinism should be true, and suppose that determinism is in fact true. Then it would be inappropriate, because it would be unfair, to hold people to any moral obligations we accept, in the way that is connected with the reactive emotions—including the obligation of fairness itself. But if we cannot appropriately hold people to obligations of fairness, then we cannot very well criticize ourselves for holding people responsible in the face of determinism, on the grounds that it would be unfair to do so. Because it is reflexive in the way I have described, incompatibilism, on this account of it, seems to lose its critical animus as soon as we imagine it to be correct. But this conclusion would be far too swift. Suppose that determinism is true. Then the incompatibilist could be thought of as confronting us with a dilemma. Either we hold people to obligations of fairness, in which case the consistent application of those obligations will give us an important reason to stop holding people to any moral obligations at all (so that responsibility ushers itself from the scene), or we simply don't hold people to moral obligations that we accept in the first place. Both horns would spell trouble for our practice of holding people morally responsible.

Before we can determine whether we are in this dilemmatic predicament, however, we need to get clearer about the content of our norms of fairness. One notion of fairness that does not seem particularly relevant to responsibility has to do with our participation in cooperative practices. Thus we have the view that people who benefit from participation in a cooperative practice act unfairly if they do not play by the rules that constitute or define the practice in question. Fairness in this sense seems to be a source of basic moral obligations: we are obligated to play by the rules of a practice if we have gained from the practice by voluntarily participating in it. This is what Rawls calls the "principle of fairness," and it seems to capture a large part of our thinking about fairness and the moral obligations it generates.[29] But it is not the notion of fairness to which the incompatibilist appeals. If it would be morally wrong to hold people responsible for actions that are determined, this is not because doing so would violate the rules of a cooperative practice that we voluntarily participate in and benefit from; it is because it would be unfair in some different sense. But what might this different sense be?

One possibility is that the incompatibilist is relying on a notion of fairness as *desert*.[30] Thus the incompatibilist may be seen as appealing to the idea that people never really deserve to be blamed or sanctioned for what they do, if they lack strong freedom of the will. Take, for example, a case of forcible constraint, where an agent is physically prevented from carrying out some moral obligation that we accept. The incompatibilist might say that it would be unfair to hold the agent

29. See John Rawls, *A Theory of Justice* (Cambridge, Mass.: Harvard University Press, 1971), secs. 18 and 52. In Rawls's formulation of the principle of fairness, it is also required that the practice that we voluntarily participate in and benefit from must itself be just.

30. Compare Glover, *Responsibility*, pp. 70–73.

responsible in this case, because the agent does not deserve to be blamed or sanctioned in the absence of alternate possibilities. It might then be argued that determinism would deprive all agents of alternate possibilities, on all occasions, so that it is never the case that people deserve to be blamed or sanctioned for their actions. Determinism would thus make it unfair to hold people responsible for their actions, in the sense that people would never really deserve to be blamed or sanctioned for what they do in the absence of strong freedom of the will.

This possibility seems to me to capture at least part of what is meant when incompatibilists suggest that determinism would make it unfair to hold people responsible for their actions. Note, however, that the notion of desert is itself unusually complex. Claims of desert notoriously take a variety of forms: it is said, for instance, that people deserve punishment because of their *actions,* deserve success because of their *effort,* deserve to win games or contests because of their *talent* or *skill,* deserve happiness because of their *character.*[31] This apparent variety does not necessarily impugn the notion of desert, but it raises a question as to the kind of desert claim the incompatibilist should be understood to be advancing. Here two points may be remarked. First, considerations of desert, as they bear on questions about responsibility and freedom, seem to come into play in connection with responsibility for particular actions or omissions. The incompatibilist wishes to say that people do not deserve to be blamed or sanctioned for the individual actions they perform, if determinism is true. In the terms proposed earlier, this is most naturally interpreted as the claim that strong freedom of the will is a B-condition of responsibility, a condition for the appropriateness of holding people to blame for the particular things they do. Second, note that in attempting to support this claim by appealing to the notion of desert, the incompatibilist is advancing a thesis that is both basic and negative. The contention is not that we deserve to be blamed for the wrongs we commit if we have strong freedom of will, still less that we deserve to suffer a specific quality or degree of harm because of what we have done, but rather that we do *not* deserve to be held to blame for our acts in the absence of such freedom. Even those who are suspicious about appeals to desert in other contexts (as, for instance, providing a preinstitutional basis for conclusions about social justice) may be willing to concede that we have legitimate, considered convic-

---

31. On the variety of desert claims, see George Sher, *Desert* (Princeton, N.J.: Princeton University Press, 1987), chap. 1.

tions about such basic, necessary conditions of desert.[32] Furthermore, we may endorse such basic convictions without committing ourselves to the different and problematic thought that wrongdoers positively deserve to suffer.

But desert does not seem to be the only concept of fairness that the incompatibilist could be relying on. A second candidate is the concept of fairness as *reasonableness*. Consider an example: a young child does something morally wrong—lies to her parents, say, about whether she has cleaned her room. There may well be good reason to scold or punish the child in this situation, but I take it we would think it unfair to hold the child fully responsible for her deed, in the way we would ordinarily hold morally responsible an adult who lies for personal advantage. It would not be unfair to the child in the sense that we would be failing to play by the rules of some practice from which we ourselves had gained, nor in the sense that the child does not deserve to be punished or blamed. Rather, it would be unfair roughly in the sense that it would be unreasonable to treat the child as fully accountable in the first place. Similarly, the incompatibilist might try to show that it would be unfair to hold people responsible if determinism is true, roughly in the sense that it would be unreasonable for us to hold people morally accountable if they lack strong freedom of the will.[33]

The notion of reasonableness, like that of desert, is both complex and elusive. Indeed reasonableness is among our most basic moral notions, and a responsiveness to considerations of reasonableness is among the most fundamental forms of moral motivation.[34] How might the incompatibilist call on this basic moral concept to support the conclusion that strong freedom of the will is a condition of responsibility? The discussion in the preceding paragraph provides a clue. There, I suggested that the incompatibilist appeals to reasonableness in connection with concerns about accountability. The thought is that it would

32. For example, Rawls, though he rejects preinstitutional appeals to desert as a basis for conclusions about social justice, relies on the moral conviction that people do not deserve their natural advantages and abilities—a basic, negative claim about the conditions of desert; see Rawls, *A Theory of Justice,* p. 104.

33. See Morton White, "Oughts and Cans," in Alan Ryan, ed., *The Idea of Freedom: Essays in Honor of Isaiah Berlin* (Oxford: Oxford University Press, 1979), pp. 211–219, at pp. 217–218, for an explicit appeal to reasonableness as the moral basis of the incompatibilist position.

34. Compare the fundamental role that reasonableness plays in the moral theories of Rawls, as explained in "The Powers of Citizens and their Representation," lecture 2 in his *Political Liberalism* (New York: Columbia University Press, 1993), pp. 47–88, and T. M. Scanlon, "Contractualism and Utilitarianism," in Amartya Sen and Bernard Williams, eds., *Utilitarianism and Beyond* (Cambridge: Cambridge University Press, 1982), pp. 103–128.

be unreasonable to hold people accountable if they lack freedom of the will, in a way perhaps analogous to that in which it is unreasonable to hold young children or the insane morally accountable. This suggests the following conclusion: whereas considerations of desert provide potential support for the claim that strong freedom of the will is a B-condition of responsibility, considerations of reasonableness potentially support the claim that strong freedom is an A-condition of responsibility, a necessary condition for moral accountability. Thus, the incompatibilist could argue that it would not be reasonable to hold people morally accountable if they do not have freedom of will in the strong sense.

So far, then, I have identified two distinct kinds of claims that the incompatibilist might wish to endorse: that people do not deserve to be blamed or sanctioned for their doings if they lack strong freedom of the will; and that it would be unreasonable to hold people accountable if they lack strong freedom of the will. It remains to consider how claims of these kinds might be defended or challenged.

4.4   Strategies

On the interpretation I have developed in this chapter, resolving the debate about responsibility will require that we venture into normative moral theory. In particular, we need to investigate the content of our concepts of fairness—construed as reasonableness or desert—and determine what those concepts imply about the conditions under which it would be fair to hold people responsible. This is an extremely significant conclusion. It means that claims about the conditions of responsibility cannot be advanced in abstraction from normative reflection about our substantive moral views. Rather, such claims must be treated as hypotheses in normative moral theory and be subjected, accordingly, to the standards of argument that prevail within such theory. This is the distinctive premise from which my argument in the remainder of the book will proceed.

Seen in this way, the controversy about responsibility centers on competing claims about the moral principles to which we are committed. I will understand moral principles to be propositions that isolate the features of situations or actions that justify particular claims of moral right; they specify the reasons that a given course of action is obligatory or prohibited. As I suggested earlier (in section 2.3), particular conclusions about moral obligation must be supported by some principle or other, in this sense of "principle." Thus, when incompatibilists say that it would be unfair (and hence wrong) to hold people responsible if determinism is true, their claim must be backed up by an appeal to a principle of fairness that explains what it is about determinism that would make this form of treatment unfair. And conventional incompatibilist positions can indeed be expressed as appeals to moral principles in this way. Incompatibilists have often alleged, for instance, that determinism would undermine responsibility by depriving us of alternate possibilities for action. We can unpack such assertions as appeals to one of the following principles of fairness: (1) that people do not deserve to be blamed or sanctioned for what they do if they lack alternate possibilities for action; and (2) that it would be unreasonable to hold people accountable if they lack alternate possibilities for action. To challenge an argument of this kind, the compatibilist, too, will have to engage in normative moral reflection, by either disputing the assertion that we are committed to (1) or (2), or by offering an interpretation of those moral principles that denies their incompatibilist implications.

How, in general, are claims about the content of our moral principles to be defended? One strategy would be to ground such principles in a higher-order moral principle, such as the principle of utility in one of its versions, or in a higher-order procedure that tests candidate moral principles for their acceptability, such as Kant's categorical imperative procedure. Certainly once the debate about responsibility is correctly framed in the normative terms I have proposed, it has to be conceded that disputes about the content of our higher-order principles and procedures of moral justification may have a bearing on what the conditions of responsibility turn out to be. For my present purposes, however, I propose to try as far as possible to resolve the issue about responsibility without entering into disputes concerning the content of our ultimate moral principles and procedures. The considerations that seem most directly to support incompatibilist claims about fairness are largely independent of higher-order disputes in normative ethics, and so we will most effectively come to terms with such claims if we bracket the higher-order disputes and focus on understanding the sources of incompatibilist pictures in our ordinary moral reflection and experience.

To expand briefly on this point, suppose for the moment that the principle of utility is accepted as the supreme principle of morality. It would follow from this, perhaps, that incompatibilist pictures must be mistaken, but the route by which one would arrive at this conclusion would not even engage the considerations that lead people to be attracted to incompatibilism, and so it would be unlikely to persuade any but the most ardent utilitarians. The principle of utility is a forward-looking principle, enjoining us to maximize expected overall utility (on some interpretation of utility), but the kind of lower-order principles that incompatibilists rely on are backward-looking principles (or at least "straight-ahead looking" ones). Principle (1) just described, for instance, tells us that people do not deserve to be held to blame for their actions if they lacked alternate possibilities when they acted; (2) says that agents who lack such alternate possibilities cannot reasonably be held morally accountable. If we accept that the principle of utility is the supreme moral principle, it is hard to see how a serious argument could be mounted by appeal to lower-order principles of this sort. Most likely, such principles would be rejected out of hand, as underivable from the forward-looking principle of utility, since it is doubtful that a forward-looking concern to maximize utility would give us reason to accept a backward-looking principle of alternate possibilities—especially one that tolerates an incompatibilist interpretation. Even if such principles could be justified in this way, however, their normative force would be entirely derivative from the principle of utility, and so they would have to give way to that highest-order principle in cases where they might conflict with it. Hence any incompatibilist appeal to principles such as (1) and (2) would be vulnerable to being undermined, if (as seems likely) it should turn out that there are good forward-looking reasons for holding people responsible.

Consider, for instance, the position of the sophisticated utilitarian adverted to in section 3.1, who abandons the economy of threats interpretation of responsibility, taking blame and moral sanction instead to be part of the natural repertoire of human responses (at least under certain cultural conditions). A utilitarian of this stripe might plausibly regard the practice of holding people responsible as beneficial to human welfare on the whole—in part because of its deterrent effects, but also, perhaps, because its connection to the reactive emotions makes possible the more subtle riches of interpersonal relationship that figure in Strawson's pragmatic argument. For the utilitarian, however, these pragmatic considerations would not engage an interest that is external to our moral practices; rather, they would appeal to a basic moral interest, indeed to our most fundamental moral concern, the concern that determines our highest and overriding standard for deciding what we ought morally to do. But if pragmatic considerations tell in favor of holding people responsible, on the whole, and if pragmatic considerations answer to our highest, overriding moral concern, then the incompatibilist's appeal to fairness *cannot* succeed. By assigning a derivative status (at best) to considerations of fairness, utilitarianism presents a secure defense against incompatibilist arguments before they even get off the ground.[35]

This brings out, I think, how deeply inhospitable to incompatibilism a utilitarian conception of morality would be. It is commonly thought that utilitarians tend toward compatibilist positions on account of their revisionist interpretations of responsibility. They advocate some version of the economy of threats strategy for explaining what it is to hold people responsible (see, again, section 3.1), and responsibility, so understood, clearly is compatible with determinism. This is historically accurate as an account of how utilitarians have tended to treat the question of the relationship between determinism and responsibility, but it does not capture the depth of the opposition between utilitarian conceptions of morality and incompatibilist interpretations of responsibility. The argument just sketched shows that even if the utilitarian abandons the aspiration to account for responsibility itself in utilitarian terms, and accepts the reactive account of responsibility I have proposed, it will remain difficult to formulate the incompatibilist position in a way that would trouble the utilitarian. Indeed, this inability to so much as make sense of incompatibilist worries is one of the many ways in which utilitarianism fails to do justice to ordinary moral consciousness, for the temptation to think about responsibility in incompatibilist terms is surely one of the most familiar features of the moral point of view.

For this reason I should prefer to bracket disputes between utilitarians and their opponents about our higher-order moral principles. Instead, I want to focus directly on subordinate principles of fairness such as (1) and (2); this should enable me both to formulate and to assess the strongest possible arguments that can be made for the incompatibilist position. But if justifications that appeal to higher-order moral principles or procedures are eschewed, how should claims about the content of our subordinate principles of fairness be assessed? It might be suggested that claims of this sort are simply self-evident, such that we have a direct

35. This is not to say that utilitarians would necessarily approve of the practice of holding people responsible, in the end. For instance, those persuaded by the cruelty objection canvassed in Chapter 3 might be skeptical that the gains of the practice outweigh its costs. The point is that considerations of fairness have no direct bearing on the calculation of gains and losses, which is what will ultimately decide the issue for the utilitarian.

intuition of their truth. This style of intuitionist argument does not seem very promising, however—not, at any rate, if it means that we may ignore the considered convictions in which competent moral judges have a high degree of confidence. A plausible candidate for a subordinate principle of fairness has to be anchored somehow in considered convictions of this kind; otherwise there will be good reason to question whether we are really committed to it, whether it represents one of *our* moral principles.[36] The attempt to anchor candidate principles of fairness in our considered moral convictions is a local application of the method of reflective equilibrium, and it seems to me the only way to proceed if one is not going to appeal directly to some higher-order principle or procedure of justification.[37] Proposed subordinate principles should be assessed on the grounds of their ability to account for considered convictions in which we have a high degree of confidence. One must ask whether a given principle is needed to explain or express such considered convictions, or whether it more successfully explains and expresses our considered convictions than other principles that are available.[38]

By far the most promising application of this approach in the incompatibilist's cause would start with a set of fairly concrete moral convictions. These are our considered judgments about the circumstances that

36. Indeed, I believe that most serious appeals to the self-evidence of moral principles are best seen as attempts to characterize some of our more abstract considered convictions. This brings out the important point that considered moral convictions can be of varying levels of concreteness or abstraction.

37. For important expositions of the method of reflective equilibrium, see Rawls, *A Theory of Justice*, sec. 9, and his "The Independence of Moral Theory," *Proceedings and Addresses of the American Philosophical Association* 48 (1974–75), pp. 1–22. It is not possible here to go into the many questions that Rawls's statement and use of this method raise; for my purposes what is important is the rudimentary idea that claims about the content of moral principles must be anchored in considered convictions in which we have a high degree of confidence, and that our understanding of those convictions is in turn subject to revision as a result of moral theorizing. This is an idea that can and should be accepted by proponents of very different philosophical accounts of the nature of morality; on this point, see Rawls, "Political Constructivism," lecture 3 in *Political Liberalism*, pp. 89–129, at pp. 95–97, and also T. M. Scanlon, "The Aims and Authority of Moral Theory," *Oxford Journal of Legal Studies* 12 (1992), pp. 1–23.

38. Of course, the method of reflective equilibrium allows for the possibility of revising our initial considered convictions as a result of theorizing about them. This might, in turn, seem to render the method peculiarly ill-suited for defending an incompatibilist view. Thus, suppose some initial set *r* of considered convictions supports an incompatibilist principle of fairness, and suppose also that determinism is true. It would apparently follow that we should rescind a massive number of other considered convictions, namely those whereby we judge particular people blameworthy or accountable. Faced with this prospect, it might seem that equilibrium would best be achieved by revising the initial set *r* of incompatibilist convictions rather than by giving up all of our

we acknowledge to excuse or exempt people from moral responsiblity in particular cases. It is our considered moral view that such conditions as physical constraint, coercion, insanity, hypnotism, behavior control, and childhood render it unfair to hold people morally responsible. The incompatibilist might try to show that the truth of determinism would render it unfair to hold people responsible in just the way that these kinds of conditions are already accepted as making it unfair to hold people responsible, in the concrete circumstances of the moral life. An approach of this kind needs to be formulated carefully, however, if it is to have any chance of supporting the incompatibilist's position. In particular, the proponent of the approach should not insist that legitimate appeals to fairness must be tied rigidly to the criteria that actually guide us in our moral judgments about the standard cases of exemption and excuse.[39] That would represent an implausible denial of the generality implicit in such moral judgments.

Clearly, the kinds of causal influences operative in cases of constraint, coercion, hypnotism, and the like differ in many ways from those operative in more ordinary cases. The truth of determinism would not entail that such differences are altogether negligible, so that our actions would always be just like those of a person who has been hypnotized or coerced (say); nor does the incompatibilist strategy I am sketching say otherwise. The strategy maintains, rather, that our acknowledgement that it would be unfair to hold people responsible in such cases presupposes that there are *reasons* for not holding people responsible in those cases, and that those reasons might generalize beyond the standard exemptions and excuses. To return to the model of reflective equilibrium, think of our considered judgments about the standard cases as being supported by principles of fairness, principles that both explain those considered judgments, specifying what it is about the cases that excuses or exempts the people in them from responsibility, and that

---

judgments of responsibility. But this seems doubtful to me. Our considered judgments of responsibility are premised on the assumption that those held responsible are free agents, in some sense. If the convictions in set r support an incompatibilist interpretation of this kind of agency, the truth of determinism would not really require us to rescind all our judgments of responsibility, for it is part of the content of those very judgments that assignments of responsibility should be revised if those held responsible turn out not to be free agents, in the relevant sense.

39. For this suggestion, see the "paradigm case" method sketched and applied in Antony Flew, "Divine Omniscience and Human Freedom," in Antony Flew and Alasdair MacIntyre, eds., *New Essays in Philosophical Theology* (New York: Macmillan, 1955), pp. 144–169. Further doubts about this method are raised by Peter van Inwagen, *An Essay on Free Will* (Oxford: Clarendon Press, 1983), pp. 106–114.

potentially generalize to apply to other cases as well. Thus, the incompatibilist might argue, we think it unfair to hold those responsible who are physically constrained, or insane, or under the influence of a drug or hypnotic treatment that has been forcibly administered, and these judgments rely at least implicitly on moral principles that specify what it is about these kinds of conditions that makes it unfair to hold people responsible when they obtain. The incompatibilist may then try to show that some such principle of fairness, required to account for concrete judgments of excuse in which we have great confidence, would equally tell against holding people morally responsible if determinism should be true.

I shall call this kind of argument the generalization strategy, since it tries to show that determinism would amount to a generalization of reasons already accepted in moral practice as making it unfair to hold people responsible. This strategy represents the most straightforward way to deploy the method of reflective equilibrium in support of the incompatibilist conclusion. It starts with our considered convictions about the kinds of conditions that undermine or block moral responsibility, anchoring in those concrete convictions general principles of fairness whose consistent application entails that we should never hold people responsible, if determinism is true.

As I shall try to show in Chapters 5 and 6, however, the generalization strategy does not succeed. Incompatibilists have traditionally supposed that the excuses and exemptions we acknowledge in practice commit us to principles like (1) and (2) described earlier, to the effect that we should not hold people morally responsible unless they have the ability to act otherwise. Indeed most compatibilists have also accepted such principles, granting that we are committed to them by our considered convictions about excuses and exemptions from responsibility. Accepting these principles of alternate possibilities (as they may be called), compatibilists have traditionally focused their efforts on devising analyses of the concept of alternate possibility, analyses that secure the compatibility of such possibilities with determinism. These analyses have brought to light important unclarities and equivocations in our notions of ability, power, and possibility. By themselves, however, they do not constitute a satisfying response to the incompatibilist's generalization argument. As I explain in Appendix 2, once it is conceded that moral responsibility requires alternate possibilities, attempts to block the incompatibilist conclusion by invoking a competing analysis of ability or possibility tend to seem ad hoc and unconvincing. I therefore follow a different approach in Chapters 5 and 6, engaging the generalization strategy on its own terms by showing that our considered judgments of exemption and excuse are best explained not by the principles of alternate possibilities, but by quite different principles of fairness, ones that do not even threaten to generalize if determinism should be true. The argument to this conclusion will draw particularly on the account of holding people responsible that was developed in the preceding chapter, focusing on the role of the reactive emotions in that account to explain why alternate possibilities are not a genuine condition of the fairness of holding people responsible, and identifying the different principles actually at work.

Once the generalization strategy has been dispatched, the remaining options for defending incompatibilism are reduced to two. First, the incompatibilist could try to mount a different argument within the method of reflective equilibrium, appealing to a class of considered moral convictions distinct from those at the center of the generalization strategy. Alternatively, the incompatibilist could abandon the method of reflective equilibrium altogether, attempting to support a suitable principle of fairness not by anchoring it in our considered moral convictions, but by appealing to direct intuition—the brute self-evidence of the conclusion that determinism would make it unfair to hold people responsible. This last option has an air of desperation about it and does not need to be taken seriously. But we cannot so quickly dismiss the possibility that there are other considered moral convictions, outside the contexts in which we excuse or exempt people from responsibility, that might give some comfort to the incompatibilist. There is, after all, the phenomenon that I referred to in Chapter 3 as the seductiveness of incompatibilism, the profound pull that incompatibilist pictures have on ordinary thinking about responsibility. This phenomenon may manifest itself in the persistence of an abstract conviction that certain consequences of determinism would make it unfair to hold people responsible, if they actually obtained. Thus even after the generalization strategy has been dealt with, it can continue to seem that it would be unfair to hold people responsible if they lack alternate possibilities, or if they cannot avoid the harms to which we expose them by blaming them for moral wrongs. Incompatibilist principles of fairness might then be defended on the grounds that they are required to express and explain these high-level considered convictions.

Moral principles that are defended in this way have the peculiar feature of not being applicable outside the context in which we are considering the implications of determinism for responsibility; for this reason, one might refer to them as "one-off" principles of fairness. Do our abstract moral convictions really provide support for incompatibilist principles of this sort? The first thing to note is that these abstract convictions are not among the moral convictions in which we have the highest degree of confidence; this becomes plain when we isolate the abstract convictions from our more particular judgments about excuses and exemptions, with which they are apt to be confused. But if we are not very confident about these abstract moral convictions, we should accept the one-off principles they support only if we have no other plausible way of accounting for the convictions as aspects of moral consciousness.

As I argue in the chapters to follow, however, there is an alternative explanation for the troublesome moral convictions. Specifically, it is possible to *diagnose* these convictions, by tracing them to natural and unsophisticated errors that we are apt to make about the conditions of responsibility. Once we are provided with a diagnostic explanation of this sort, we will be in a position to grant the seductiveness of incompatibilism while denying that the abstract convictions that voice our sense of this seductiveness have probative force in moral theorizing. Diagnostic considerations therefore play a large role in the moral argument I am developing; they are the primary topic of Chapter 7. Among the themes that will emerge from my diagnostic discussion is the importance of systematicity in the study of our considered convictions about fairness. Only when we look for principles that account for all of our concrete judgments of excuse and exemption will it become apparent that principles of alternate possibilities are not firmly anchored in those convictions. And only once we have a systematic account of this kind in place will we be able to diagnose effectively the seductive lure of incompatibilist pictures in ordinary moral consciousness.

5

Blameworthiness and the Excuses

※

In this chapter and the next I wish to argue against the generalization strategy. As explained in the preceding chapter, the generalization strategy attempts to anchor incompatibilist principles in a class of considered moral convictions in which we have an especially high degree of confidence. These are the judgments whereby we acknowledge the presence of conditions that make it unfair to hold people responsible in moral practice. I wish to show that these concrete judgments can best be accounted for in terms of principles of fairness that provide no comfort to the incompatibilist, so that the reasons that support the judgments would not generalize, if determinism is true.

We may distinguish two kinds of conditions that are acknowledged to block or inhibit responsibility: excuses, which function locally (examples include physical constraint or coercion); and exemptions,[1] which operate more globally (such as insanity, childhood, or perhaps addiction). To make this distinction more precise, it will help to recall the distinction I earlier drew between two different conditions of responsibility: B-conditions make it fair to hold people morally to blame for particular things they have done, while A-conditions make it fair to hold people morally accountable. In these terms, excuses indicate the absence of a B-condition of responsibility, while exemptions indicate the absence of an A-condition. We need to clarify which conditions the excuses and exemptions deprive people of, and to explain why these are conditions of responsibility. I focus on excuses in this chapter, saving the topic of the exemptions for Chapter 6.

The account of the excuses that I defend builds on and develops

---

1. I borrow this useful term from Gary Watson, "Responsibility and the Limits of Evil: Variations on a Strawsonian Theme," in Ferdinand Schoeman, ed., *Responsibility, Character, and the Emotions: New Essays in Moral Psychology* (Cambridge: Cambridge University Press, 1987), pp. 256–286, at pp. 259–261.

some suggestions made by J. L. Austin and P. F. Strawson. Austin draws the following distinction between justifications and excuses: whereas a justification for doing *x* shows that *x* is not really wrong, an excuse grants that *x* would be wrong, but shows that the agent did not really do *x* intentionally. This suggests that doing *x* intentionally is a condition of blameworthiness for *x,* a condition that is defeated by the excuses. But why does blameworthiness require intention in this way? Strawson's proposal is that an unintentional *x*-ing is not really a moral wrong in the first place, because the demands to which we hold people regulate not just bodily movements but also the qualities of will expressed by such bodily movements. I explain these points in section 5.1, arguing that two things are needed if one is to work up Strawson's and Austin's suggestions into a satisfactory account of the excuses: first, an explanation as to why the demands we hold people to should be focused on qualities of will, in the way Strawson supposes; and second, a demonstration that the full range of excuses can all be accounted for as conditions that defeat the presumption that the agent has done something morally wrong.

I take up the first of these tasks in section 5.2, drawing on the reactive account defended in earlier chapters to explain why our moral obligations regulate the qualities of will expressed in action, and isolating which qualities of will are important. The basic idea is that the stance of holding people to moral obligations one accepts involves a commitment to the existence of justifications that support those obligations, specifying reasons that can motivate compliance with them. It follows from this that moral obligations must be focused on states that are directly susceptible to the influence of reasons, and I argue that these states should be understood as choices that are expressed in action. If this is correct, however, then one can only count as having violated a moral obligation if one has done something that expresses the right kind of choice. As I show in section 5.3, the standard excuses can all be understood as conditions that defeat this presumption. They undermine blameworthiness by blocking the inference from outward behavior to the conclusion that the agent really has violated the obligations we hold her to. But if this is how the excuses function, then determinism would not represent a generalized excuse, since determinism would not entail that people never act on choices that violate the obligations we hold them to (section 5.4).

If successful, the argument in this chapter will deprive incompatibilist principles of fairness of their foothold in our considered judgments of moral excuse; in particular, it will show that those judgments are not best explained in terms of the principle of alternate possibilities. This is not the only way one might essay to refute incompatibilist proposals about our moral principles. A different approach may be found in the work of Harry Frankfurt, who has developed an influential style of counterexample to the principle of alternate possibilities. As I explain in Appendix 2, however, Frankfurt's counterexamples are problematic, and doubts about them are bound to persist so long as we lack an alternative and systematic account of the ordinary excuses and exemptions that identifies the actual principles of fairness latent in our considered judgments of exemption and excuse, and that shows why those princi-ples do not support the incompatibilist's generalization. The goal of this chapter and the next is to provide a systematic account of this kind.

5.1   Excuses and Intentions

My topic is the set of conditions that are commonly judged to block or undermine moral responsibility for what people do. To home in on this territory, let me begin by recalling J. L. Austin's distinction between *justifications* and *excuses.*[2] Suppose that agent *s* apparently does *x,* where *x* is an act that is, on the face of it, morally wrong. Austin suggests that a justification for *s*'s act would grant that *s* did *x,* but try to adduce reasons for thinking that *x* is not morally wrong after all (either in general, or in the circumstances in which it was performed). An excuse, by contrast, would grant that *x* is morally wrong but adduce reasons for thinking that *s* did not really do *x* after all. For instance, *s* might have done *x* only accidentally or inadvertently; *s* might have been pushed, or have been acting in response to coercive threats or under duress; or *s* might have done *x* while asleep, or as a result of reflex muscular contractions (brought about, say, by an epileptic fit, or the attack of a swarm of bees).

Several points should be noted about Austin's distinction between justifications and excuses. First, excuses are unlike justifications in blocking or inhibiting responsibility for whatever action was performed. If *s* offers a justification for doing *x* then *s* does not mean to deny responsibility for the act; rather, *s* accepts responsibility for doing *x,* and tries to show why *x* was a morally permissible (or even obligatory) thing

2. See Austin's "A Plea for Excuses," as reprinted in J. L. Austin, *Philosophical Papers,* J. O. Urmson and G. J. Warnock, eds., 3rd ed. (Oxford: Oxford University Press, 1979), pp. 175–204.

to do. Excuses, by contrast, aim precisely to challenge the claim (or suspicion) that *s* was morally responsible for *x;* they adduce conditions that make it unfair to hold *s* morally responsible for *x.* Now, to hold a person responsible for a particular action *x* that is morally wrong is to regard the person as having done something blameworthy; so excuses, on Austin's account of them, may be considered "blameworthiness inhibitors."[3] The crucial question, of course, is why excuses inhibit blameworthiness. As I have noted, the incompatibilist has an answer to this question ready to hand, one that has also been accepted by many compatibilists. Many of the accepted excuses (such as coercion, physical constraint, and reflex bodily movement) apparently cite circumstances that deprive an agent of alternate possibilities. Registering this fact, compatibilists and incompatibilists alike have proposed that the excuses rely implicitly on a moral principle of fairness, to the effect that an agent does not *deserve* to be blamed for an action if the agent could not have done otherwise.

Austin's distinction between justifications and excuses suggests a different account of what ties the excuses together as a class. Granting that *x* would be morally wrong, excuses, on Austin's interpretation, apparently show that agent *s* did not really do *x* intentionally: *s* may have made the bodily movements that normally constitute *x*-ing, but without the attitudinal conditions (whatever they are) that turn such bodily movements into cases of doing *x* intentionally. Thus if one does *x* as the result of being pushed, or because of a muscular twitch or spasm, then one hasn't really *acted* at all; if one does *x* inadvertently, or by accident, then—though one may have acted—one didn't do *x* intentionally; and if one does *x* as a result of coercion or duress, then— though one may have done *x* intentionally—one hasn't *merely* done *x* intentionally, one has done *x*-rather-than *y.*

This is so far only a tentative hypothesis. It remains to be shown in detail that the full range of excusing conditions are all conditions that defeat the presumption that an agent intentionally did something wrong. One potential problem for the account, for instance, is the case of responsibility for omissions. Austin's hypothesis seems to take for granted that there is a connection between doing *x* intentionally and

3. It is perhaps worth stressing that what is at issue are *moral* excuses, that is, claims that may be advanced on behalf of an agent who would otherwise be subject to moral blame. There is a use of the word "excuse" in etiquette that does not signal a moral excuse in this sense, and that therefore does not fall within the range of Austin's proposal (as in: "Excuse me, Madame, but you appear to have dropped your glove").

being responsible for doing *x,* a connection that is severed by the excusing conditions. But it is not clear that responsibility for omissions really does require that one intentionally omitted doing what one is held to blame for failing to do—thus one can fairly be blamed for *neglecting* or even *forgetting* to keep an appointment. It remains to be seen whether Austin's general approach can be adapted to handle cases of this kind, and whether it covers all of the conditions accepted as excuses in ordinary moral practice.

Even if it can meet these burdens, however, it is not clear that Austin's proposal would equip us with an account of our excusing judgments sufficient to defeat the incompatibilist's rival hypothesis. For the factor that is isolated by Austin might merely be correlated with some different blameworthiness inhibitor (such as the absence of alternate possibilities), rather than itself being a factor that makes it unfair to blame the agent for her action. To work up Austin's hypothesis into an account of the excuses, therefore, we need an explanation of the normative force of the excuses, as he characterizes them. As I said, Austin seems to presuppose that there is a connection between doing *x* intentionally and being morally responsible for doing *x.* Specifically, on Austin's account it looks as if doing *x* intentionally is ordinarily a condition of responsibility for *x,* such that if *s* has not done *x* intentionally, then it is unfair to hold *s* morally responsible for doing *x.* But *why* should it be a condition of *s*'s blameworthiness that *s* has done *x* intentionally? *Why* would it be unfair to hold *s* responsible for *x* if *s* has not intentionally done *x* in the first place?

A tempting answer to this question is suggested by Hume.[4] Defending the view that causal determination of actions is not only compatible with responsibility but also necessary for it, Hume notes that the actions for which we hold people responsible are transitory phenomena. This raises a puzzle: how can we be justified in holding the continuing agent responsible for a transitory action, long after the action has been performed? The solution, Hume believed, is that we can be justified in holding the agent responsible for the transitory action if the action was caused by some persisting trait in the character of the agent. This in turn suggests an answer to the question of why the recognized excusing conditions excuse. Those conditions, it appears, defeat the presumption that agent *s* performed an act of morally prohibited kind *x,* showing instead that *s* did not really do *x* intentionally. But if *s* did not do *x*

---

4. See Hume, *A Treatise of Human Nature,* bk. 2, pt. 2, sec. 2.

intentionally, then whatever *s* did cannot be taken as evidence of some persisting undesirable character trait of *s*'s, in the way that an intentional performance of *x* normally could be.[5]

This is, as I said, a tempting account. But it seems misleading in its insistence on the need to connect transitory actions to continuing traits of character on the part of the agent who is held responsible. Hume's puzzle, as he presents it, is in fact a superficial one, presumably encouraged by his empiricist conception of personal identity. Of course there must be some connection between the continuing agent and the act for which the agent is held responsible. But it seems overly literal to suppose that the act need be connected with some trait of the continuing agent that itself persists, at the time when the agent is held to blame. People can fairly be held morally responsible even for spontaneous acts whose motives are extinguished after the deed is done. The lack of a persisting malicious motive or character trait might mitigate the degree of blame that would be appropriate, as would the presence of subsequent guilt and remorse; but guilt, remorse, and the absence of persistent malice are not themselves excusing conditions. On the contrary, guilt normally implies the acceptance of responsibility.

Even if we do not require a connection between the action and a literally persisting character trait, however, Hume seems correct to suppose that we require some sort of connection between an agent and an act for which the agent is held responsible. Moreover, he also seems correct to suppose that this connection must tell us something about the state of mind of the agent, at least at the time when the action was performed. As I have said, the accepted excusing conditions all appear to sever this connection, showing that whatever the agent might have done, it did not amount to an intentional doing of *x* (where *x* is an act of a morally impermissible type). The further question, however, is why we should insist on this kind of connection between the action and the attitudes of the agent, as a condition of moral responsibility for an action.

Of course, if *s* did not do *x* intentionally, then there is a clear sense in which there is no action that *s* performed at all; precisely because *s* did not do *x* intentionally, we may conclude that *x* was not really

---

5. Of course, even an unintentional performance can provide evidence of some persisting trait on the part of the agent—for instance, unintentionally treading on someone's toes might be evidence of a general tendency to negligence or thoughtlessness or even recklessness. But it is, at best, evidence of a kind of general trait different from those that a deliberate act of stepping on someone's toes would normally disclose.

something that *s did*. Hence, it seems that there is no action to be assessed one way or the other. But this observation, though correct, does not really address the problem I have raised: to account for the unfairness of holding *s* responsible for something *s* has not intentionally done. To note that we do not hold *s* responsible in these cases because there is no intentional action to be assessed presupposes the unfairness of holding people responsible in the absence of intention; it does not explain that assumption.[6]

But perhaps the problem has no interesting solution; perhaps it is simply a fact about people that they care about the intentions that are expressed in human action. The importance attached to intention for moral responsibility might merely reflect this basic fact about us. A view of this sort is suggested by the following quotation from H. L. A. Hart: "Persons interpret each other's movements as manifestations of intention and choices, and these subjective factors are often more important to their social relations than the movements by which they are manifested or their effects. If one person hits another, the person struck does not think of the other as *just* a cause of pain to him; for it is of crucial importance to him whether the blow was deliberate or involuntary. If the blow struck was light but deliberate, it has a significance for the person struck quite different from an accidental much heavier blow."[7]

Hart's view seems to be that it is a brute fact about people that they attach significance to the intentions expressed in action.[8] Even if this is a brute fact about people, however, I do not think we can explain in terms of it the kind of importance that intention has for moral responsibility and blame. After all, it is equally a brute fact about people that they attach significance to the qualities of emotion and desire that are expressed in human action. For example, it will matter greatly to me whether the object of my affections reciprocates my love, or whether a colleague I admire holds me in high esteem and wants to see me

6. Similar remarks apply to Jonathan Glover's suggestion that the importance attached to intention in action can be traced to an underlying view of the self; see *Responsibility* (London: Routledge and Kegan Paul, 1970), pp. 64–66. Glover proposes, more specifically, that we identify people with their intentions, for purposes of praising or blaming them. But the claim about the self, so qualified, does little more than restate the point that whether *s* did *x* intentionally bears on the question of whether *s* is morally responsible for *x;* it does not explain why blameworthiness depends on intention in this way.

7. H. L. A. Hart, "Punishment and the Elimination of Responsibility," as reprinted in his *Punishment and Responsibility: Essays in the Philosophy of Law* (Oxford: Clarendon Press, 1968), pp. 158–185, at pp. 182–183.

8. See Hart, "Punishment and the Elimination of Responsibility," p. 183.

advance in the profession. Yet the absence of such emotions is not necessarily a moral failing, nor would it interfere with moral responsibility for particular actions in the way the lack of intention seems to do. The point is that humans attach great importance not only to intentions, as these are expressed in action, but also to qualities of emotion and desire. Intention, however, appears to have a significance for questions of moral responsibility and blame that emotion and desire do not. Granting that it is a fact about us that we attach great importance to intentions in action, we still want to know why intention matters to us in the way it does.

An approach to the excusing conditions that begins to answer this question is sketched by P. F. Strawson in "Freedom and Resentment." Strawson notes that the conditions I have referred to as excusing conditions all seem to operate locally: they make it inappropriate to hold an agent responsible for a particular action, but they do not make it inappropriate to view the agent as morally responsible in general.[9] Strawson then proceeds to account for the force of the excusing conditions, so understood, in terms of the reactive attitudes. Given the connection between responsibility and the reactive attitudes, a condition will make it inappropriate to hold an agent responsible for a given action if the condition makes it inappropriate to respond to the action with one of the reactive emotions. Whether one of the reactive emotions will be an appropriate response to a particular action will in turn depend on the expectations with which the reactive emotions are connected, for it is these expectations that fix the proper objects of the reactive emotions.

More specifically, Strawson contends that the reactive attitudes are bound up with expectations concerning, in the first instance, the attitudes and feelings of other people, and of ourselves, as expressed in action: thus we demand that people should display toward each other a degree of respect, consideration, kindness, and so on, and we tend to resent or blame people to the extent that they fail to satisfy these demands.[10] Excusing conditions, then, show that a person who appeared to violate such expectations did not in fact violate them after all. If I

9. See P. F. Strawson, "Freedom and Resentment," as reprinted in Gary Watson, ed., *Free Will* (Oxford: Oxford University Press, 1982), pp. 59–80, at pp. 64–65, 72–73. This is the "internal" strand of argument in Strawson's essay to which I alluded at the beginning of sec. 4.2. (In presenting Strawson's suggestion, I adapt it slightly to fit into the framework of my alternative account of the reactive emotions.)

10. See Strawson, "Freedom and Resentment," pp. 62–63, 67, 70.

learn that someone who has stepped on my foot did so inadvertently, or because she was coerced into doing so, then I will have a reason for withdrawing the resentment I would ordinarily feel. For what I demand of people is that they display a degree of respect and consideration toward others in their behavior, and someone who has acted out of ignorance or coercion will generally not have violated this expectation—even if it initially appeared that she did.[11]

This intriguing proposal suggests a way of developing Austin's approach to excuses different from those previously sketched. Austin proposes that the excusing conditions give us grounds for doubting that s did x intentionally, where x is a kind of action that is admitted to be morally wrong. The challenge confronting this proposal was to explain why the fact that s did not do x intentionally should make it unfair to hold s responsible for x. The other accounts I have considered trace the importance of intention to an interest in connecting action with persisting motives in the agent, or to underlying conceptions of action and the self, or to the brute fact that we care about the attitudes of others. By contrast, Strawson seems to be suggesting that the importance of intention lies in determining whether agent s has really done x, a morally impermissible act, in the first place. If the moral expectations we place on other people are primarily expectations concerning their attitudes toward us and toward others, as manifested in action, then what will be prohibited and required of people will not be types of bodily movement per se, but rather the attitudes expressed in bodily movements.

There is a sense, however, in which this proposal merely *relocates* the problem, shifting it onto the question of why our moral demands should concern the attitudes expressed in action. Why do we demand that people not express hostility or ill will in their actions, instead of demanding simply that they not move their bodies in ways that cause others harm or pain? Why are our reactive emotions specially concerned with what Strawson calls the "quality" of peoples' will,[12] and not merely with the effects of their actions? A further problem is to explain precisely which qualities of will should matter to us, for purposes of ascribing responsibility and apportioning blame. Strawson himself suggests that we care about the "attitudes" and "feelings" that people express in their actions. But while this is no doubt true, not all the attitudes and feelings so expressed seem to matter equally when we

11. Strawson, "Freedom and Resentment," pp. 64–65, 72–73.
12. See, for instance, Strawson, "Freedom and Resentment," p. 70.

are deciding whether a person has done something morally wrong. As was seen in considering Hart's remarks, the quality of intention seems to have a bearing on questions of responsibility and blame that the different qualities of emotion and feeling do not have. A satisfying development of the approach I have sketched should not only tell us why moral demands are focused on the qualities of will expressed in action; it should also explain why some qualities of will are much more important than others.

I address these questions in the following section, arguing that by developing the account of holding people responsible proposed in earlier chapters, one can explain both our general moral concern with the qualities of will expressed in action, and the special importance attached to intention. Once this has been done, however, it will still remain to show that the resulting framework can account adequately for the full range of conditions accepted as excuses in moral practice. If the account is to help in defending against the generalization strategy, it must be established that all of our considered judgments of excuse can be explained without appealing to a principle of fairness that supports incompatibilism, such as the principle of alternate possibilities. To show that this is the case, I need to identify an alternative principle of fairness that explains why people do not deserve to be held to blame when they have not violated the moral demands to which we hold them. I then need to consider the various excuses in sufficient detail to establish that all of our judgments of excuse can be accounted for in terms of this alternative principle; and finally, I need to show that this principle would not support the incompatibilist's conclusion that determinism is a kind of generalized excuse. This is my agenda in the sections to follow.

5.2   Qualities of Will

On the general approach I have extracted from Austin and Strawson, excuses serve to show that an agent has not really done anything wrong. In Strawson's terms, excuses show that *s*'s action, though it may have appeared to violate our moral demands, did not really violate any moral demand that we accept. The approach further claims that excuses perform this function by showing that *s* did not really do *x* intentionally, where it is intentional performances of *x* that are, in the first instance, prohibited by the moral demands we accept. To flesh out the account, something more needs to be said about at least two topics. First, why do moral demands concern themselves with intentional performances?

Second, why would it be unfair to blame someone whose behavior does not express the right quality of intention? What principle of fairness is at work?

As was seen in the preceding section, not all qualities of will that might be expressed by our actions are of equal moral significance. On the account I have proposed, the stance of holding someone to blame for an action is connected with a special class of demands, namely the moral *obligations* one accepts; qualities of will are therefore important to blameworthiness only insofar as they bear on the question of whether such moral obligations have been violated. But for this purpose, the qualities of will that matter would seem primarily to be an agent's *choices*.[13] Only if an action expresses a choice of some sort can we say that a moral obligation has either been violated or complied with. Consider the moral obligation of nonmaleficence, for instance: this is not simply an obligation not to make bodily movements that harm other people. Rather it is an obligation not to act in ways that express the choice to harm other people, in the ordinary pursuit of one's own ends. Accordingly, the primary target of moral assessment in terms of this obligation is not bodily movement per se, nor is it the emotions and desires to which we are subject; rather it is the quality of choice expressed in what we do. Thus we are not blamed for violating the duty of nonmaleficence except when what we do results from a choice to harm someone. Indeed, the degree of our moral fault is determined essentially by the quality of the choices on which we act, regardless of whether we succeed in achieving the ends fixed by these volitional states. If I set out to harm someone, but fail because, say, the knife slips out of my hand, I am no less blameworthy (from the moral point of view) than I would have been had I succeeded in inflicting harm.[14] Similar remarks apply to the other classes of moral obligation that we accept and hold people to—a point Kant acknowledged by treating maxims of action as the primary target of moral assessment.[15]

The fact that the stance of holding people responsible is connected

13. I shall use the term "choice" generically, to refer to a basic volitional element in human action; other expressions that might be deployed include "intention" or "decision." For purposes of my discussion, nuanced differences between these volitional concepts will not be important.

14. Of course, there may be very good reasons to distinguish between these cases in the law, but that is a different story—something Thomas Nagel apparently neglects in his influential essay "Moral Luck," reprinted in Watson, ed., *Free Will*, pp. 174–186.

15. It would be out of place here to launch a discussion of choice (or of Kant's notion of a maxim). But three points may be noted. First, as I construe them, choices are subject to the direct

to the notion of moral obligation thus helps to explain the special importance of an agent's choices, for as we ordinarily interpret them, moral obligations are focused on just these qualities of will. But why do moral obligations have this peculiar focus? To answer this question, and hence to deepen our understanding of the importance of intention to responsibility, it will help to further develop the account I have offered of the stance of holding people to moral obligations we accept. As I have said, moral obligations are supported by reasons, of the sort that may be expressed in the form of principles. To take a simple example: one's moral obligation to pick up a friend at the airport might in the first instance be justified by appealing to the fact that one has promised to pick up the friend, and to the principle that it is wrong to break the promises one has made. This principle may in turn admit of further justification, in terms of more general moral principles. It might be that the obligation to keep one's promises derives from a general principle to the effect that we must not disappoint expectations that we have deliberately induced in other people, or it might instead derive from considerations about the conventional nature of promising, and from a principle enjoining us to play by the rules of conventions that we have voluntarily participated in and benefited from. Deciding between these accounts requires systematic reflection about a wide range of cases, with the aim of isolating the kind of wrong that promise breaking involves,[16] and it is plain that most of us hold ourselves and others to obligations of promise keeping without having undertaken a philosophical investigation of this kind. Still, if one genuinely accepts a specific moral obligation for purposes of practical deliberation and public discourse, there will have to be *some* justification one could cite in support of the obligation. In the promising case, one should be able to say at least that a given course of action is an instance of promise keeping, and that it is wrong to break the promises one has made— even if one has not worked out more exactly what kind of wrong it is that promise breaking involves, and even if one is skeptical that there

---

influence of practical deliberation about one's reasons for action. Second, I contend that every intentional action open to moral assessment involves a moment of choice. Of course, many morally significant actions are spontaneous, not preceded by an episode of prior deliberation. It follows— third—that choices, as I understand them, are not necessarily episodes in one's mental life, prior to and phenomenologically distinguishable from the intentional actions to which they lead.

16. See Thomas Scanlon, "Promises and Practices," *Philosophy and Public Affairs* 19 (1990), pp. 199–226, for an example of this kind of inquiry.

is anything more general to say about why promise breaking is impermissible.[17]

I will take this as a further specification of the distinctively *moral*
stance of holding people to moral obligations we accept. Reflecting the
special connection between moral obligations and the reasons expressed
in principles, the moral stance of holding people to such obligations
involves a commitment to the possibility of justifying the obligations
by appealing to moral principles. These principles articulate reasons for
acting in conformity with the obligations we accept. In the case of
genuinely moral attitudes, they will be the very reasons that explain
why we strive to comply with the obligations to which we hold
ourselves. They are also reasons that could be cited to others to support
the obligations to which we hold them, and that could move others
who accept those reasons to comply with such obligations themselves.
The stance of holding people to moral obligations one accepts in this
way incorporates a commitment to justifications, identifying reasons
that could move both the judge and the agent held responsible to
comply with the obligations in question.

This is not to say that those we hold to moral obligations must
already have a motive for complying with those obligations, supplied
by their prior acceptance of the very reasons we take to justify them.
The point is, rather, that moral reasons are of a sort that, *if* accepted by
those we hold responsible, could motivate the compliance of those
agents with the obligations they justify; this is the role that moral reasons
play in the deliberations of the agents who accept them.[18] Note also
that when we hold other people to moral obligations we accept, we
do not literally demand that they comply with the obligations because
they grasp the moral reasons for doing so. At least for purposes of
apportioning blame, we generally do not care so much why people
comply with the moral obligations to which we hold them, so long as

17. As this example illustrates, the principles that justify particular obligations (such as the
obligation to pick up one's friend at the airport) may themselves take the form of slightly more
general statements of obligation (for example, that we are required to keep the promises we have
made). The commitment to justification incorporated in the stance of holding people to obligations
one accepts is thus fairly minimal; it is a commitment to *some* general statement of obligation that
isolates a right-making feature of particular cases.

18. Acceptance of obligations and their supporting justifications, as I construe it, thus has a
motivational dimension. For my present purposes, it may be left an open question whether this
motivational element is somehow tied to the content of moral justifications (as "internalists"
maintain) or is, rather, supplied by the psychological stance that I have called "acceptance." (For
more on this stance, see sec. 2.4.)

they do comply with those obligations in fact.[19] Thus, though I would resent someone who deliberately set out to harm me, I would not necessarily resent a person who refrained from harming me for non-moral rather than moral reasons (out of a fear of legal sanctions, say). Nevertheless, insofar as my stance is a genuinely moral one, I commit myself to the availability of reasons that support and motivate my compliance with the obligations in question, and that could move those I hold responsible to do so as well.[20]

This has implications for the content of moral obligations. Specifically, it suggests that such obligations can properly be focused only on phenomena that are susceptible to being influenced directly by reasons. That is, *what* one is obligated to do must be the sort of thing that could be motivated by one's grasp of the reasons expressed in moral principles; otherwise the commitment to justification that is inherent in the stance of holding people responsible cannot be sustained. But neither emotions and feelings nor mere bodily movements appear to be phenomena of this sort. Emotions and feelings have their reasons of course, in the sense that they often have propositional objects, which are explained by their privileged connection to certain sorts of beliefs (a point I have had extensive opportunity to confirm in this book, in connection with the reactive emotions). Particular states of emotion or feeling, however, are not the sorts of states that can directly be controlled by the reasons expressed in moral principles: such states as love,

---

19. It is of course otherwise when questions of character assessment are at issue: there we do care very much what an agent's reasons for acting really were. There may also be a disanalogy between the first- and third-person cases, with respect to questions of blame. Thus, though it would be strange for others to resent or be indignant with me when I comply with moral obligations for the wrong reasons, it would not necessarily be strange for me to feel guilt in such cases. Compare Kant's suggestion that we have a duty to ourselves to strive to act from purely moral motives, in the *Metaphysics of Morals*, "Doctrine of Virtue," pt. 1, secs. 21–22.

20. Compare Gary Watson's suggestive proposal that the reactive attitudes are incipiently forms of moral communication, in "Responsibility and the Limits of Evil," pp. 264–265. As Watson is of course aware, we often hold people responsible for what they do without literally communicating our attitude toward them. In what way, then, are our attitudes incipiently forms of communication? Watson may be pointing toward the feature of the moral reactive attitudes I have been describing in the text, namely that the obligations they are connected with are supported by moral justifications. Since those justifications, in turn, are expressed in moral principles, we might say that the moral reactive attitudes are "incipiently" connected with the communication of reasons by means of principles. See also T. M. Scanlon's suggestion that morality is a "system of co-deliberation"; Scanlon, "The Significance of Choice," in Sterling M. McMurrin, ed., *The Tanner Lectures on Human Values,* vol. 8 (Salt Lake City: University of Utah Press, 1988), pp. 149–216, at pp. 166–167.

esteem, and goodwill are generally not states that could be produced simply by the belief that there are moral considerations that make them obligatory.[21] This is why we cannot plausibly interpret moral obligations as governing the quality of peoples' will, where such qualities are construed broadly, to encompass emotions and feelings quite generally.

The reasons expressed in moral principles are *practical* reasons, or reasons for *action*. This suggests that such reasons should regulate what we do, the bodily movements that we make. But it is not bodily movements considered merely as such that are subject to the direct influence of moral reasons. Rather it is bodily movements insofar as they manifest a choice that is made by the agent. We make choices precisely on the basis of reasons we grasp and accept; it is only through the mediation of our choices that the reasons expressed in moral principles may influence either our emotions or feelings, or the bodily movements we make.[22] This means that one can be said to have *complied* with a moral obligation only when there is present a relevant quality of choice. Someone who inadvertently bumps into me, thereby knocking me out of harm's way, has in no sense complied with the obligation of mutual aid; by contrast, a person can be said to have complied with the obligation if she acted out of a choice to save me from harm—even if the choice was based on reasons of a self-interested rather than a moral nature. Similarly, one cannot be said to have *violated* a moral obligation in the absence of a relevant quality of choice.

We have, then, an explanation of the idea that the moral obligations we hold people to concern qualities of will as expressed in action. This idea does not simply record a brute fact about the objects of our moral attitudes, as Hart and Strawson seem to suppose (see section 5.1). Rather, one can make sense of this idea by relating it to the distinctively moral stance of holding people to obligations we accept, a stance that reflects, in its turn, the defining role that reasons play in supporting

21. This is not to rule out the indirect influence of these emotional states by moral justifications: believing, for instance, that goodwill is morally desirable, and pride or patriotism morally objectionable, one might take steps to cultivate the one emotion and to rid oneself of the others. Indeed, one might even have a moral duty to take such steps: for this view, see (for instance) Kant's remarks on the indirect duty to cultivate sympathetic feelings in ourselves, in the *Metaphysics of Morals*, "Doctrine of Virtue," pt. 2, sec. 35.

22. I here echo some remarks of Scanlon's, in "The Significance of Choice," pp. 170–172. Scanlon's remarks are offered in the context of a discussion of the "special force" of judgments of moral responsibility, but as I explained in sec. 3.3, it is obscure how the susceptibility of choices to the direct influence of reasons might account for the special force of moral judgments. Scanlon's remarks, it seems to me, are better taken as locating one of the conditions of responsibility. (This theme is developed further in Chapter 6.)

moral obligations. But with this explanation in place, it also becomes clear why we should attach so much moral importance to the question of whether the bodily movement that a person has made was or was not intentional. If such a movement was not intentional, it will generally not express any particular choice that the agent has made, and so it will not provide grounds for thinking that a moral obligation we hold the agent to has been violated. Take the obligation of nonmaleficence, not to harm people in the ordinary pursuit of one's ends. In accordance with the remarks just made, this must be construed as an obligation not to make bodily movements that harm someone, as the result of a choice to bring about such harm. Now if *s* makes a movement that harms someone (treading on another's hand, say), but it turns out that *s* did not tread on the person's hand intentionally, then what *s* did will not constitute a case of harming someone as the result of a choice to bring about such harm. Hence *s* will not have breached the obligation of nonmaleficence, and it would be inappropriate to hold *s* responsible for a violation of that duty.

In what way would this be inappropriate? What kind of reason would the fact that *s* did not do *x* intentionally give us not to hold *s* responsible for *x*? This is the second topic I said I would address, and I am now in a position to turn to it. At issue are the conditions in which it would be appropriate to hold someone morally responsible for a particular act, in the sense of viewing the action as morally blameworthy. To hold someone responsible in this way, I have proposed, is to be subject to a reactive emotion because one believes the act to have violated a moral obligation one accepts, or it is to believe that the person's having violated such an obligation would make it appropriate for one to be subject to such a reactive emotion.[23] If this is right, then holding someone morally responsible for a particular act presupposes a state of belief, namely the belief that the act violates a moral obligation one accepts. It is this belief, for instance, that determines the propositional object of a particular state of reactive emotion such as resentment or indignation, fixing what it is that the resentment or indignation is *about*. But I have suggested that excuses function by showing that the agent did not really violate the moral obligations we accept after all. It follows that excuses make it inappropriate to hold an agent responsible for a

---

23. In what follows, I take this second clause to be understood. This will not affect the discussion of excuses, since the conditions that make it appropriate to be subject to a reactive emotion are precisely the conditions that make it appropriate to *believe* that it would be appropriate to be subject to a reactive emotion.

particular action, by undermining a belief that is incorporated in the stance of holding the agent responsible for the action. To hold *s* morally responsible for *x*, when an excusing condition obtains, would involve the false belief that *s's* *x*-ing violated a moral obligation we accept; this gives us a reason for not holding people to blame when the excusing conditions are present.

This conclusion is slightly puzzling, however. I have maintained that it is a condition of moral blameworthiness for a given action—a B-condition of responsibility—that the action violates some moral obligation that we accept.[24] But why is this a condition of blameworthiness for a given action? The account just sketched traces the answer to our theoretical interest in the truth: to hold *s* responsible for *x* is (in part) to believe that *x* has violated a moral obligation we accept, and this belief would be false if *x* did not in fact violate a moral obligation of this kind. Excuses function precisely by removing this important B-condition of responsibility. The reason they give us not to hold people to blame for specific actions thus appears to derive primarily from our theoretical interest in the truth.[25] But what about the moral issue of fairness? It has been a leading idea of my discussion that it would be not only theoretically improper but also morally wrong to hold people to blame when an excusing condition is present. Furthermore, incompatibilists would appear to be well positioned to explain this moral aspect of the excuses. The principle of alternate possibilities, for instance, can be represented as a moral principle, latent in our considered judgments of excuse, to the effect that people do not deserve to be blamed for their actions if they could not have done otherwise.

The approach I have sketched, however, also has the resources to

24. I thus demur from the account of culpability offered by Michael J. Zimmerman, in *An Essay on Moral Responsibility* (Totowa, N.J.: Rowman and Littlefield, 1988); see especially sec. 3.1. Zimmerman contends that one may be culpable even if one has not done something wrong, so long as one *believed* that what one was doing was wrong. On my account, this may not be the case. What matters is whether the agents we hold responsible have in fact violated the obligations we hold them to, and this condition might not be satisfied even when the agents believe they have done something wrong. (Consider the concentration camp guard, who violates what he takes to be his duty with an act of kindness to a prisoner in his charge.) Of course, it may be that among the moral obligations we hold people to is a "metaobligation" that they should follow their conscience, never doing what they believe to be wrong. In that case, believing oneself to have acted wrongly would be a sufficient condition for culpability. But this would follow not from a general analysis of blameworthiness, but from a specific claim about the *content* of our moral obligations.

25. The possibility of assessing the stance of holding someone responsible in this way, in light of theoretical norms, was anticipated in sec. 4.1.

account for the moral dimension of the excuses. Indeed, it can explain this aspect of the excuses in terms whose moral significance is much more secure than is the principle of alternate possibilities. On my approach, excuses function by showing that an agent has not really done anything wrong. When this is the case, it will not merely be theoretically improper to hold the agent to blame (because doing so would involve a false belief); it will also be morally unfair, for it is surely the case that people do not deserve to be blamed if they have not done anything wrong in the first place. As I have shown, to hold someone blameworthy is to be subject to a reactive emotion on account of what the person has done, where such emotions naturally find expression in sanctioning behavior—condemnation, reproach, avoidance, and the like. These emotions and sanctions are essentially reactions to a moral wrong on the part of the agent who is held to blame. Hence those who have not in fact done anything wrong clearly do not *deserve* to be subjected to the reactive emotions and the forms of sanctioning treatment that express them. This is a fundamental principle of desert; it expresses an abstract moral conviction in which reflective moral judges have the highest degree of confidence. By drawing on this fundamental principle—I will call it the principle of no blameworthiness without fault—the approach I have sketched suggests an absolutely compelling account of the moral force of the excuses. By contrast, the principle of alternate possibilities does not have nearly so secure a place in the scheme of our moral convictions. That principle derives its primary force from its claim to be implicit in our particular, concrete judgments of excuse and exemption; considered in abstraction from those judgments, the principle is not one that we would be very confident in endorsing.

Suppose, then, that we can account for the full range of excuses in terms of the framework I have proposed, showing that they are all conditions in which an agent has not done anything wrong, because of the absence of the necessary quality of choice. This would yield a unified and persuasive account of our concrete moral judgments of excuse, explaining in straightforward terms why people do not deserve to be blamed when the excusing conditions obtain. Furthermore, the explanation provided would leave no basis for the incompatibilist's generalization argument, since it is doubtful in the extreme that the truth of determinism would entail that people never act on choices that violate moral obligations we accept. This in turn would deal a severe blow to the principle of alternate possibilities. That principle derives its primary appeal from its claim to be necessary to account for our concrete judgments of exemption and excuse; but with respect to the excuses, at least, it would have been shown that those judgments can all be explained—and powerfully explained—without appealing to the principle of alternate possibilities, or to any other principle that would generalize if determinism is true.

5.3   A Typology of Excuses

To confirm the adequacy of the general framework I have just sketched, I will now look in some detail at the variety of excuses actually accepted in moral practice. As was seen in section 5.1, it is an important test of an account of excuses that it yield a plausible explanation of all the main kinds of excusing conditions. For analytical purposes these may be divided into four broad classes: inadvertence, mistake or accident; un-intentional bodily movements; physical constraint; and coercion, necessity, and duress.[26]

(a) Inadvertence, Mistake, or Accident

Intentions are sensitive to beliefs. To do something of a certain kind intentionally, one must know that one is doing something of that kind. More precisely, to do something of kind *x,* as the result of the choice to do something of kind *x,* one must believe that what one is undertaking to do is of kind *x,* at the time that one makes the choice to do it.[27]

Suppose I do something that happens to be of kind *x*. The first class of excuses defeats a presumption that I did *x* intentionally, by showing that I did not know that I would be doing something of kind *x* at all

26. I have left out of this classification dilemmas, which are sometimes included on lists of the ordinary excuses, because an adequate treatment of the issues they raise would take me too far afield. The basic difficulty is that those who believe there are moral dilemmas also tend to deny that dilemmas function as excuses; on the contrary, they take the appropriateness of guilt in situations of moral conflict to indicate that such situations involve genuine dilemmas. Those who accept the principle that ought implies can, on the other hand, tend to deny that there are genuine conflicts of obligation. (For some remarks on the principle that ought implies can, see sec. 7.4.)

27. This is not to imply that the choice is necessarily a mental episode prior to the act that is explained in terms of it. But when it is prior to the act, the point at which ignorance functions as an excuse is the time when the choice is made, not the time when the action is carried out. (One may know perfectly well what is happening as the ice gives way under one's feet and one falls into the lake. But this may still be an accident, if one did not anticipate that it would happen when one decided to cross the ice.)

when I chose to do whatever it was that turned out to be of kind *x*. Thus if I tread on *s*'s hand inadvertently, while walking to the refrigerator to get a beer, then I must not have anticipated that I would be treading on *s*'s hand when I made the choice to get a beer. If I tread on *s*'s hand by mistake, I may have known that I would be treading on a hand, but not that it was *s*'s hand that I would be treading on (perhaps I took the hand for *p*'s, where *p* was a thief trying to reach for the weapon on the floor). And if I tread on *s*'s hand accidentally (say, while trying to stomp out the flames), I may know that I am treading on a hand at the time when my treading motion occurs. But again, I will generally have lacked the foreknowledge that I would be treading on *s*'s hand, at the time when I made the choice that led to the treading activity.[28]

As with actions, so with omissions. At least with the cases of inadvertence and mistake, one could omit to do something of kind *x* out of ignorance that what one has chosen to do would amount to a failure to do *x*.[29] For instance, while working in my office I might omit to extinguish the fire in the office next door inadvertently, not knowing that there is a fire in the next office at all (and so not knowing that, by choosing to go on working, I am failing to put out the fire). Or I might omit to extinguish the fire by mistake, pushing a button that I falsely believe will remove all the oxygen in the neighboring office (in fact it activates an air conditioning unit in the men's room).[30] Notice that in all these cases—actions as well as omissions—the effect of excusing conditions on blameworthiness will be highly localized. Treading on *s*'s hand by mistake or accident or inadvertence at most blocks one's responsibility for treading on *s*'s hand; it does not affect at all one's responsibility for the other things one knowingly undertook

28. With accidents, it may be the case that the agent recognized some low probability that something of kind *x* would occur, at the time when the choice was formed. But if the agent actually anticipates that something of kind *x* will occur, we would no longer say that *x* occurred by accident. Rather *x* would be, at best, a foreseen but unintended consequence of what the agent does.

29. Whether one could accidentally omit to do something in this way seems to me doubtful. In *Responsibility*, p. 60, Jonathan Glover suggests otherwise, proposing that "[i]t was an accidental omission if I set off to go and do it, but on the way the car broke down." This case seems to me better described, however, as a case in which physical constraint is the excusing condition, and the physical constraint, in turn, is caused by an accident: one did not accidentally omit to do the thing in question, one was physically prevented from doing it by an accident.

30. I say a bit more about the topic of responsibility for omissions in my discussion of the third class of excusing conditions: physical constraint.

to do at the same time (walking to the refrigerator, trying to thwart a thief, stomping out the flames).

Furthermore, excuses in this first class may not be accepted at all if the ignorance that makes what one did unintentional is itself culpable. In that case it will be taken not for a valid excuse, but for evidence of one of a different family of moral faults that includes negligence, carelessness, forgetfulness, and recklessness. Thus if the *s* whose hand I tread on is a baby I am supposed to be looking after, then I am presumably under an obligation to keep track of where the child is and what he is up to, and so my ignorance that I would be treading on the child's hand by going to the refrigerator would not excuse my treading on his hand. More precisely: it might excuse me from responsibility for directly treading on the child's hand, but only by making me vulnerable to the different charge of negligence, which led to the hand's being damaged. In cases of negligence or carelessness, I take it, the agent does not anticipate a consequence of her action that she ought to have anticipated, where the consequence is a matter of some moral significance. With recklessness, by contrast, the agent will have known that there was some risk that the undesirable consequence would occur, and this level of risk ought to have been taken as a sufficient ground for refraining from undertaking the course of action in question.[31]

Both negligence and recklessness can be taken to reflect qualities of will, as expressed in action, and so to be appropriate grounds for blame, on the account I have been developing. But the qualities displayed when negligence or recklessness leads to *x* are different from those involved in intentionally doing *x*. Recklessness, as I have construed it, involves a cavalier attitude toward risk that shows itself in the relation between one's choice and one's awareness of the risk in acting on that choice. One does something that brings about *x*, without intending to do so or even knowing that *x* would occur, but in the awareness that there was some risk that *x* would occur. This is an aspect of choice that is subject to being controlled directly by reasons (thus one might undertake to act more carefully, accepting that it is wrong to take a cavalier attitude toward risk), and so recklessness can itself be a blame-

---

31. Compare the Law Commission definition of recklessness, quoted by Anthony Kenny in *Freewill and Responsibility* (London: Routledge and Kegan Paul, 1978), p. 63. So construed, recklessness is never really a question of culpable ignorance, but of a known or anticipated risk that is not sufficiently taken into account. Hence, though recklessness may perhaps lead one to do something accidentally, it seems it cannot lead one to do something inadvertently or by mistake.

worthy quality of will.[32] Negligence and forgetfulness are slightly harder cases, perhaps, because there may not even be awareness of the risks involved at the time when one acts negligently or forgetfully. Here one may have to trace the moral fault to an earlier episode of choice: agreeing to look after the child, for instance, I may then have failed to take steps sufficient to ensure that I would uphold this agreement, where this led to the child's negligently being harmed.[33] Once again, this feature of my earlier choice—whether or not I took precautions to ensure that my agreement would be carried out—is subject to the direct influence of reasons, since I might have chosen to take precautions because I recognized this to be required by my agreement to care for the child. In this way, negligence and forgetfulness may also be traced to a blameworthy quality of will.[34]

But when neither negligence nor recklessness is at issue, it seems clear that excusing conditions of the first class function to render what one did (or an aspect of what one did) unintentional, where this in turn means that one has not in fact violated a moral obligation after all. When I step on *s*'s hand, you at first take me to have violated the duty of nonmaleficence, which you both accept and hold me to; learning that I stepped on *s*'s hand only inadvertently, or accidentally, or by mistake, you no longer hold me responsible for stepping on *s*'s hand, because you no longer believe that in doing so I violated the duty of nonmaleficence—though you may continue to hold me responsible for other intentional aspects of what I did, or possibly for negligence or recklessness.

32. The same kind of explanation will apply to responsibility for foreseen but unintended consequences of one's actions. Thus moral obligations may prohibit not just choosing to do *x* directly, but also choosing to do something that one knows will lead to *x*, as well as choosing to do something when one is aware that there is a risk of *x*'s resulting. I may blame my neighbor for undertaking an excavation that he knew would cause my house to collapse, or that he knew to risk this outcome, even if it was not his direct intention to damage my property at all. (Of course, the kind of wrong involved will be different in these various cases.)

33. For a defense of this way of accounting for the moral fault of negligence or forgetfulness, see Barbara Herman, "What Happens to the Consequences?" as reprinted in her *The Practice of Moral Judgment* (Cambridge, Mass.: Harvard University Press, 1993), pp. 94–112, especially secs. 2 and 3.

34. Moral principles may thus intelligibly regulate not just the content of choices, but also the way those choices are arrived at and executed. Neglecting this point leads H. L. A. Hart sometimes to downplay the role of the "subjective element" of intention and choice in accounting for responsibility for particular acts; see his "Negligence, *Mens Rea*, and Criminal Responsibility," as reprinted in his *Punishment and Responsibility*, pp. 136–157. For a brief discussion of differences in the legal and moral uses of the terms "negligence," "carelessness," and "recklessness," see *Punishment and Responsibility*, pp. 259–260.

(b) Unintentional Bodily Movements

A second class of excuses singles out cases in which it would be natural to say that the agent did not really *do* anything at all, though the agent's body may have moved in ways that harmed someone else or otherwise appeared to violate our moral obligations. Examples include reflex bodily movements caused by disease (say, an epileptic fit or St. Vitus's dance); reflex bodily movements caused by external stimuli (flailing movements provoked by the attack of a swarm of bees, or by being severely tickled); bodily movements that occur while one is unconscious (rolling over and smothering one's child while asleep or in a drunken stupor, or entering a neighbor's house while sleepwalking); and bodily movements caused by external forces or agents (being pushed onto someone else by the surge of the crowd, or having one's hand used as an implement to beat a third party, by the forcible exertions of another agent—"main force," as it is sometimes called).

In all of these cases it seems quite clear that there is no intentional action at all to be held responsible for. One's body may have moved in a way that caused harm, or that otherwise appeared to violate the moral obligations we accept. But the bodily movements in question did not express any quality of choice, and so they cannot be taken, strictly speaking, to violate the moral obligations we hold people to (taking moral obligations, again, to govern the choices expressed in action). To say that a choice is expressed in an agent's action is generally to say that the action results from the agent's choice.[35] But in the cases where excuses of the second class obtain, there is typically no state that could be described as a choice to move one's body in the way that it moves;[36]

---

35. Except in cases of negligence, this is a B-condition of moral responsibility. It follows that there is usually a volitional element, additional to foreknowledge of consequences, that is required for responsibility for those consequences. H. L. A. Hart argues against such a volitional condition of responsibility, in "Acts of Will and Responsibility," as reprinted in his *Punishment and Responsibility*, pp. 90–112. But if we deny the volitional condition, it is hard to account plausibly for the excusing force of conditions such as automatism and reflex movement; for this point, see J. L. Mackie, "The Grounds of Responsibility," in P. M. S. Hacker and J. Raz, eds., *Law, Morality, and Society: Essays in Honour of H. L. A. Hart* (Oxford: Clarendon Press, 1977), pp. 175–188. More basically, as I have suggested, we presuppose that volitional states (such as choice) directly influence action when we hold people to moral obligations we accept; this is what led me to say that such states are the proper target of moral assessment in terms of moral obligations.

36. A precious exception to this generalization would perhaps be a case where one wants a reflex movement to occur, and so contracts to have oneself violently tickled or attacked by a swarm of bees.

and even when there is such a mental state, it is never true, in these cases, that the bodily movements result directly from such a choice.

As with the first class, excuses of the second sort may not fully deprive one of responsibility if one was negligent or reckless in getting oneself into the situation in which the excuses were operative. This is clearest with the drunken stupor case that I mentioned above: usually one is fully responsible for taking the steps that lead to one's being inebriated to the point of stupefaction, and if one does this knowing that the condition of stupefaction presents some risk of harm, one can fairly be held responsible for recklessness. Similarly, if one knows oneself to be an exceptionally deep sleeper, it is probably reckless to go to sleep knowing that there is a baby lying next to one; and if one has a history of sleepwalking, it is probably reckless not to take steps to prevent oneself from straying into the neighbor's house. But even when reck-lessness of this sort is present, one should be held responsible not for the unintentional bodily movements one made, but for the recklessness that led one to be in a condition in which those movements were made. The reason, again, is that the bodily movements in question do not themselves violate moral obligations we hold people to, because they do not directly express the agent's choices.

(c) Physical Constraint

Excuses in the third category involve cases where one omits to do something morally obligatory because one is physically constrained from moving one's body in the way that is necessary to fulfill the obligation. The physical constraint in question is often external: thus one may be prevented from keeping a promise to rendezvous with a friend by being handcuffed, hit over the head, restrained by the police, stuck in a traffic jam or a derailed subway car, or locked in one's office. But the physical constraint might equally be "internal" to the agent's body, as one might say, due for instance to paralysis or physical collapse, or to a stroke or heart attack.[37]

On the account I have sketched, obligations are concerned with the choices expressed in action. There are two ways in which omissions

---

37. Some of these cases will provide us simultaneously with multiple grounds for not holding the agent responsible: the victim of a severe stroke, for instance, might not only have an excuse for particular acts of omission, but also an exemption from being treated as a morally accountable agent, at least in the immediate aftermath of the stroke.

might express this quality of will, and hence be the sorts of things that may properly be said to violate moral obligations. First, the failure to do *x* might be the result of a choice not to do *x,* but to do something else instead (hearing cries for help in my neighbor's office next door, I may decide to stay in my office rather than go next door to investigate). Or the omission may result from negligence or recklessness, where negligence and recklessness may be traced to different aspects of choice: a failure to take reasonable precautions, perhaps on an earlier occasion of choice (negligence), or a cavalier attitude toward risk (recklessness). In this way, one can see how the claim that blameworthiness requires intention can be accommodated to cases of blameworthy omissions that are not themselves intentional (a problem I raised in section 5.1). The idea is that in cases of this sort, there are different choices the agent has made that may exhibit the qualities of negligence (as in cases in which one carelessly forgets to keep an appointment) or recklessness.

But when an omission is due solely to physical constraint, it will generally not involve either of the two kinds of culpable choice that I have described. If *s* fails to keep a promise because of a subway derailment, or because he is locked in his office by a malicious student, or because of the sudden onset of paralysis, then his failure to keep the promise is not due to a choice to break the promise in order to do something else instead. Nor will such cases typically reflect qualities of negligence or recklessness (unless, for instance, the subway derails frequently enough that the decision to travel by that means of locomotion itself betrays a failure to take reasonable care, or a cavalier attitude toward risk). But if the failure to do something because of physical constraint is not a case of an omission that expresses some quality of choice, then it cannot be said to violate any moral obligation we accept. Again, it appears that excuses function by defeating a presumption that the agent has breached such a moral obligation.

Of course if physical constraint is to function in this way, it must be the case that the omission is genuinely due to the physical constraint alone. If, for instance, one decides not to meet one's obligation to rendezvous with the friend, but one discovers that one has all along been handcuffed to one's chair or locked in one's office, these forms of constraint will not be valid excuses for the failure to meet the obligation. In these cases, despite the presence of physical constraints, one's omission nevertheless expresses precisely the kind of choice that our moral obligations prohibit. Here we see the grain of truth in Harry Frankfurt's contention that it is not the inability to do otherwise that deprives one of moral responsibility for one's actions, but the fact that what one does is explained solely by the circumstances that make it inevitable.[38] What I have called physical constraints all make it inevitable, in some sense, that one will omit to do something that is morally obligatory; but they will only provide valid excuses when they alone account for the omission.

Furthermore, the account I have sketched explains why moral responsibility for omissions should be sensitive in this way to the explanatory role of inevitability.[39] The reason is that it is only when physical constraints alone account for one's omission that we can infer that the omission does not express the agent's choices. Hence it is only in those cases that physical constraint defeats a presumption that one's omission has violated a moral obligation.

(d) Coercion, Necessity, and Duress

The fourth set of excuses involves intentional actions or omissions that aim to avoid some substantial harm that is threatened or anticipated. A classic example is that of the bank clerk who hands over cash to the thief, to avoid being shot. But the harm that is to be avoided need not be a harm to the agent whose action is excused, nor need it be a harm that is threatened by another agent. The teller's action would as effectively be excused if it were chosen to avoid the execution of a child, whom the thief had taken hostage and threatened to kill. Similarly, the fact that one has credibly been threatened with severe torture may excuse one's disclosing an industrial secret that one has promised to keep confidential; but such an action would equally be excused if the target of the threatened torture had instead been one's mother or husband. Finally, there are cases in which the harm to be avoided is not the result of the actual or threatened interventions of another agent. The starving victim of a plane crash may be excused for stealing food from a village shop to save his life; or—to adapt a famous example from

---

38. See Harry Frankfurt, "Alternate Possibilities and Moral Responsibility," as reprinted in his *The Importance of What We Care About: Philosophical Essays* (Cambridge: Cambridge University Press, 1988), pp. 1–10, at pp. 9–10. The point is also implicit in Frankfurt's influential treatment of addiction, in "Freedom of the Will and the Concept of a Person," as reprinted in *The Importance of What We Care About,* pp. 11–25. I discuss Frankfurt's views about alternate possibilities in more detail in Appendix 2, and take up his account of addiction in Chapter 6.

39. Frankfurt also suggests an explanation of this point, but it turns on the problematic and undeveloped idea that higher-order identification is a necessary condition of moral responsibility for one's actions; see, again, the discussion in Appendix 2.

Aristotle—someone who has agreed to transport goods across the ocean may be excused for throwing them overboard, if that act is necessary to prevent the ship from capsizing in a storm.[40]

It is a common feature of all these cases that the agent does something intentionally that to all appearances violates a moral obligation: flouting one's obligations to the bank, or to the colleagues in the firm whose confidence one betrays, or to the shop owner whose food one steals, or to the friend whose goods one has agreed to transport. And yet in all of these cases it would seem unfair to hold the agent blameworthy for violating moral obligations. Why? The answer, I believe, is the very answer I arrived at in considering the other classes of excusing conditions, namely that the agent has not really violated the moral obligations that we accept. To see this, it is important to note a complexity in the structure of moral obligations that I have not hitherto had occasion to mention. Take, for example, the bank teller's obligation not to distribute the bank's funds to those who are not authorized to have access to those funds. This obligation would be violated by the teller's intentionally giving the bank's money to his friends, in order to please them, or by his stealing the money himself, for the purpose of personal enrichment. But the choice expressed in those actions is quite different from the choice expressed in the teller's giving the bank's money to a thief, in order to avoid his own death or the death of a hostage. Moreover, the difference is such that only actions of the former sort express a choice that violates our moral obligations, for we do not generally require bank tellers to perform their ordinary professional role if the result will be their own death or the death of a hostage.

More formally, one may say that moral obligations generally rule out doing actions of kind x, as a result of the choice to do something of kind x. Excuses in the final class function by showing that agent s's doing x actually expressed a different kind of motive: not merely a choice to do x, but a choice to do x-rather-than-y, or x-in-order-to-avoid-y. Of course, for nearly any case in which an agent s does x intentionally, there will be some y such that s could truly be said to do x as the result of a choice to do x-rather-than-y: the embezzling bank clerk, for instance, chooses to violate his professional duties rather than engage in honest toil. Whether an explanation of this form will serve as an excuse will then depend on the content of our moral obligations— in particular, whether they prohibit intentionally doing x-rather-than-y.

40. See the Aristotle, *Nicomachean Ethics*, bk. 3, chap. 1. Such cases are sometimes referred to as cases of necessity, and are distinguished from coercion or duress, where the harm or penalty is threatened or administered by another agent.

This in turn will depend on the action descriptions that are substituted for the variables x and y: stealing food to avoid starvation may be morally permissible, but it is not clear that killing and eating another human being to avoid starvation is permissible;[41] it is clearly not permissible to kill or torture someone in order to avoid, say, the theft of a postage stamp or having someone step on one's toe.

For this reason not all cases of doing something to avoid an anticipated or threatened harm will constitute valid or successful excuses.[42] Whether they do or not will depend on the principles that support the moral obligations we accept, since these principles determine the range of actions that can be justified by the need to avoid a given level of harm. Presumably a rough rule of thumb is that the avoidance of a given harm y can justify doing an otherwise prohibited act x only if the moral significance of y is at least as great as that of x; but this is rather uninformative, and there is bound to be controversy about many of the particular cases that may arise.[43] For my present purposes it is enough to observe that controversies of this sort will be substantive moral controversies, about the content of the moral obligations we accept. Furthermore, when there is agreement about these matters—as I think there is in the sorts of cases I have described—excuses of the fourth class function by showing that the agent's action did not express a choice that violates our (considered) moral obligations. In these cases, doing x because of a choice to do x-rather-than-y is not really a case of doing anything morally impermissible at all.

With excuses of the fourth class, as with those of the first class, it is

41. For discussion of an actual case of this sort—*R v Dudley and Stephens* (1884)—see Kenny, *Freewill and Responsibility*, pp. 37–39.

42. Even when a threatened or anticipated harm or injury does not constitute a successful excuse, it may still serve to mitigate blameworthiness. In these cases doing x-rather-than-y will be impermissible, but the fear of y may be so strong as to impair the agent's ability to do what is morally required (consider, for instance, the survivors of a shipwreck who kill and eat one of their number to avoid starvation, or the case of a soldier ordered to kill a group of civilians on pain of his own death). Here the threatened or anticipated harm would function rather like a localized exempting condition (as I explain in Chapter 6). In this section I am trying to account only for cases in which such factors provide a successful excuse—though it is important to acknowledge that they may modify our responses in other ways as well, and that it may not always be clear how a given case is to be characterized.

43. This brings out the fact that the question of the validity of excuses of the fourth class will turn on broader issues of moral justification, of a sort that arise even outside contexts of coercion, duress, or necessity—for example, under what circumstances, if ever, is it morally permissible to perform such ordinarily prohibited kinds of acts as telling a lie, harming another person, killing another person, and so on? As a result, Austin's distinction between excuses and justifications may blur a bit in these kinds of cases. Coercion excuses s's doing x, by justifying s's doing x in the circumstances (where harm y is threatened).

important to be careful in describing what we do or do not hold the agent morally responsible for. Thus, though we do not hold *s* responsible for *x* (stealing food, handing over the money, throwing the goods overboard), we still hold *s* responsible for what *s* did when it is more circumspectly described as *x*-rather-than-*y;* this functions as an excuse because *x*-rather-than-*y* turns out not to violate a moral obligation. Frankfurt contrasts cases of this sort (what he calls cases of duress) with genuine coercion, where the motive on which *s* acts (the desire to avoid the harm or injury *y*) is beyond *s*'s ability to control, and its being beyond *s*'s ability to control explains *s*'s acting on the motive.[44] In these coercive cases, Frankfurt suggests, *s* has not acted freely at all, and there is nothing *s* did for which *s* can be said to be morally responsible.

It seems to me artificial, however, and at odds with standard usage, to draw this kind of rigid distinction between coercion and duress or necessity. No doubt the victims of coercion often report that they were "compelled" to do what they did, or that they "had no choice." But similar claims are made by the victims of duress or necessity (such as the bank teller, or the starving survivor of a plane crash). Surely what is meant by these claims is not that the victim's action was literally unavoidable—still less that it was explained solely by the circumstances that made it inevitable—but that the victim had no *reasonable* alternative, at least from the moral point of view; that, in the circumstances, there was no other action the agent was morally obligated to perform. Coercion differs from other cases of duress or necessity only in that the victim of coercion is placed in a situation of this sort by another agent or set of agents, who threaten the imposition of serious harms as a way of getting the victim to do what they want.[45]

What Frankfurt calls "coercion" seems to me better treated as a different kind of case altogether. Coercion, in his sense, involves a situation in which the agent *s* intentionally does something of a certain kind (say, *x*-rather-than-*y*), and yet, by contrast with the cases I have discussed, we would allegedly not hold *s* responsible for doing *x*-rather-than-*y*. The best way to make sense of this description, it seems to me, is to suppose that *s*'s condition at the time of the action is such that it

44. See Harry Frankfurt, "Coercion and Moral Responsibility," as reprinted in his *The Importance of What We Care About,* pp. 26–46, at sec. 2; also his "Three Concepts of Free Action," as reprinted in *The Importance of What We Care About,* pp. 47–57, at pp. 48–50, 55–56.

45. This is at odds with legal usage, where duress is often understood simply as coercion by another agent who threatens serious injury or harm: see H. L. A. Hart, "Prolegomenon to the Principles of Punishment," as reprinted in his *Punishment and Responsibility,* pp. 1–27, at p. 16; and Kenny, *Freewill and Responsibility,* pp. 35–36.

would not be appropriate to treat *s* as a morally accountable agent at all. That is, what I have called an *exempting* condition is present, which indicates the absence of an A-condition of responsibility. For only when an exempting condition is present will an agent who has done something intentionally be morally responsible for nothing that he has done (however carefully described). In these terms, Frankfurt's further suggestion is that what constitutes the exempting condition, in the situations he considers coercive, is the fact that *s*'s action is due solely to the factors that make it unavoidable; this in turn rules out the agent's identifying with the action, at the level of higher-order assessment. But the issue of whether this is an adequate explanation must be postponed until I have made a more systematic examination of exempting conditions in the chapter to follow.

5.4 Determinism and Excuses

The discussion in the preceding section has established that whenever people are genuinely excused from responsibility for their actions, those actions will not have been morally wrong. Obligations regulate the choices that are expressed in action, but when a valid excuse obtains, it turns out that what an agent has done did not express a choice at odds with the moral obligations to which we hold that agent.

If one understands the excuses in these terms, however, then one can see immediately that the truth of determinism would not constitute a generalization of the accepted excusing conditions. Take determinism to be the thesis that a complete physical description of the world at a given time, together with a complete description of the laws of nature, entails every truth as to the physical state of the world at later times.[46] To say that determinism is a generalization of accepted excusing conditions is to say that determinism would make it unfair to hold any agent responsible for anything the agent does, and that this conclusion is supported by the same reasons that back up ordinary moral excuses in particular cases. In light of the account of excuses I have offered, this amounts to saying that determinism would make it the case that no agent ever does anything that violates the moral obligations we hold people to. But it is clear that determinism would not have this consequence. If agent *s* stamps on my foot, out of a choice to inflict pain on

---

46. For further discussion of this now fairly standard way of characterizing determinism, and references to more detailed treatments, see Appendix 2.

me in the ordinary pursuit of his ends, and in the absence of coercion or duress, then *s* will have violated the moral obligation of non-maleficence that I both accept and hold *s* to—regardless of whether *s*'s bodily movement is entailed by the laws of nature together with facts about the earlier state of the world.

A number of responses to this rather easy argument come to mind. Some of these focus on my assumption that the truth of determinism would be compatible with explanations of actions in terms of an agent's choices. Against this, it might be maintained that deterministic explanations of behavior would preempt *all* explanations of human activity by reference to psychological states that have propositional content, so that in a deterministic world nothing we do could express an intentional quality of will. Alternatively, it might be suggested that though determinism would not undermine all intentional explanations, it would preclude us from explaining actions in terms of choices, because there would be no *genuine* choices in a deterministic world. The first of these objections raises very difficult issues about the status of intentional explanations of human activity. These issues do not, however, depend especially on the truth or falsity of determinism: it is not determinism per se that allegedly threatens intentional explanations, but mechanism or (more broadly) naturalism. I therefore set this issue to the side at the very start of this book (in section 1.1), assuming the legitimacy of intentional explanations of what we do in order to focus on the more specific issue of what sets apart certain kinds of agents as responsible.

Here, however, the second objection may be pressed. Even if one grants the existence and explanatory efficacy of such intentional states as beliefs, desires, and reactive emotions, it might be urged that a deterministic world would not leave room for *choices*. It is tempting to suppose that choice—or, at any rate, genuine choice—itself requires the availability of alternate possibilities.[47] In that event the truth of determinism would, after all, amount to a kind of generalized excuse, entailing that none of our actions express our choices in the way required for moral blameworthiness. But this line of argument seems to beg the central question. It conflates the issue of whether choices would exist in a deterministic world with the separate issue of whether choices

47. See, for example, Alan Donagan, *Choice: The Essential Element in Human Action* (London: Routledge and Kegan Paul, 1987), p. 170: "choosing presuppose[s] that you have the power either to choose in accordance with any conclusion you may reach or not, your situation and the person you are being the same." (A similar claim might be made about the genuineness of decisions or intentions in a deterministic world.)

would really be free in such a world. That choice would survive the truth of determinism is shown by the fact that we confidently ascribe choices to ourselves and others, and explain what we do in terms of these choices, without knowing whether determinism is (already) true; furthermore there is nothing to suggest that these kinds of explanations are defeasible, such that we ourselves would take them to be undermined by the confirmation of determinism. The truth of determinism would not render it *false* that I chose to take some exercise yesterday afternoon, and then proceeded to run in the park as a result of making that choice.[48]

When it is objected that determinism would undermine genuine choices, probably what is meant is that it would render our choices unfree, depriving us of real alternatives from which to choose. But it cannot simply be assumed that "genuine" choice, in this sense of free choice, is a condition of responsibility, since that is precisely what is at issue. Moreover, I have shown in this chapter that our concrete judgments of excuse do not commit us to the view that "genuine" choice of this kind is a condition of blameworthiness. Excuses function not by defeating the freedom of our choices, but by indicating the absence of an ordinary choice whose content violates the moral obligations to which we are held.

The argument for this conclusion may be summarized as follows. I have identified a basic principle of fairness, the principle of no blameworthiness without fault, which itself expresses an abstract moral conviction in which we have the utmost confidence. This principle says that people do not deserve the responses of blame and moral sanction if they have not done anything wrong in the first place. I have then showed how all of our concrete judgments of excuse can be accounted for in terms of this principle, insofar as the accepted excuses all indicate the absence of a culpable choice. At this point, however, a different and more fundamental worry suggests itself—not about the survival of choice in a deterministic world, but about the account of the normative

---

48. A different suggestion would be that we could *no longer* make choices once we knew the world we inhabit to be deterministic—either because we would then know that our choices make no difference, or because we would then be in a position simply to predict what we are going to do. But if one grants that determinism would not undermine the general efficacy of intentional states, there is no special reason to draw the fatalistic conclusion that our choices would make no difference in a deterministic world. As to the issue of predictability, I have already noted (sec. 1.1) that issues of metaphysical and epistemic determination must be kept distinct, and that the truth of determinism would almost certainly not deprive us of the epistemic openness required for deliberation and choice.

force of the excuses I have developed. As I have just said, that account turns on the claim that we can explain all our concrete judgments of excuse in terms of a basic principle of desert, which would not generalize if determinism is true. But even if we can explain these judgments in this way, it does not follow that this is the only way to explain them, still less that it is the best explanation. Perhaps the principle of alternate possibilities provides a more illuminating account of our standard judgments of excuse than the account I have offered.

To expand on this suggestion, note that our judgments of excuse often incorporate a rudimentary understanding of how the excuses operate. Thus when we invoke moral excuses on our own behalf, we frequently use expressions that appear to indicate that alternate possibilities are conditions of blameworthiness: "I couldn't help it," "The car wouldn't start," "It was too heavy to move," "I just couldn't keep my eyes open any longer," and so on. It might be thought that judgments of this sort would best be explained by citing principles that give systematic expression to the normative considerations directly signaled by those very judgments. On this score, the principle of alternate possibilities may seem superior to the principle of no blameworthiness without fault. Not only does it agree extensionally with our concrete judgments of excuse (so to speak), it also provides insight into the content of those judgments, harmonizing with our sense that blameworthiness somehow requires alternate possibilities.

But this line of argument does not stand up to closer inspection. Note first that the argument, even if cogent, does not simply displace the explanation I have already offered of how the excuses operate. If it is true, as I have claimed, that the agents whom we excuse from blame have not really done anything wrong, this already gives us one very good reason for concluding that those agents do not deserve to be blamed for what they have done. It is an independent and firm moral conviction of ours that those who have not really done anything wrong do not deserve the responses of blame and moral sanction (which, being bound up with the reactive emotions, are essentially responses to a moral wrong). The fact that this basic moral principle applies to the excusing conditions provides an exceptionally compelling explanation for the conclusion that people do not deserve to be blamed when those conditions obtain, an explanation that any serious moral judge would have to endorse. The argument just sketched for the principle of alternate possibilities does not undermine that explanation—how could it?—but at best proposes an additional reason for thinking that it would be unfair to hold people to blame when they have a valid excuse.

Note further that the explanation I have offered accounts for all of our concrete judgments of excuse. As I have shown, all of the excuses indicate the absence of a culpable quality of will; hence the principle of no blameworthiness without fault offers a unified treatment of the moral force of the full range of excusing conditions. The same cannot be said of the principle of alternate possibilities. Some of the ordinary excuses might plausibly be described as cases in which an agent could not have done otherwise, in some sense; the best examples of this fall under the second and third categories I have described, and involve such phenomena as reflex bodily movement and physical constraint. But other standard excuses do not even appear to deprive a person of alternate possibilities for action or choice. Thus if I harm someone inadvertently, the natural way to beg for excuse would be to say not "I couldn't help it," but rather "I didn't mean to hurt you." Similarly, a coercive threat of torture if I do not open the safe would not ordinarily be thought to prevent me from taking some other course of action, but only to make such alternatives extremely unattractive.

Taking these points together, it seems most implausible that the principle of alternate possibilities offers a superior account of our concrete judgments of excuse than the principle of no blameworthiness without fault. We require the latter principle to account for a good number of excusing judgments, to which the principle of alternate possibilities does not even appear to apply. Furthermore, the same principle that is needed to account for these cases also applies to the other kinds of excuses, providing a supremely compelling explanation of why it is unfair to blame a person whenever an excusing condition of any kind should obtain. Against this background, the most that can be said for the principle of alternate possibilities is that it identifies an additional reason for judging it unfair to blame a person—a reason that is at play only in a subset of cases of excuse. But why should one believe this claim? As I have said, the principle of alternate possibilities is not a principle that we have an independently strong commitment to; it derives its appeal from its claim to be grounded in our concrete judgments of excuse and exemption. So it would have to be maintained that there is some aspect of the selected subset of excusing judgments that is left unexplained by the principle I have invoked, and that *requires* us to appeal to the principle of alternate possibilities.

Here the point I made earlier will be recalled: that many of our excusing judgments incorporate a nascent understanding of the excuses as conditions that deprive people of alternate possibilities. It might be suggested that *this* is the aspect of those judgments that can adequately be accounted for only in terms of the principle of alternate possibilities. Given the explanatory power of the principle of no blameworthiness without fault, however, this last-ditch argument for the principle of alternate possibilities looks very feeble. The nascent interpretations implicit in our judgments of excuse are not in any case themselves unequivocal. If I request an excuse by saying that my car wouldn't start, for instance, I am not merely registering the absence of alternate possibilities, I am just as plausibly making a point about my quality of will: namely that I tried to get to the airport in time to meet your plane.[49] Once equipped with the systematic account I have offered, it becomes extremely natural for us to interpret all of our concrete judgments of excuse in this way, treating such remarks as "I couldn't help it," "It was too heavy to move," and so on as abbreviated redescriptions of our quality of will. This is an example of the perfectly general phenomenon whereby our understanding of our considered moral convictions can be refined and adjusted as a result of moral reflection that begins from those very convictions. But if our judgments of excuse tolerate and even invite this style of interpretation, it can no longer seriously be maintained that they provide any basis for the principle of alternate possibilities.

Still there is apt to be some residual tendency to think that the availability of alternate possibilities must be a condition of blameworthiness—even once it has been granted that this conclusion is not anchored in our concrete judgments of excuse. The persistence of this thought is one manifestation of the phenomenon I have referred to as the seductiveness of incompatibilism, and if not addressed it can leave us vaguely dissatisfied with any compatibilist interpretation of responsibility. But my argument in this chapter suggests a way of removing this residual source of incompatibilist unease, insofar as it points toward a *diagnosis* of the thought that alternate possibilities are conditions of

---

49. In this context it may be helpful to consider an application of Frankfurt's style of counterexample to the principle of alternate possibilities, in which an agent acts out of a choice to do something wrong, but circumstances are present that allegedly make it inevitable that she will act in this way; see Frankfurt, "Alternate Possibilities and Moral Responsibility," for this general strategy of argument. It would not count as a valid excuse for such an agent to plead that she could not help it or that she had no choice, and this may reinforce the thought that such pleas do not ordinarily function merely by registering the absence of alternate possibilities. In Appendix 2 I contend that Frankfurt's counterexamples cannot bear the brunt of an argument against the principle of alternate possibilities by themselves. But against the background of an alternative explanation of our judgments of excuse, the counterexamples may have some auxiliary use, helping to refine our understanding of how the excuses operate.

responsibility. As I have noted, many of the excuses in the second and third categories can accurately be described as cases in which an agent could not have done otherwise, in some sense: consider, for instance, bodily movements caused by reflex stimulations (being stung by a swarm of bees), or omissions due to such internal and external constraints as paralysis or the derailment of one's subway train. The fact that these are cases of valid excuse, and that they involve a lack of alternate possibilities, can make it very natural to infer that this fact about the cases is what accounts for their excusing force. In endorsing the principle of alternate possibilities, one identifies a genuine and even salient feature of some of the excusing conditions, and draws the conclusion that that feature is what it is about the excuses that makes it unfair to hold people responsible when they obtain. The intuitive pull of the principle of alternative possibilities is thus explained by the fact that it is an obvious way of generalizing from a central class of cases.

If my argument in this chapter is sound, however, this extremely natural generalization is also a false one. It is false because the condition to which it traces the force of the excuses is not normatively significant in itself. Rather, that condition is correlated, in at least a subset of cases, with a different factor that makes it clearly unfair to hold people to blame, and that is present in all cases of legitimate excuse. This is the fact that the agent who is excused has not done anything morally wrong.

6

Accountability and the Exemptions

My task in this chapter is to complete the defense against the generalization strategy by working out a compatibilist interpretation of the recognized exempting conditions. As explained in Chapter 5, exemptions are unlike excuses in being less localized: whereas excuses block responsibility for particular acts an agent has performed, exemptions make it inappropriate to hold the agent accountable more generally. One could say that the excuses indicate the absence of a B-condition of responsibility, while exemptions indicate the absence of an A-condition. A satisfactory account of the recognized exemptions must identify the relevant conditions of accountability, explaining why it is unfair to hold people accountable when these conditions do not obtain. It must also show that the accepted exemptions all function by blocking the A-conditions that have been identified. This is my agenda in the present chapter.

A-conditions make it fair to treat someone as a morally accountable agent. Given the normative approach I have adopted (see Chapter 4), it follows that an account of the A-conditions will describe a certain kind of moral agency; specifically, it will yield an interpretation of what it is to be a morally accountable agent. On the normative approach, to be an accountable agent simply is to be someone who can fairly be held morally accountable.[1] But what are the conditions under which it is fair to hold someone morally accountable? The approach I sketch in section 6.1 builds on the idea that the moral obligations we accept admit of justification. Thus, as I explained in the preceding chapter, the stance of holding people to moral obligations one accepts involves a commitment to reasons that support those obligations, and that can motivate compliance with them. If this is right, however, then it will be reason-

1. Recall schema (N), presented and discussed in sec. 4.1.

able to adopt this stance only toward people who possess what I refer to as powers of reflective self-control: the general ability to grasp and apply moral reasons and to regulate their behavior by the light of such reasons. Possession of these powers is thus a basic condition of the fairness of holding people accountable, and in section 6.2 I try to show that all the standard exemptions can be construed as impairing or depriving a person of these conditions of accountability. But as incompatibilists themselves agree, general powers such as those of reflective self-control would not be undermined by the truth of determinism. Hence determinism would not amount to a generalization of the standard exemptions, any more than it would constitute a generalized excuse. I explain these points, and compare my approach to other compatibilist strategies, in the final two sections of this chapter.

6.1 Exemptions and Abilities

I noted in Chapter 5 that excuses operate locally: they give us a reason to withdraw the attitudes we would ordinarily take in response to a particular *action,* but they do not give us a reason to view the *agent* as anything other than an ordinary, accountable person in general. There are other responsibility-inhibiting conditions, however, that function precisely by inviting us to suspend our reactive attitudes altogether toward a person—to stop holding the person morally accountable, in the terms introduced earlier. I have called these conditions exemptions, to set them apart from the excusing conditions. Following Strawson, one may distinguish two subgroups of exempting conditions, in this sense.[2] First, there are conditions—such as hypnotism, extreme stress or physical deprivation, and the short-term effects of certain drugs—that make it unfair to hold a person accountable during a restricted segment of the person's life. Second, there are more systematic and persistent states that render a person's normal condition one in which it would be unfair to hold the person morally accountable; here one might include, for example, insanity or mental illness, extreme youth, psychopathy, and the effects of systematic behavior control or conditioning.

Both excuses and exemptions may make it unfair to hold an agent responsible for some specific action (say, *x*), but they function very differently in bringing about this result. As I have explained, an excuse

2. P. F. Strawson, "Freedom and Resentment," as reprinted in Gary Watson, ed., *Free Will* (Oxford: Oxford University Press, 1982), pp. 59–80, at pp. 65–66, 73.

differs from a justification in the following way: whereas a justification for *s*'s doing *x* will admit that *s* did *x* (intentionally), and will try to show why *x* was a morally permissible or even obligatory thing to do, excuses grant that *x* would be an impermissible thing to do, but provide grounds for doubting that *s* really did *x*. Refining this distinction, I have suggested that what are morally impermissible or obligatory in the first instance are not mere bodily movements but actions that express certain qualities of will, and that excuses defeat the presumption that *s* has an impermissible state of will by showing that *s* did not intentionally do *x* at all.

Exemptions are like excuses—and unlike justifications—in granting that doing *x* intentionally is morally impermissible. By contrast to excuses, however, exemptions do not inhibit responsibility for a particular action *x* by providing grounds for doubting that *s* did *x* intentionally. Young children or the insane may intentionally do *x*, where that indicates the presence of a morally impermissible choice, and yet the psychological condition of such persons nevertheless makes it unfair to hold them morally responsible for doing *x*. Thus, whereas excuses inhibit responsibility for a particular act by showing that a morally accountable agent has not done anything morally impermissible in the first place, exemptions block responsibility for a particular act by showing that an impermissible act has been done by someone who is not, in general, a morally accountable agent.[3] To put the point a different way, excuses indicate the absence of a B-condition of responsibility, whereas exemptions indicate the absence of an A-condition of responsibility. And where such A-conditions are absent—where it is not fair to hold an agent morally accountable in general—it will, a fortiori, not be fair to hold the agent responsible for the particular acts that agent may perform.

But how do exemptions function? Which A-conditions of responsibility are absent when the exemptions obtain? To begin to answer these questions, it will be helpful to recall a point made in the preceding chapter. When we hold *s* to a moral obligation we accept, we of course

3. Understood in this way, the distinction between exemptions and excuses appears to mirror the distinction drawn in Continental legal codes between questions of "imputability" (concerning defects of general psychological capacity) and questions of "fault" (concerning defects of knowledge or intention on particular occasions of action). Anglo-American legal codes, by contrast, tend to treat all questions concerning the psychological conditions of legal responsibility under the single rubric of mens rea. See H. L. A. Hart, "Postscript: Responsibility and Retribution," in his *Punishment and Responsibility: Essays in the Philosophy of Law* (Oxford: Clarendon Press, 1968), pp. 210–237, at pp. 218–220; see also p. 266.

demand that *s* will comply with the obligation. But as I suggested earlier, the moral obligation that we thus expect *s* to comply with will be supported by justifications of the sort that might be expressed in moral principles. These justifications provide moral reasons for complying with the obligations in question, reasons that explain why we ourselves strive to comply with these obligations, and that provide terms for justifying and criticizing both our own behavior and that of others. Consideration of this connection between moral obligations and reasons has led me to treat moral obligations as governing the choices expressed in action, for it is these qualities of will that are subject to the direct influence of reasons. The same point, however, may now help to illuminate the conditions of accountability. These conditions must make it fair to demand that *s* comply with moral obligations we accept, where the obligations are supported by distinctively moral reasons. But it would seem fair to demand this of a person only if the person possesses what I shall refer to as the powers of reflective self-control:[4] (1) the power to grasp and apply moral reasons, and (2) the power to control or regulate his behavior by the light of such reasons. I will look at each of these conditions in turn.

To grasp the reason expressed in a moral principle is a more complex task than it might at first appear to be. The understanding required is a kind of participant understanding that goes well beyond the ability to parrot the moral principle in situations in which it has some relevance. What is needed, rather, is the ability to bring the principle to bear in the full variety of situations to which it applies, anticipating the demands it makes of us in those situations, and knowing when its demands might require adjustment in light of the claims of other moral principles. This in turn requires, at a minimum, a grasp of the concepts that figure in the moral principle in question. Take the principle of nonmaleficence: that one should not deliberately harm other people in the ordinary pursuit of one's own ends. One will only be able to apply this principle to a wide array of situations if one has a sophisticated understanding of the concept of *harm,* knowing what kinds of treatment would count as harmful to another person (inflicting physical pain, causing psychic anguish or distress, damaging a person's reputation or interests, and so on). Furthermore, one must have some appreciation for the considera-

---

4. I borrow this expression (loosely) from T. M. Scanlon, "The Significance of Choice," in Sterling M. McMurrin, ed., *The Tanner Lectures on Human Values,* vol. 8 (Salt Lake City: University of Utah Press, 1988), pp. 149–216; at p. 174 Scanlon refers to similar abilities under the rubric of "the capacity for critically reflective, rational self-governance."

tions that make it wrong to harm other people in these ways. These considerations need not take the form of a further justification for the principle of nonmaleficence itself—for present purposes, I should like to leave it open whether this principle requires or admits of a further justification. But if there are such further justifications available, one should have at least the ability to grasp the reasons that those justifications cite (perhaps as a result of the kind of reflection prompted by "hard cases"). And if there are no such justifications, so that the principle of nonmaleficence is itself basic, that too should be the sort of point one is able to understand. Otherwise one's deployment of the principle of nonmaleficence will have a wooden quality, rendering it ill-suited to guide one through the complexities of the moral life. Beyond this basic ability to appreciate the concepts and values involved in moral justifications, one will also need ancillary abilities of attention, concentration, and judgment, to bring moral principles accurately to bear on particular situations of action, and to focus effectively on the conclusions they support in deliberating about what to do.

Turn now to the second condition mentioned above, the power to regulate one's behavior by the light of the moral reasons one grasps. This too is a more sophisticated ability than it may at first appear to be. It involves, to begin with, a capacity for critical reflection: the ability to step back from one's immediate desires and assess the actions they incline one to perform, in light of the moral reasons one has grasped and accepted. For example, someone who lacks this capacity to reflect critically on her malevolent impulses can hardly be credited with the ability to control her behavior in accordance with the principle of nonmaleficence. She will simply act on whichever of her desires happens to be strongest at a given time, and if one of those should be a malevolent impulse, she will lack the power to refrain from acting on it. In addition to this capacity for critical reflection, the ability to control one's behavior by reasons also requires the capacity to make choices as a result of deliberation. As I have already noted, it is choices that are subject to the direct influence of reasons for action. Someone who lacks the capacity for deliberated choice will therefore lack the ability to control what she does *by* grasping moral reasons. Indeed, possession of this ability requires not just the basic capacity for deliberated choice, but also the capacity to make certain kinds of choices: namely choices that accord with the moral reasons one grasps. Finally, it is necessary that the agent should have some capacity to translate her choices into behavior. Reasons for action, after all, regulate qualities of choice, as expressed in behavior; but someone without this last capacity will hardly have the power to act in ways that express her choices at all.

The division of these various abilities into two broad classes suggests a distinction between cognitive and affective powers. The power to grasp moral reasons appears to be made up of a set of essentially cognitive abilities, which enable one to understand and to apply the justifications expressed in moral principles, whereas the abilities collected under the power to regulate one's behavior by the light of moral reasons appear essentially to concern the will. It would be misleading, however, to construe this distinction too literally, interpreting it, say, in the rigid terms of faculty psychology. No doubt each of the classes of powers I have distinguished has cognitive and affective aspects, and the two sets of abilities will generally develop together and reinforce each other. For instance, it is likely that one's attainment of a participant understanding of moral reasons will at least be facilitated if one has some motivational responsiveness to those reasons; and the ability to regulate one's behavior in light of moral reasons presupposes that one has some ability to grasp those reasons in the first place. Furthermore, the powers in question seem to admit of degrees. These powers are matters of general psychological competence or capacity, and it is in the nature of such general capacities that they admit of various levels of development. Just as one may distinguish between rudimentary and more developed abilities to speak a foreign language, play squash, or solve differential equations, so one might in principle distinguish different levels of development of the powers to grasp moral reasons and to control one's behavior accordingly.

Against this idea, it might be suggested that the notion of choice is such that we cannot really make sense of a partial impairment of the power to choose in a certain way; many conditions present obstacles to the implementation of our choices, others operate by moving us to act without engaging our power to choose at all, but nothing could impair the basic power of choice itself.[5] There is an important grain of truth here, namely that it is hard to conceive of an obstacle or impediment to the activity of choosing (as opposed to an obstacle to the successful implementation of choice). "Willing is necessarily successful," as Gary Watson has said.[6] It follows that we cannot construe impairments of the

---

5. For a probing statement of this idea, see Rogers Albritton, "Freedom of Will and Freedom of Action," *Proceedings of the American Philosophical Association* 59 (1985–86), pp. 239–251.

6. Gary Watson, "Free Action and Free Will," *Mind* 96 (1987), pp. 145–172, at p. 163 (footnote 28); pp. 161–164 of this article are very helpful on the question of freedom of will.

powers of reflective self-control on the model of obstacles to the activity of choosing. But such impairments can be thought of in other ways. Note first that the powers of reflective self-control do not simply involve the bare power to choose: rather, they require the power to choose in a certain way (namely in accordance with moral reasons). There are a number of things that might potentially impair this power without constituting obstacles to the activity of choice. Intense emotions and desires, for instance, might make certain actions so superlatively attractive or unattractive that it becomes extremely difficult to choose to act in the way one believes to be morally required. Consider the soldier ordered to kill innocent civilians on pain of his own death: the emotion of fear might impair the soldier's ability to choose to do the right thing, not by erecting an impediment to the activity of choice, but by coloring the potential object of choice in an extremely unfavorable light.[7] But even when the power to choose is not in this way diminished, the broader powers of reflective self-control may nevertheless be impaired. One's ability to appreciate and focus on the moral reasons in favor of an obligatory course of action may be reduced (either in general, or for a limited period of time); or internal conditions of emotion and desire may render it difficult to translate one's moral choices effectively into action.

Whether a given person has the powers of reflective self-control will therefore not be an all-or-nothing affair. Nevertheless it seems clear that a certain level of development of these powers (no doubt hard to specify exactly) is an A-condition of responsibility. Moreover I believe that the reactive account of responsibility helps us to see why these powers are conditions of accountability. On the reactive account, to treat someone as a morally accountable agent is to hold the person to moral obligations that one accepts, in the dispositional sense of holding people to obligations. This stance involves a disposition to respond to the person's violation of moral obligations with the reactive emotions, and as I have shown, these emotions naturally find expression in adverse forms of treatment that sanction the person held to blame (such as avoidance, reproach, condemnation, and scolding). It is this connection to adverse

---

7. Of course, fear might additionally present an obstacle to the soldier's ability to execute the choice he realizes to be morally required, but I see no reason to deny that it could render it difficult to *make* the choice in the first place. Consider a different example: someone with an intense aversion to snakes may find it supremely difficult to choose to pick up a boa constrictor. There may thus be empirical as well as conceptual limitations on one's freedom or power to choose in a certain way. (Contrast Albritton, "Freedom of Will and Freedom of Action.")

forms of treatment that brings the stance of holding people accountable within the scope of moral principles, making it a candidate for assessment as fair or unfair. But the stance also involves a commitment to the existence of reasons that support the obligations to which accountable agents are held, and that can motivate compliance with those obligations, and this aspect of the stance points toward the conditions of accountability. Given the commitment to moral reasons that support the obligations we accept, it does not seem fair to demand that people comply with such obligations unless they have the general ability to grasp those reasons and to regulate their behavior accordingly.

Why would it be unfair to hold someone accountable in the absence of these powers? One is tempted to say that the stance of holding people to moral obligations fits together with the powers of reflective self-control the way a key fits into a lock. But of course this image, however tempting, is not very informative; the question remains, what kind of "fit" is there between the stance and the powers that make the stance fair? The answer, I would suggest, is the following: it would be unfair to hold someone to moral obligations one accepts, in the absence of the powers of reflective self-control, in the sense that it would be *unreasonable* to hold the person to moral obligations under these conditions. To make this proposal is, in effect, to postulate a moral principle of reasonableness, namely that it is unreasonable to demand that people do something—in a way that potentially exposes them to the harms of moral sanction—if they lack the general power to grasp and comply with the reasons that support the demand. I take this to be a principle of reasonableness that any competent moral judge would endorse, on reflection; like the principle of desert appealed to in Chapter 5 ("no blameworthiness without fault"), it expresses an abstract moral conviction in which we have the utmost confidence.

Consider the following simpler analogies. It would presumably be unreasonable to demand that a foreigner (a newly landed political refugee, say) should speak and understand one's language like a native, because such a person lacks the basic ability to do what we are demanding. Similarly, it would seem unreasonable to demand that a child should be a star athlete if the child lacks the basic physical talents that are necessary to excel in school sports. In these cases, what makes the stance of holding someone to an expectation unreasonable is the fact that the agent lacks the basic power to do the sort of thing that we demand of him (speak English fluently, excel at sports). Notice that the abilities in question in these judgments seem to be *general* psychological or physical competences or capacities: what makes it unreasonable to expect these things of the child or the refugee is not the fact that they lack the opportunity to exercise such abilities as they may possess, but rather the fact that they lack the general competence to do what we expect of them. Someone in this condition will thus lack the basic capacity to avoid the sanctions to which violating a demand normally exposes one.

The examples just described suggest one way in which such general powers are conditions for the reasonableness of holding people to expectations. It is reasonable to adopt this stance only if the target of the stance has the general power to do the sort of thing demanded and thereby to avoid the sanctions associated with failure to meet the demand. To hold someone accountable, however, also involves a commitment to moral reasons that support the obligations we accept and that can motivate compliance with them. But where the stance of holding someone to expectations is supported by reasons of this sort, it will be reasonable to adopt the stance only toward people who possess the following further general powers: the power to grasp moral reasons and the power to control their behavior in accordance with them—the forms of normative competence that I have referred to as powers of reflective self-control. In their absence, people will be fundamentally unable to understand why they should comply with moral obligations; or if they can understand this, they will be fundamentally unable to translate their understanding into action and thereby to avoid the responses of moral sanction. Such basic incapacities would plainly make it unreasonable to hold people to moral obligations we accept.

This is a fundamental point but also a subtle one, with far-reaching implications; to attain a deeper understanding of the kind of reasonableness involved, it may be instructive to compare the stance of holding people accountable with our disposition to sanction animals (dogs, say). Both of these stances expose the creatures at whom they are directed to risks of harm, and this brings both of them, at least potentially, within the scope of moral principles. Thus, it would seem unreasonable to insist that one's dog should spend the whole weekend locked indoors without relieving itself on the carpet. To scold one's dog in such a case would be to sanction it for failing to do what it anyway lacked the general ability to do, and this would be objectionable in a way at least analogous to the unreasonableness of blaming the refugee for failing to speak one's language like a native. The parallel ends, however, when we consider the reasons that support the different standards. The dog owner, for instance, may have very good reasons for wanting her dog to relieve itself outdoors—at least when it is allowed out of the house at regular intervals—and may adopt a disposition to sanction the dog in ways designed to bring about this result. But the reasonableness of this disposition seems in no way dependent on the dog's having the general power to grasp the owner's reasons and to control its behavior accordingly.

Two factors seem relevant to explaining this disanalogy with the case of moral accountability. First, the dog owner's reasons—unlike those that support the moral obligations we accept—are not reasons for the owner to comply with the standards to which the sanctions are attached. It is not that the owner has reason to relieve herself outdoors, but that she wants her dog to do so, and she adopts a disposition to sanction the dog as a strategy to bring this result about. In this way, the dog owner's reasons stand in a relation to the standards of behavior she enforces that is very different from the relation between moral reasons and the obligations they support. Second, there is an important difference between the sanctions involved in the two cases. The dog owner's sanctions are purely forward-looking and strategic; their point is fully achieved if they succeed in making salient to the animal a pattern of behavior that is to be avoided and associating with such behavior a clearly negative signal. The sanctions bound up with holding people accountable, by contrast, cannot be construed exclusively in forward-looking, strategic terms. As I have argued, such moral responses as censure, reproach, denunciation, and avoidance have an essentially expressive function, giving voice to the reactive emotions. But where those emotions are connected to moral obligations we accept, they will be fully intelligible only to people who are themselves capable of grasping the reasons that support those obligations. Hence possession of the powers of reflective self-control on the part of the people to whom moral sanctions are addressed is a condition of the success of those sanctions.

I take it that we generally view normal, mature adults as possessing the various general abilities collected under the heading of powers of reflective self-control. These are the sorts of abilities one tends to acquire in the course of a normal upbringing, and in the absence of some specific reason to think otherwise, we presume that the adults we deal with are in possession of these abilities. I also take it that—at least in principle—a given agent may have the powers of reflective self-control without actually accepting all of the moral obligations that we accept and hold people to. This explains our willingness to hold accountable those who are not members of our moral community, in that they reject outright some of our most basic moral obligations: racists and torturers and rapists, for example. For—assuming that such people are not psychopaths, or victims of severe childhood deprivation or social indoctrination—they may possess the general *ability* to grasp the reasons that support our moral obligations, and to regulate their behavior in light of such reasons, even if they have rejected those obligations in fact; so long as they satisfy this condition, it would seem reasonable to hold them to our moral obligations, and so to treat them as morally accountable agents.

It is often said that accountability renders one fit to participate in interpersonal relationships of some sort.[8] This seems suggestive, but given the remarks just made, we need to be careful in specifying the kind of relationships that accountability enables one to participate in. What matters for accountability is not merely one's capacity for ordinary or normal interpersonal relationships, since immoral but culpable behavior may disqualify one from these;[9] it is, rather, one's suitability for a certain kind of moral relationship. The relevant kind of moral relationship is a relationship defined by the successful exchange of moral criticism and justification. This is not to say that in holding people responsible we are always engaged in such an exchange—clearly we can hold people accountable even if we do not communicate with them at all, and even if we have no interest in literally exchanging criticism and justification with them. But it will be reasonable to hold accountable only someone who is at least a candidate for this kind of exchange of criticism and justification. As I just noted, the stance of holding people accountable involves a susceptibility to sanctioning behavior whose function is essentially to express the reactive emotions. Insofar as these responses are bound up with the moral obligations we accept, they will only be fully intelligible as forms of expression when addressed to people who are capable of grasping moral reasons. Furthermore, unless those held accountable have the further ability to control their behavior by the light of the reasons in question, they will lack the capacity to take steps to avoid the potentially harmful responses of moral sanction.

8. See, for instance, Strawson, "Freedom and Resentment," pp. 68–69, 73.

9. This is a problem for Strawson's account, which interprets accountability as rendering one suited to participate in "normal" interpersonal relations. For similar complaints about Strawson's treatment of accountability and the exemptions, see Scanlon, "The Significance of Choice," p. 165, and Gary Watson, "Responsibility and the Limits of Evil: Variations on a Strawsonian Theme," in Ferdinand Schoeman, ed., *Responsibility, Character, and the Emotions: New Essays in Moral Psychology* (Cambridge: Cambridge University Press, 1987), pp. 256–286, at pp. 262–263.

The community of morally accountable agents is thus the set of people who are capable of successfully exchanging moral criticism and justification: grasping the reasons behind moral criticism, and responding constructively on the basis of such reasons.[10]

Now, I do not suppose it is always entirely clear which people actually have the powers of reflective self-control that equip them for participation in this form of moral relationship. There are conceptual difficulties, independent of the theory of moral responsibility, that cloud our understanding of these powers. For instance, I take it to be a truism that certain sorts of moral education greatly facilitate the development of the powers of reflective self-control; conditions important in this connection include love and emotional support of the sort that encourage self-esteem, and freedom from hypocrisy and arbitrariness in the promulgation and enforcement of moral standards. It is not clear, however, whether any particular set of such educational conditions is strictly necessary to the acquisition of a level of reflective self-control sufficient for minimal moral responsibility. A related issue concerns the degree to which the power to grasp and respond to moral reasons is culturally specific. Resolution of this issue may depend in part on the success of the philosophical project (pursued in different ways by Hume and Kant, for instance) of describing a basis for moral understanding and concern in universal features of human nature or practical reason. If an objectivist account along these lines could be made out, then we would be unlikely to regard mere cultural variation as an obstacle to acquiring the basic powers of reflective self-control; ignorance of moral principle, in other words, would not constitute a valid exemption from accountability for moral wrong.[11] If, on the other hand, an objectivist interpretation of morality cannot be defended, then we may have reason to doubt whether the members of some thoroughly racist or sexist cultures

10. Consider, in this connection, Scanlon's suggestion that morality is a "system of co-deliberation," in "The Significance of Choice," pp. 166–167; also Watson's idea that the reactive attitudes are "incipiently" forms of moral address or communication, in "Responsibility and the Limits of Evil," pp. 264–265.

11. Do the powers of reflective self-control, with respect to a given obligation, require that one have some *reason* to comply with the obligation? I have already shown that there is reason to comply with such obligations, insofar as the obligations are supported by *justifications;* these justifications identify moral reasons capable of moving those who accept them to comply with the obligations they support. I have also shown that the powers of reflective self-control do not require that one have some occurrent *motive* for complying with the obligations, insofar as these powers may be possessed by people who actually reject the obligations. Whether the powers of reflective self-control require that one have reason to comply with the obligations in a sense different from these seems to me obscure; the notion of a reason is not sufficiently well-understood to permit us to return a clear answer to this question.

(say) should be credited with the power to grasp the moral reasons against the injustices that prevail within their societies.[12]

These unclarities in the powers of reflective self-control are reflected in moral practice, insofar as we are easily pulled in different directions when considering whether to hold fully accountable the victims of childhood deprivation, or those who have accepted the immoral values prevalent within their society.[13] There are, however, plenty of other cases in which it seems clearer to us that the powers of reflective self-control are substantially impaired. These are the cases in which the acknowledged exempting conditions are present, for what unifies and accounts for those conditions, I now want to argue, is that they deprive people of the powers of reflective self-control. More precisely, the conditions in question are accepted as exemptions insofar as they are believed to deprive people of the powers of reflective self-control, and their interference with these powers is what accounts for their exempting force.

Accepted exemptions include cases of childhood, insanity or mental illness, addiction, posthypnotic suggestion, behavior control, psychopathy, and the effects of extreme stress, deprivation, and torture. The following section develops the framework I have just proposed for understanding these accepted exempting conditions. My aim is not to provide a detailed account of how these conditions actually operate—that would be beyond the scope of this book—but rather to show how their presence may be supposed to impair the powers of reflective self-control. The question is not what is in fact true about the nature and effects of these conditions, but what is believed to be true about them insofar as they are taken to constitute legitimate exemptions from accountability.

6.2   Exemptions: Some Cases

Young children, to begin with, are clearly not taken to have developed fully the powers of reflective self-control. Cognitively, they are at the stage where they are learning how to apply moral principles and the

---

12. Of course, we could still view the members of such cultures as "responsible for their actions," in the different sense that their actions stem from values that they accept. (This is the autonomy condition to which I made reference in sec. 3.1.) We could also continue to *hold* them morally responsible, with respect to other moral obligations we accept: as I explained in sec. 3.2, the dispositional stance of holding people accountable is implicitly relative to a set of obligations, so that it is possible to hold someone *selectively* accountable, with respect to some obligations but not others.

13. I return briefly to the topic of childhood deprivation in Chapter 8.

often very complicated concepts (such as harm or reciprocity) that the principles incorporate. Affectively, they have not yet acquired the ability to control their behavior reliably in accordance with such moral principles. This may be true even if children succeed much of the time in acting in conformity with the moral obligations we accept. Reflective self-governance requires the capacity to comply with moral obligations because one grasps the moral reasons in support of those obligations, and young children may not yet have the ability to act from motives of this sort. In that event their compliance with moral obligations will be due to quite different sorts of motives: the wish to avoid punishment, say, or the desire for parental approval. Thus it should not always be inferred from the fact that *s* intentionally acts in a way that conforms with moral obligations that *s* has acquired the powers of reflective self-control. Because children lack these abilities, or are still in the process of acquiring them, it would be unreasonable to hold them fully accountable with respect to the moral obligations we accept.[14] But of course we often treat them *as if* they were accountable agents when they violate those obligations. This is partly because we do not believe even very young children completely lack the powers of reflective self-control (recall that possession of such abilities can be a matter of degree). And partly it is because treating children as if they were responsible is believed to be the most effective way to stimulate the development of their powers of reflective self-control.

Turn next to cases of insanity or mental illness. There are, of course, conflicting views about the nature of insanity or mental illness, and about whether these conditions (supposing them to exist) constitute legitimate exempting conditions; these complexities are beyond the scope of my discussion. What I wish to claim is only that, to the extent insanity and mental illness are taken to be legitimate exemptions, it is because they are believed to interfere with the powers of reflective self-control. This may be confirmed by a brief look at legal discussions of insanity as a condition that may exempt a defendant from responsibility under the law. Consider, for instance, the M'Naghten Rules, which formulated the conditions believed by the judges of the House of Lords in 1843 to be necessary if mental abnormality is to constitute a successful defense to a criminal charge: "to establish a defence on the ground of insanity it must be clearly proved that, at the time of committing the act, the accused was labouring under such a defect of

---

14. Similar remarks apply to people who are mentally retarded, who may be seen as having perpetually undeveloped capacities for reflective self-control.

reason, from disease of the mind, as not to know the nature and quality of the act he was doing, or, if he did know it, that he did not know he was doing what was wrong."[15]

Though these rules are meant to formulate conditions of nonliability in the law, they seem equally to express a natural view about the effect of mental illness on moral accountability. The rules refer to a "defect of reason" resulting from a "disease of the mind," suggesting that the underlying condition will generally be a long-standing one, and in this way different from an ordinary excuse (which functions only to block responsibility on particular occasions).[16] Furthermore the defect of reason must be such as to deprive the agent either of knowledge of the nature and quality of her acts, or of knowledge that they are wrong. Now, cases in which a mentally ill person literally has no idea about the nature and quality of her acts seem quite rare. More commonly, when someone in the grip of such conditions as depression or paranoia does something wrong (attacking a relative, say), she will know perfectly well that she is attacking the person; indeed, such actions are sometimes elaborately premeditated.[17] But there will often be present a "defect of reason" that prevents the agent from accurately assessing the moral quality of her act. The agent who is severely depressed, for instance, may believe—falsely, and against all reasonable evidence—that she has infected her children with an incurable disease, and that she must therefore destroy them to save them from greater torments ahead; or the person in the grip of a paranoid delusion might falsely be convinced that her husband is unfaithful to her, so that an attack on the husband is seen as a means of self-defense or revenge.[18]

15. "The Rules in M'Naghten's Case," as reprinted in Herbert Morris, ed., *Freedom and Responsibility: Readings in Philosophy and Law* (Stanford: Stanford University Press, 1961), p. 395.

16. Cases in which insanity is said to be temporary will come closer to the excusing conditions, especially insofar as insanity deprives the agent of knowledge of the moral quality of the act, and so affects the intention with which the act was performed. Even in these cases, however, there is a difference between exemptions and excuses: exemptions affect the intentionality of one's actions by impairing—at least temporarily—one's powers of reflective self-control, whereas excuses affect the intentionality of one's action without impairing such general powers.

17. The cases that prompted the formulation of the M'Naghten rules were of this type. M'Naghten himself was in the grip of the paranoid delusion that Prime Minister Robert Peel was part of a conspiracy to ruin him; he shot and killed Peel's secretary, believing him to be Peel. Thus there was no question that M'Naghten knew that he was undertaking to kill someone. On this point, see C. L. Ten, *Crime, Guilt, and Punishment: A Philosophical Introduction* (Oxford: Clarendon Press, 1987), pp. 124–125.

18. These examples are loosely borrowed from Angus Macniven, "Psychoses and Criminal Responsibility," as reprinted in Morris, ed., *Freedom and Responsibility,* pp. 396–410, at pp. 398, 404. Two points should be noted in connection with such cases. First, the delusions they involve

But a defect of reason of this sort would effectively deprive the agent of the powers of reflective self-control, at least with respect to behavior that touches directly on her delusion. Even if the agent retains the ability to grasp the moral principles we hold her to, she will lack the ability to apply them correctly in the situations she actually confronts. To apply moral principles in this way, it is not sufficient that one should know the nature and quality of one's actions under some description (for example, that one is undertaking to kill one's children). One must also be able to attain a clear and accurate view of the morally relevant features of the situation in which one is acting, and this is something that a delusion would appear to preclude. Someone falsely and pathologically convinced that she has mortally infected her children, or that her husband is cheating on her, will not be able to judge correctly how moral principles apply to the circumstances she actually finds herself in (as distinguished from the circumstances she believes herself to be in).

Of course, a delusion need not thoroughly deprive a person of the ability to apply moral principles in this way.[19] It may be that, outside her "delusional system," the mentally ill agent has a perfectly normal capacity to judge the morally relevant features of situations and to apply moral principles in those situations. In that event the mental illness would function only as a selective exemption from accountability: the presence of the illness would not make it completely unreasonable to treat the person as a morally accountable agent, in all situations and areas of conduct, and there might be individual actions that we could fairly hold the mentally ill agent morally responsible for.

---

must be genuinely pathological if their presence is to count as an exemption (for a brief discussion of what might distinguish delusions from nonpathological false beliefs, see Jonathan Glover, *Responsibility* [London: Routledge and Kegan Paul, 1970], pp. 133–135). Second, precisely because of the role of delusion in explaining the agent's action in these cases, the quality of will expressed by the action will not be that which a morally wrong action would normally express: killing your children with the intention of saving them from greater doom is different from killing them with malicious intent. These cases thus have something in common with the cases where excuses are present. The difference is that the delusion is a persisting condition, which not only affects the quality of the agent's will in particular situations, but also deprives the agent of the general powers of reflective self-control.

19. See Anthony Kenny, *Freewill and Responsibility* (London: Routledge and Kegan Paul, 1978), pp. 81–83, on this point. Kenny describes the case of an academic suffering from the paranoid delusion that his colleagues are plagiarizing his work, who methodically sets out to kill his mother-in-law to attain an inheritance; surely, Kenny suggests, the fact that the academic is suffering from the paranoid delusion would not make it unreasonable to hold him responsible for this act, which seems to have nothing to do with the delusion.

The M'Naghten Rules seem to express a common view about at least some of the conditions present in cases of insanity or mental illness that make it unreasonable to hold people accountable for what they do. The preceding discussion has shown that these conditions can be accounted for within the framework I have provided. Specifically, the kinds of cognitive defects that mental illness is often believed to involve seem to deprive one of the powers of reflective self-control, by depriving one of the ability to apply moral principles correctly in the circumstances one actually confronts. Whether this is the *only* way in which mental illness or insanity might interfere with accountability is more controversial. Almost from the time of their first formulation, the M'Naghten Rules have come under fire for their exclusive focus on cognitive defects or defects of reason in mental illness and insanity.[20] It has been argued that mental illness may equally cause defects of the will, such as a susceptibility to irresistible impulses, and that Continental legal codes are superior in their acknowledgment that such affective or motivational defects may also render it unreasonable to hold an agent accountable.

Much of the controversy about this question turns on the issue of whether irresistible impulses really are among the symptoms of mental illness; whether, that is, people in the grip of insanity or mental illness are plausibly regarded as acting from irresistible impulses.[21] Even if we are skeptical about the claim that irresistible impulses are genuine symptoms of insanity or mental illness, however, I think we can agree that susceptibility to such impulses would often be an exempting condition. Moreover the exempting force of this condition would be due to its interfering with the powers of reflective self-control. To see this, consider the quite different case of addiction, which is often thought to involve a susceptibility to impulses that cannot be resisted. Suppose that the impulses in question are such as to lead the agent to do things that

20. For a brief account of English criticism of the M'Naghten Rules, see H. L. A. Hart, "Changing Conceptions of Responsibility," as reprinted in his *Punishment and Responsibility,* pp. 186–209, at pp. 189–192.

21. For a generally skeptical discussion of the idea of irresistible impulses, and of the suggestion that such impulses would provide independent grounds for legal excuse, see Stephen J. Morse, "Diminished Capacity," in Stephen Shute, John Gardner, and Jeremy Horder, eds., *Action and Value in Criminal Law* (Oxford: Clarendon Press, 1993), pp. 239–278, at pp. 250–265. In accordance with the discussion in sec. 6.1, one should not think of irresistible impulses on the model of obstacles to the activity of choice. They would have to operate by making certain objects of choice so attractive that we completely lack the power to choose any other object, or by presenting obstacles to the successful *execution* of any contrary choices we might be able to make.

are consistently at variance with the moral obligations we accept (say, spending his money on drugs rather than family support). If these impulses are truly irresistible, then the agent will not genuinely have the ability to control his behavior in light of the moral obligations that the impulses lead him to violate. Even if he can perfectly grasp and apply the principles that support those obligations, so that he knows that what he is doing is wrong, the irresistibility of the impulses deprives the agent of the capacity to act in conformity with them. Of course the resulting impairment of the powers of reflective self-control may be selective rather than total, leaving aspects of the addict's behavior, or periods in the addict's life, in which he retains the general power to control his behavior by the light of moral obligations. But to the extent that irresistible impulses deprive the agent of those abilities, it would seem unreasonable to hold the agent morally accountable.[22]

Whether addictive desires really are irresistible is a further question, beyond the scope of my discussion. What is clear is that addiction is widely believed to involve a susceptibility to irresistible desires; taking this idea seriously, I have suggested that such impulses would interfere with the powers of reflective self-control and so constitute exempting conditions, according to the account of those conditions that I have been developing. But even if addictive desires are not literally irresistible, it is plausible to suppose that they are very difficult to resist. If this is right, then it seems safe to conclude that addiction would, at the very least, involve a substantial (if possibly selective) reduction of one's capacity to regulate one's conduct in light of the moral obligations that the addictive impulses incline one to breach. Recalling that general capacities admit of degrees, we might say that addiction largely impairs one's powers of reflective self-control. Hence addiction would seem to make it unreasonable to hold the agent *fully* accountable for the range of behavior that it affects, even if it does not deprive the agent altogether of accountability for that behavior.

But what if the addict really wants to do what his addiction leads him to do (say, to consume drugs at the expense of supporting his family)? What if he *values* such activities more than the alternatives available to him, or *identifies* with those activities, at the level of his highest-order commitments? The fact that the addict is in this way

---

22. Here and throughout my discussion of addiction, I bracket the issue of whether the addict is responsible for becoming addicted in the first place. Of course we may hold an agent morally responsible for getting himself into a state in which he is no longer fully responsible for what he does.

"willing" to engage in the activities his addiction leads him to favor would not necessarily make it less true that the addiction deprives him of the powers of reflective self-control. Assuming that these activities are morally wrong, and that addiction functions the way we ordinarily take it to function, the willing addict may lack the power to control his behavior in accordance with our moral principles—just like his unhappy counterpart, the unwilling addict. On the account I have been developing, it should therefore be unreasonable to treat either kind of addict as morally accountable, at least with respect to those activities that the addiction leads them to engage in. Yet Harry Frankfurt has influentially contended that the willing addict acts freely and can be considered morally responsible for the acts that his addiction leads him to perform.[23] Is this a plausible claim, and if so, can it be reconciled with the account of the exemptions that I have been developing?

To answer these questions it will be helpful to distinguish between two different models of the case of the willing addict; whether we think it reasonable to hold such an addict morally accountable will depend, I think, on which of these models we take to apply. On the first model, addiction is pictured as functioning (as it were) continuously through a person's life. It is not merely a source of desires that are practically irresistible. Rather, the condition of being addicted is taken to affect the agent's capacities for practical reasoning, depriving the addict of the power to think clearly about those aspects of his life affected by the addictive desires. On this model, it may well be the case that the addict is substantially and persistently deprived of the ability to choose to refrain from engaging in the activities that the addictive desires lead him to find attractive. Thus, the addict's inability to think clearly about his addictive activities may make him unable to accept the reasons that count against those activities, and so unable to make choices in accord with those reasons.[24] Assuming (as I have been) that the addictive

23. See his "Freedom of the Will and the Concept of a Person," as reprinted in Frankfurt, *The Importance of What We Care About: Philosophical Essays* (Cambridge: Cambridge University Press, 1988), pp. 11–25, especially pp. 24–25; compare his "Identification and Wholeheartedness," also in *The Importance of What We Care About*, pp. 159–176, which speaks of higher-order commitments and decisions rather than higher-order volitions. For purposes of the present discussion, it does not matter whether one follows Frankfurt in construing the willing addict as subject to higher-order volitions or commitments that endorse his addictive desires, or rather as *valuing* the activities to which he is addicted; for the latter proposal, see Gary Watson, "Free Agency," as reprinted in Watson, ed., *Free Will*, pp. 96–110.

24. The addict might still know that what his addiction leads him to do is morally wrong, but for the reasons given he would lack the ability to take this consideration seriously in practical reflection.

activities violate moral obligations that we accept, it will follow that the addict is substantially and persistently deprived of the power to govern his behavior in light of our moral expectations. Hence it will not be reasonable to hold such an agent morally accountable: even if the agent is "willing" to be subject to his addiction, the addictive circumstances in which he came to identify with this condition are circumstances in which the agent lacked the powers of reflective self-control. The fact that an addict identifies with his condition does not by itself make it reasonable to hold him morally accountable for the actions to which the condition gives rise.

Consider now a second model of how one might come to be a willing addict. On this model, addiction is a source of desires that are irresistible or extremely difficult to resist, but these desires affect the addict only episodically, and during the periods when the addict is not in their grip they have no influence on the addict's capacity to reason effectively about what to do. A willing addict who meets this description would thus have the capacity, at least intermittently, to grasp the principles that support our moral obligations and to regulate his behavior in light of those principles. He can, for instance, understand the moral reasons that count against developing and sustaining an addiction to drugs, and he is able to make choices in accordance with those reasons. He is even able to translate his choices into action—though it might require extraordinary, Odysseus-like measures to bring this result about. (The addict might, for instance, have to turn himself over to the care of relatives or to the officials of a treatment center, who would see to it that he is prevented from obtaining the substance to which he is addicted when the addictive desires again become active.[25]) On the second model, then, the addictive condition would not continuously deprive the agent of the powers of reflective self-control. But if, retaining these powers, the addict endorses his addictive condition, reaching the decision to continue to take the substance to which he is addicted (rather than, say, supporting his family), it would seem reasonable to

25. This assumes, of course, that the addict knows that he is subject to a latent addiction, and that the addictive drives will substantially impair his power to resist them on his own, should they become active. Note too that this possibility of taking extraordinary measures to control behavior in accord with moral demands might also be open to the unwilling addict who realizes he is addicted (assuming that there are friends or institutions he could turn to for help). On the second model, then, it might equally be appropriate to hold even an unwilling addict accountable: in the momentary grip of addictive drives, such an agent might not have the powers of reflective self-control, but those powers are available to the unwilling addict at other times, and would enable him to take steps to overcome his addictive condition.

treat him as morally accountable—even on the account of exemptions that I have been developing.[26]

Thus we may agree with Frankfurt's contention that a willing addict can be morally accountable for the actions his addiction would lead him to perform. But though we may agree with this conclusion, the considerations that support the conclusion are different from those that Frankfurt himself relies on. On Frankfurt's view, what makes the willing addict morally responsible is a structural fact about the addict's higher-order attitudes, namely the fact that the willing addict identifies with the activities to which he is addicted, at the level of his higher-order commitments. When this structural condition is present, it is not the case that the addict's activities are explained solely by the state of addiction that allegedly makes such activities inevitable; this sets the willing addict apart from the unwilling addict, whose activities are solely explained by his state of addiction.[27]

I have suggested, by contrast, that the presence of Frankfurt's structural condition is not by itself sufficient to make the willing addict morally accountable for what he does. What is important is not the mere fact that the addict identifies with the activities to which he is addicted, but the circumstances in which he has come to be in this condition, and here it will matter greatly which model of addiction we take to apply. Specifically, if the first model is adopted, then the state of addiction will be taken to influence the process whereby the addict came to identify with the activities to which he is addicted, and so the presence of that structural condition will not render him morally accountable for engaging in those activities. Frankfurt might agree with this conclusion, arguing that, on the first model, it turns out that the state of addiction that makes what the addict does unavoidable alone accounts for the addict's behavior (since it in some sense determines the process of deliberation that leads the addict to approve of the activities to which he is addicted). But even if it is true, on the first model, that

26. Some of Frankfurt's own descriptions of willing addiction strongly suggest this second model. For instance, in "What We Are Morally Responsible For," as reprinted in his *The Importance of What We Care About,* pp. 95–103, at p. 96, he describes a condition of "dormant" addiction, which plays no role in bringing about the addict's actual decision to take a given drug, but which would have caused the addict both to decide to take the drug and to act on that decision if he had not reached such a conclusion independently.

27. Of the willing addict, Frankfurt writes: "Given that it is . . . not only because of his addiction that his desire for the drug is effective, he may be morally responsible for taking the drug" ("Freedom of the Will and the Concept of a Person," p. 25). Compare the discussion of Frankfurt's views about the moral relevance of alternate possibilities in Appendix 2.

the addiction alone accounts for the addict's behavior, this does not yet explain *why* we should not hold the willing addict morally accountable when the model obtains. The reason, I have suggested, is that according to the first model, the willing addict is deprived of the powers of reflective self-control, where those powers are conditions of accountability.

Other cases in which these powers are taken to be substantially impaired include posthypnotic suggestion and behavior control, as well as cases of psychopathy and the effects of extreme stress and deprivation. Take hypnotism, to start with: someone who does something as a result of a posthypnotic suggestion may act fully intentionally, taking steps to satisfy a desire that she has, and with knowledge of what she is doing. Granted, the desire on which such an agent acts may be thought of as having been "implanted" by the hypnotist, and to that extent not really the agent's own desire. But this alone would not seem to make it unreasonable to hold the agent morally accountable—after all, people who are fully accountable act all the time on desires adopted from other sources (friends or advertisements, for instance), often without being aware that they have taken over goals that others would like them to advance.[28] What is distinctive about hypnotism is that the desire on which the agent acts becomes effective in a way that disables the agent's powers of reflective self-control. If posthypnotic suggestion leads the agent to violate our moral obligations, we will suppose that the agent lacks the power to control her behavior in light of those obligations at the time when she acts. But even if the agent is led to act in accordance with our moral obligations, it will not be because she has grasped the reasons that support those obligations and has chosen to comply with them. Rather, such powers of reflective self-control as the agent possesses will seem to be disengaged at the moment when the hypnotic suggestion becomes effective, resulting in intentional behavior that bypasses the will. Hence the common image of the hypnotized person as being subject to a kind of automatism: acting to satisfy desires to which she is subject, but disconnected from her ordinary capacity to

28. I have in mind here cases of "straightforward" influence by acquaintances or advertisements, as when one adopts a preference to imitate or flatter a friend, or because an advertising campaign has created a pleasing image for a product. These forms of influence may not engage one's powers of reflective self-control directly, but they do not disable those powers. There may, however, be less straightforward forms of manipulation that come closer to hypnotism and the other kinds of exemptions: for instance, subliminal advertising, or systematic deception by an acquaintance to cause one to adopt a certain end.

step back from those desires and control her behavior reflectively. It is this disengagement of the powers of reflective self-control that explains why hypnotism (as it is ordinarily taken to function) should be an exempting condition.

Like hypnotism, behavior control involves the manipulation of one agent by another. Here too, however, it is not the mere fact of influence by another agent that makes it unreasonable to treat the victim of behavior control as morally accountable, but rather the way in which such influence is exerted.[29] In particular, what seems to matter morally is whether influence is exerted in a way that deprives the victim of the normal powers of reflective self-control. For instance, systematic disinformation or indoctrination could deprive one of the capacity to apply moral obligations, by making one unable to judge accurately the morally relevant features of the situations one confronts; the result of such a process might thus resemble the effects of delusion as discussed in the case of mental illness or insanity. Aversive behavioral conditioning— such as that to which the character Alex is subjected in *A Clockwork Orange*—would seem to affect the powers of reflective self-control in a different way. Here certain kinds of behavior are negatively reinforced by being associated with visceral emotions or sensations, such as fear, anxiety, or nausea. Such associations may not deprive one altogether of the ability to engage in the forms of behavior that are negatively reinforced, but they would at least significantly diminish such powers to control the behavior as one may possess.[30] If the behavior in question is morally obligatory, the result will be a serious impairment of the agent's ability to control her behavior by the light of the moral reasons that support those obligations, which would make it unreasonable to expect the agent to comply with them. And if (as in Alex's case) the behavior is morally prohibited, the result will similarly be an impairment of that ability, since the association of the behavior with visceral emotions and sensations will make it extremely difficult to avoid that behavior for the right reasons (that is, because one grasps the moral considerations that count against it).

29. For a similar treatment of what Gary Watson calls "Brave New World" cases, see his "Free Action and Free Will," pp. 151–153.

30. Compare P. S. Greenspan, "Behavior Control and Freedom of Action," as reprinted in John Martin Fischer, ed., *Moral Responsibility* (Ithaca, N.Y.: Cornell University Press, 1986), pp. 191–224, especially pp. 196–199, on the role of visceral emotions in explaining the results of aversive conditioning. Greenspan assimilates such cases to cases of compulsion, suggesting that agents such as Alex have no reasonable choice but to avoid the behavior that they have been conditioned to find repulsive. This is suggestive, but I do not think it quite locates the persistent exempting force of extreme aversive conditioning.

As I have said, in holding people morally accountable we expect that they will comply with our moral obligations, where those obligations are supported by distinctively moral reasons; accordingly, it is reasonable to adopt this stance only toward agents who are capable of grasping and acting on such reasons. But someone who complies as a result of aversive behavioral conditioning may have a diminished capacity to act on distinctively moral reasons, because of the anxiety or fear associated with the immoral behavior that the victim has been conditioned to avoid.[31] This is presumably at least part of what is disturbing about aversive conditioning, even in cases in which it is successful on its own terms. As I suggested earlier, accountability requires the capacity to enter into certain sorts of moral relationships—ones characterized by the exchange of moral criticism and justification; but aversive conditioning, as it is popularly understood, secures outer conformity with moral requirements without restoring this kind of moral status.

Consider next the case of the psychopath. Many things are presumably characteristic of those we classify as psychopaths. Such agents are, for instance, not members of our moral community, insofar as they do not accept the moral requirements that we accept and hold people to, and they may be incorrigible in their immorality as well.[32] Neither of these characteristics by itself, however, appears to provide a sufficient *reason* to exempt the psychopath from moral accountability. If not being a member of our moral community were an exempting condition, we would have to treat all evil agents as people who are not morally accountable for what they do. But this seems to go too far: as I suggested earlier, we often want to hold accountable even those who reject our moral standards, and this would seem to be a reasonable thing to do so long as those agents retain the capacity to grasp and apply those standards and to regulate their conduct accordingly. As to incorrigibility, it may in fact be the case that the psychopath is distinguished from the ordinarily evil person by being constitutionally unresponsive to moral

31. Similar remarks may apply to the cases that Frankfurt classifies as coercion, in which an agent acts intentionally but is not morally responsible for what he intentionally does, because of the role of strong emotions (such as fear and anxiety) in producing the intentional action; see the end of sec. 5.3. Frankfurt himself supposes that the role of these strong emotions is such that the factors that make the coerced action inevitable also explain the action, and he suggests that this is what makes it inappropriate to hold the coerced agent morally responsible for the actions he intentionally performs. By contrast, I would suggest that these cases be treated as localized forms of behavior control, in which an agent's powers of reflective self-control are momentarily impaired by the strong emotions that the coercing agent (in Frankfurt's sense) conjures up.

32. Both incorrigibility and lack of responsiveness to our moral standards are proposed by Herbert Fingarette, as distinctive of the psychopath; see "Acceptance of Responsibility," as reprinted in his *On Responsibility* (New York: Basic Books, 1967), pp. 17–45.

education. Certainly if it is true that psychopaths are incorrigible in this way, it is a disturbing fact about them. But it is unclear why incorrigibility by itself should give us a reason to refrain from treating the psychopath as morally accountable with respect to our moral obligations. Perhaps it would do so if the stance of holding someone morally accountable were essentially a technique of moral improvement, a way of bringing the person held accountable to understand and to accept our moral obligations. But though education may plausibly be thought integral to the legal institution of punishment,[33] it does not seem similarly essential to the practice of holding people morally accountable.

What makes it appropriate to exempt the psychopath from accountability, I would suggest, is the fact that psychopathy, as conventionally understood, disables an agent's capacities for reflective self-control. Possession of these capacities requires the ability to grasp and apply our moral obligations, where that in turn involves a participant understanding of the moral reasons that support the obligations, enabling one not merely to parrot moral discourse but also to apply moral principles intelligently from case to case. But psychopathy is often thought to deprive one of precisely this aspect of the power of reflective self-control. Thus it has been suggested that psychopaths lack the qualities of imagination and practical understanding required to bring common moral principles to bear in new cases; for instance, they often have great difficulty distinguishing between trivial and important moral concerns, and so lack the capacity to engage in intelligent critical reflection on moral issues.[34] This severe impairment of the capacity for reflective self-control would set the psychopath apart from an "ordinary" evil person (such as Adolf Eichmann, perhaps), providing us with a reason for not treating the psychopath as a morally accountable agent. Whether psychopaths are in fact deprived of the capacity for reflective self-control in this way is of course not here at issue; the point is simply that psychopathy is widely believed to affect one's capacity to grasp and apply moral principles, and that we can explain in terms of this belief why it is included among the accepted exempting conditions.[35]

33. For a discussion of this view, see Jean Hampton, "The Moral Education Theory of Punishment," *Philosophy and Public Affairs* 13 (1984), pp. 208–238.

34. See, for instance, Glover, *Responsibility*, pp. 138, 177–178.

35. For discussions that develop this general approach to psychopathy, see R. A. Duff, "Psychopathy and Moral Understanding," *American Philosophical Quarterly* 14 (1977), pp. 189–200, and Jeffrie Murphy, "Moral Death: A Kantian Essay on Psychopathy," *Ethics* 82 (1972), pp. 284–298.

Consider, finally, the effects of extreme stress, deprivation, and torture. Here there may be some overlap with the recognized excusing conditions: as I said in section 5.3, for example, torture and deprivation are often classified as cases of necessity or duress, which provide excuses for particular actions one performs by affecting the quality of choice expressed in the actions. But these conditions may also be regarded as short-term exemptions, making it unreasonable to treat an agent as morally accountable over a limited period of time. What determines whether we view these conditions as excuses or exemptions, I would suggest, is whether we see them as affecting the powers of reflective self-control.[36] Though deprivation or the threat of torture may alter the quality of intention expressed by a given action, the *effects* of prolonged torture or deprivation might wear down one's capacity to control one's behavior in accordance with moral obligations, and to this extent torture could appropriately be viewed as an exempting condition. Thus, for example, there would seem to be something grotesquely unreasonable about holding morally accountable the brutalized, exhausted, and starving inmates of a Nazi concentration camp; the treatment to which they were subjected systematically aimed to dehumanize them, and to the extent that it succeeded, it substantially deprived the inmates of the powers of reflective self-control.[37]

Less extreme conditions, such as the stress caused by the loss of one's job or by the sudden death of a family member, may not deprive one altogether of these powers, but like other mild exempting conditions I have discussed, they could plausibly be thought to impair them. To this extent an agent's moral accountability for what she does might fairly be thought to be diminished during the period when the agent is subjected to extraordinary stress. The effectiveness of this kind of mitigating condition will presumably be selective, however: the stressed-out agent may not be fully responsible for acts of rudeness, inconsideration, or minor cruelty, but stress alone would not seem to mitigate the agent's moral responsibility for, say, elaborately plotting and executing the murder of the employer who fired her. This reflects the reasonable view

36. Contrast the treatment of these cases in Watson, "Responsibility and the Limits of Evil," pp. 266–267; developing a suggestion of Strawson's, Watson proposes that conditions such as stress or strain exempt an agent by showing that the agent's behavior does not reflect the agent's "true" or "moral" self. As Watson himself notes, though, it is obscure what might be meant by the true or moral self, or why an agent's not being her true or moral self should constitute an exemption.

37. This point is made very vividly in Primo Levi, *Survival in Auschwitz: The Nazi Assault on Humanity* (New York: Collier Books, 1961).

that it is anyway much easier to comply with the moral prohibition on murder than with obligations of kindness or consideration. If the exempting or mitigating force of stress is due to its impairing the power to control one's behavior in light of moral obligations, that force will not extend to obligations that by their nature are fairly easy to obey.

6.3   Determinism and Rational Powers

In section 6.1 I argued that the powers of reflective self-control are among the conditions of moral accountability, identifying the principle that it is unreasonable to hold people to moral obligations we accept if they lack these general powers. Then, in section 6.2, I tried to show how the most important exempting conditions, as they are conventionally understood, seem to impair the powers of reflective self-control. Putting these two points together yields an account of the standard exempting conditions that singles out unifying characteristics of the accepted exemptions, showing what it is that makes them hang together as a class. Moreover, the unifying characteristics are not merely features that all of the exempting conditions happen to have in common; rather, they are characteristics that account for the exempting force of the exemptions, characteristics in virtue of which it is unfair to hold someone morally accountable when the exempting conditions obtain. For if the powers of reflective self-control are conditions of the reasonableness of holding people responsible, and if it is common to the accepted exemptions that they impair these powers, this common feature will make it unreasonable to hold people accountable when the exemptions are in place. The approach I have developed thus accounts for the normative force of the exempting conditions, *explaining* what it is about those conditions that constitutes an exemption from the status of a morally accountable agent.

It is perhaps worth stressing once again, however, that the account does not purport to offer an accurate picture of the nature and consequences of the conditions commonly accepted as exemptions. For all I have said, it is possible that many accepted exemptions do not in fact impair the powers of reflective self-control: hypnotism, for instance, may turn out not to function by inducing an episode of automatism, as I suggested we often take it to do. In that event, one should not conclude that my interpretation of the exemptions is incorrect, but rather that hypnotism may not be a legitimate exempting condition. The ordinary exempting conditions are accepted as exemptions because of widespread beliefs about how those conditions operate. I have tried to isolate which of our common beliefs about the exempting conditions, if true, would give us a reason to refrain from treating an agent as morally accountable when the exemptions obtain. These beliefs are generally plausible, but they are also subject to revision, and such revisions may force us to rethink our acceptance of certain conditions as exemptions. For this reason, the standard list of exempting conditions should not necessarily be thought of as definitive.

Before we can say how changes in our beliefs about the nature of the standard exemptions should affect our acceptance of those conditions as exemptions, however, we need an account of the exemptions. Drawing on our widespread beliefs about how the exemptions function, the account should yield a framework for deciding what must be true about a given condition if it is to count as a legitimate exemption. That is precisely what the account I have offered aims to provide. My account says that our ordinary judgments of exemption rest on the belief that the exempting conditions impair the powers of reflective self-control, and that this belief must be true if those conditions are legitimately to count as exemptions from accountability. Provided with such an account, we are in a position to say how further empirical and theoretical research about particular conditions, such as mental illness, addiction, and hypnotism, might affect the classification of those conditions as exemptions. But we are also, I now want to argue, in a position to see why determinism would not represent a generalization of the exemptions, giving us the same kind of reason to refrain from holding people accountable globally that the legitimate exemptions provide in particular cases

The argument is quite straightforward. On my account, exemptions impair the powers of reflective self-control, thereby making it unreasonable to hold an agent to moral obligations we accept, when they obtain. If determinism is to entail a generalization of the exemptions, it must be the case that determinism would impair the powers of reflective self-control of all agents, all the time. That is, it must follow from determinism that no agent ever has the general power to control what he does reflectively, by the light of the moral requirements we accept. But it seems clear that determinism would not have this consequence. I take determinism to be the thesis that a complete physical description of the world at a given time, together with a complete description of the laws of nature, entails every truth as to the state of the physical world at later times. Whether or not this thesis is true would seem to have no bearing on the question of whether or not people possess the powers of reflective self-control. Those powers are matters of broadly psychological capacity or competence, like the power to speak a given language, or to add and subtract large numbers, or to read and play music on the piano. It would be very strange to suppose that determinism per se would deprive people of psychological capacities of this sort—as if the confirmation of determinism would give us reason to conclude that Jane Austen lacked the competence to write in English, or that Maria Callas had no capacity to sing. Similarly, determinism would seem irrelevant to the question of whether people have the general psychological abilities I have referred to as powers of reflective self-control. The only reasons we might have to deny that people possess such general psychological powers would equally be reasons for questioning all intentional explanations of human activity. But for purposes of discussion in this book, I have granted from the start the legitimacy of intentional explanations of this kind, assuming that determinism per se would not pose a general threat to such explanations.

As I said, this argument is extremely straightforward. Note in particular that it does not rely on any specific analysis of the notion of a general psychological power. However we understand this notion, it seems to me that our possessing or lacking such powers must be completely independent of the truth or falsity of determinism. I would go so far as to suggest that the independence of these two questions should be a constraint on any analysis of the notion of a general psychological power one might care to propose: a candidate analysis that makes the possession of a general psychological power hang on the question of the truth or falsity of determinism cannot be a satisfactory analysis of that notion at all. Even incompatibilists, it seems, would agree with this point.[38] They do not deny that general psychological abilities—such as the powers of reflective self-control—are compatible with determinism; rather, accepting that this is the case, they attempt to show

38. See, for instance, Peter van Inwagen, *An Essay on Free Will* (Oxford: Clarendon Press, 1983), p. 13. Van Inwagen distinguishes between general abilities or skills, on the one hand, and the power to exercise the general abilities on a particular occasion, observing that "the thesis of determinism may or may not be relevant to the question of whether someone on a particular occasion can or cannot speak French; it is certainly irrelevant to the question whether that person is a French speaker." Van Inwagen concludes that the notion of general ability or skill is plainly not the notion at issue in discussions of free will and determinism. I am suggesting, by contrast, that the issue between compatibilist and incompatibilist treatments of accountability is in part precisely the issue of which kind of general ability is required for status as an accountable agent.

that there is a different kind of ability required for moral responsibility that is not similarly compatible with determinism. This is the ability to do otherwise, construed as an ability to *exercise* such general psychological powers as one possesses, in particular situations of action.

Consider, in this connection, the following remark of Don Locke's: "It is obvious that what is at issue in the free will–determinism controversy is not whether things possess powers and agents possess abilities which they do not exercise, but whether things and agents are able to exercise those powers, even at times when it happens that they are not exercising them. The 'can' of power and ability, in short, is not the 'can' of the free will controversy."[39] This seems to me absolutely correct, as a report about how the question of free will has conventionally been understood. But should we understand the question in this way? My argument in this chapter and the preceding one calls into question the received interpretation. At least so far as moral responsibility is concerned, the argument suggests that what matters is not the ability to exercise our general powers of reflective self-control, but simply the possession of such powers—powers that are widely conceded to be compatible with determinism. These are the powers that make one a morally accountable agent, and that the standard exemptions are taken to interfere with.

To block this conclusion, the incompatibilist must either reconsider the compatibility of general psychological powers with determinism, or challenge my account of our judgments of exemption. As I have indicated, the first route seems extremely unpromising, but there is one way of pursuing it that some incompatibilists may be tempted to follow. I have suggested that once general psychological powers are distinguished from the specific ability to exercise those powers in particular situations, it becomes clear that determinism would not *directly* undermine our general psychological powers. Once this point is grasped, however, there may still be some temptation to suppose that determinism would *indirectly* threaten our general powers. Thus it is a salient difference between general human powers and the powers of physical objects that the exercise of the former depends on the will in a way that has no analogue in the case of physical powers. Whether a sixty-watt bulb actually produces sixty watts of light is a function (basically) of the external conditions that are present, whereas a French-speaker's

39. Don Locke, "Natural Powers and Human Abilities," *Proceedings of the Aristotelian Society* 74 (1973–74), pp. 171–187, at p. 179.

exercise of her linguistic powers depends not just on the external conditions that obtain, but also on whether she chooses to speak French.[40] One might express this difference by saying that human powers are powers to do certain kinds of things freely, so that s can only be said to have the power to do x if it is true that s is free to choose to do x, in particular situations of action.[41] Determinism might then be thought to threaten our general powers indirectly, by undermining our freedom of action and choice in particular circumstances.

But this argument is unconvincing. The role of the will with respect to general human powers is such that whether those powers are exercised depends on whether the agent actually chooses to exercise them. It in no way follows from this that whether one possesses such general powers depends on whether one has freedom of choice, or freedom of action, with respect to the exercise of those powers. So long as determinism is compatible with the explanation of what people do in terms of their actual choices—and I have seen no reason to deny this—there will be room in a deterministic world for general human powers. What one can perhaps say is that general human powers are possessed by creatures about whom the question arises whether they have freedom of the will, in the standard philosophical sense that centers on the analysis of alternate possibilities or statements of the form "s could have done otherwise." But even if we do not have freedom of will, in this standard philosophical sense, it may still be the case that we possess the general powers of reflective self-control that make us morally accountable agents.

The second strategy of incompatibilist response focuses not on the notion of general human powers, but on my interpretation of accountability exclusively in terms of such powers. I have suggested that our judgments of exemption rely on the following principle of fairness: it is unreasonable to hold someone to a moral obligation if the person lacks the power to grasp and comply with the reasons that support the obligation. The incompatibilist might challenge my gloss on this prin-

40. There is a well-known class of counterexamples to this generalization, in the form of human powers that can be exercised only spontaneously and so without the deliberateness normally characteristic of choice. For example, I may become so nervous when I try to speak French that I cannot utter a single grammatical sentence, whereas I speak French passably well when questioned unexpectedly by a French tourist on the street.

41. A position of this sort is suggested by Ursula Wolf, *Möglichkeit und Notwendigkeit bei Aristoteles und heute* (Munich: Wilhelm Fink Verlag, 1979), p. 374: "das 'kann' der menschlichen Fähigkeiten [impliziert] das 'kann' der Handlungsfreiheit." ("The 'can' of human abilities [implies] the 'can' of freedom of action.")

ciple as being too narrow, suggesting that the principle admits of an interpretation that supports the generalization strategy. Thus, suppose that a given agent *s* fails to comply with our moral obligations on a particular occasion. The incompatibilist may say that there is a sense in which *s* lacked the power to comply with the obligation on that occasion, if determinism is true, insofar as determinism would deprive *s* of the ability to *exercise* the general powers in the particular circumstances of action. This in turn might make it unreasonable to hold *s* accountable, in the same way that the exemptions are judged to make it unreasonable to hold people accountable in particular cases.[42]

But this strategy builds into the concept of power an equivocation that is not really to be found in the principle of fairness underlying the standard exemptions. The principle says, again, that it is unreasonable to hold a person to a moral obligation if the person lacks the power to grasp and comply with the reasons that support the obligation. The incompatibilist would construe the concept of power in this principle disjunctively: as including either the general power to grasp and comply with moral justifications, or the specific ability to exercise that general power on a particular occasion. But there is no reason to think that this disjunctive version of the principle is needed to account for any aspect of our concrete judgments of exemption. From the very start I have taken the principle to require only general abilities to grasp and comply with moral reasons (see section 6.1). General abilities seem to be at issue in the analogous cases in which we judge, say, that it would be unreasonable to expect the newly landed refugee to speak and understand one's native language, or that it would be unreasonable to demand that one's unathletic child should excel in sports. In these cases the general abilities that matter are abilities to do the sort of thing that is demanded of one.

But general abilities would similarly seem to be at issue when, in moral practice, we inquire as to an agent's ability to grasp and comply with moral reasons. Thus the powers of reflective self-control that the exemptions impair are all general psychological abilities of this sort. Such conditions as insanity, youth, hypnotism, and aversive conditioning do not operate by depriving us of the ability to *exercise* such general

---

42. Strictly speaking, the argument just sketched would show only that the ability to do otherwise is required in circumstances in which an agent in fact violates our moral obligations, not—as ordinarily supposed—that the ability to do otherwise is always a condition of responsibility. This selective character of the threat determinism poses to responsibility is discussed at greater length in Chapter 7.

powers of reflective self-control as we may possess; rather, they undermine those general powers directly. If this is right, however, then there is nothing about our ordinary judgments of exemption that would motivate a disjunctive interpretation of the notion of power. Granted, some of the exemptions might perhaps be construed as conditions that make one unable to do otherwise, in some sense: we may be tempted to say this, for instance, about actions that result from addictive desires, or from posthypnotic suggestion. But there is no reason to treat such claims as referring to the specific inability to exercise one's general powers; rather, they sustain a perfectly straightforward interpretation, as a way of referring to the exempted agent's general incapacity to do that which she does not do in fact (namely, grasp moral reasons and regulate her conduct accordingly).

Incompatibilists require *some* principle of fairness to sustain their claim that there is a specifically moral objection to holding people responsible, in the absence of strong freedom of the will. Our concrete judgments of excuse and exemption implicitly rely on such moral principles. But the moral principles implicit in these judgments are not principles that support an incompatibilist interpretation of the conditions of accountability or blameworthiness. I conclude that the generalization strategy does not succeed. The conditions that render it unfair to blame people who have a valid excuse, and unfair to hold people accountable when the exempting conditions obtain, would not generalize if determinism is true. An incompatibilist interpretation of the conditions of responsibility must therefore appeal to principles of fairness distinct from those that support our concrete judgments of exemption and excuse.

The prospects for defending incompatibilism in this way are discussed in the following chapter. Before turning to that topic, however, it will be helpful to say a bit more about the powers of reflective self-control, by comparing my treatment of their nature and significance with other compatibilist accounts of the abilities that matter to responsibility.

6.4   Comparisons and Contrasts

On the account I have offered, the powers of reflective self-control are to be construed as forms of broadly psychological competence or capacity, like the general ability to speak a language, or to read musical notation and reproduce the music read on an instrument. I have argued that once it is clear that the central conditions of accountability are general psychological abilities of this sort, it also becomes clear that determinism presents no special threat to these conditions; for the question of whether a person does or does not have a given ability of this kind is completely independent from the question of whether a general thesis of determinism is or is not true. In making this move I am following a long compatibilist tradition. Many compatibilists have maintained that what really matters to moral responsibility are general psychological abilities, and that determinism would not by itself deprive us of such abilities. How, if at all, does my position differ from the positions of other compatibilists who have followed this strategy?

One important respect in which my position differs from that of many other compatibilists is in the context in which I take general abilities to be important. A common position is that responsibility requires not only general abilities of some (yet unspecified) sort, but also the opportunity to exercise those general abilities.[43] These two conditions—ability plus opportunity—are together taken to characterize the principal conditions of moral responsibility. On the account I have offered, however, no mention has yet been made of the idea that the opportunity to exercise one's general abilities should be a condition of moral responsibility. Presumably reference to opportunity is meant as a way of capturing the condition that is interfered with by many of the standard excuses. As I have shown, excuses function locally, blocking responsibility only in particular circumstances of action; whether one has the opportunity to exercise one's general powers would similarly seem to be a function of the particular circumstances in which one finds oneself. Furthermore some of the accepted excuses could accurately be described as cases in which one is deprived of this sort of opportunity: consider, for instance, cases of physical constraint, or automatic muscular contraction. But even if these cases can be described as cases in which one lacks the opportunity to exercise one's general abilities, it does not follow that this is what accounts for their excusing force. I have offered a different explanation of how the ordinary excuses operate, one that does not make the opportunity to exercise one's general powers a condition of responsibility. For the present it suffices to call attention to this departure from common compatibilist strategy; in the next chapter I defend this departure at greater length, arguing that the inclusion of opportunity among the conditions of responsibility is a

---

43. Philosophers who have endorsed this kind of position include H. L. A. Hart, Jonathan Glover, Anthony Kenny, and Susan Wolf; for references, see the extended discussion of opportunity in sec. 7.2.

potentially fatal mistake for compatibilists to make, and that the source of this mistake lies in a misunderstanding of the way excuses operate.

A further departure from many compatibilist accounts is my specification of the *kinds* of general psychological ability that are held to be conditions of responsibility. Compatibilists have sometimes supposed that the general ability that matters to moral responsibility is none other than the general ability to do otherwise.[44] That is, they have apparently agreed with incompatibilists that responsibility requires alternate possibilities, but offered compatibilist analyses of the kind of alternate possibilities required; according to these analyses, whether one has alternate possibilities in the relevant sense will in part be a matter of whether one has the general ability to do otherwise. By contrast, I have suggested that the general abilities that matter to responsibility are distinctively rational powers: the power to grasp and apply the principles that support the moral obligations we accept, and to control one's behavior by the light of such principles. These powers of reflective self-control are clearly relevant to the practice of holding people responsible, and equally clearly believed to be interfered with by the acknowledged exempting conditions. The general ability to do otherwise, on the other hand, does not seem to be similarly anchored in our practice of holding people morally responsible. Indeed it is very obscure what might be meant by speaking of a *general* ability to do otherwise: "doing otherwise" does not look at all like an action kind of the sort that one might possess a general competence or capacity to engage in.

Other philosophers have held that the general powers important to responsibility include not the ability to do otherwise but distinctively rational abilities. For instance, H. L. A. Hart writes that the abilities that matter to moral responsibility "are those of understanding, reasoning, and control of conduct: the ability to understand what conduct legal rules or morality require, to deliberate and reach decisions concerning these requirements, and to conform to decisions when made."[45] Similar emphasis has been placed on distinctively rational abilities in this context by a number of philosophers, including Stuart Hampshire, T. M. Scanlon, and Susan Wolf.[46] These philosophers come closer to the position I have been trying to stake out on the conditions of accountability. Still,

44. This is affirmed explicitly, for instance, by Kenny, in *Freewill and Responsibility*, pp. 30–32, and by Glover, in *Responsibility*, pp. 73, 86.

45. Hart, "Postscript: Responsibility and Retribution," p. 227.

46. See Stuart Hampshire, *Freedom of the Individual*, expanded ed. (Princeton, N.J.: Princeton University Press, 1975); Scanlon, "The Significance of Choice," lecture 1; and Susan Wolf, *Freedom within Reason* (New York: Oxford University Press, 1990), and "Sanity and the Metaphysics of Responsibility," in Schoeman, ed., *Responsibility, Character, and the Emotions*, pp. 46–62. Other

there are important differences that need to be emphasized and explained.

One of these differences concerns the kind of rational powers that accountability requires. A number of philosophers have urged that the rational powers that matter to freedom and responsibility are general abilities to respond to practical reasons, irrespective of the content of such reasons. Thus, John Martin Fischer and Mark Ravizza hold that "[a]n agent is morally responsible for performing an action insofar as the mechanism that issues in the action is reasons-responsive."[47] A mechanism is reasons-responsive, in turn, if the operation of that mechanism would have led the agent to do otherwise, in the presence of some sufficient reason to do otherwise.[48] This proposal clearly makes responsibility dependent on possession of some general ability to engage in practical reasoning and to regulate one's conduct in accordance with the results of such reasoning. But the abilities it singles out do not necessarily include the ability to grasp and respond to specifically moral reasons. Thus, it would seem that psychopaths or young children often act on processes of thought that are reasons-responsive, in the sense specified by Fischer and Ravizza, insofar as their ability to reason practically would have led them to do otherwise in response to *some* sufficient reason to do otherwise (for example, a sufficiently blatant threat or bribe). Yet it would still seem unreasonable to hold such agents morally accountable. What matters is not the ability merely to respond to (some) practical reasons, but the ability to grasp and respond to specifically *moral* reasons, of the sort that support the moral obligations we accept and hold people to.

Furthermore, where the specifically moral powers of reflective self-control are present, it would often seem reasonable to hold an agent responsible even if those moral powers are not exercised in fact. The powers of reflective self-control, as I have characterized them, are positive or "unidirectional" general abilities: abilities to grasp and apply

---

philosophers who have recently emphasized the importance of rational powers for freedom and responsibility include Bernard Gert and Timothy J. Duggan, "Free Will as Ability to Will," as reprinted in Fischer, ed., *Moral Responsibility*, pp. 205–224; John Martin Fischer, "Responsiveness and Moral Responsibility," in Schoeman, ed., *Responsibility, Character, and the Emotions*, pp. 81–106, and (with Mark Ravizza) "Responsibility and Inevitability," *Ethics* 101 (1991), pp. 258–278; and Ernst Tugendhat, "Der Begriff der Willensfreiheit," as reprinted in his *Philosophische Aufsätze* (Frankfurt am Main: Suhrkamp Verlag, 1992), pp. 334–351.

47. Fischer, "Responsiveness and Moral Responsibility," pp. 85–86; compare Fischer and Ravizza, "Responsibility and Inevitability."

48. This is the notion of "weak reasons-responsiveness," explained in Fischer, "Responsiveness and Moral Responsibility," pp. 88–90. Compare Gert and Duggan, "Free Will as Ability to Will," pp. 210–211.

moral reasons, and to act in conformity with them.[49] Strictly speaking, then, people will succeed in exercising these abilities only when they actually comply with moral obligations, and when they do so because they grasp the reasons that support them. To require actual exercise of these abilities as a condition of responsibility would therefore rule out responsibility in cases in which people do things that are morally wrong. What matters is not the exercise of the general powers of reflective self-control, but the possession of such powers. Indeed, where people possess these general powers, it will often be reasonable to hold them responsible even if they do not exercise any powers of practical reflection at all. Fischer and Ravizza apparently think otherwise, holding moral responsibility to require that one's action result from some process of practical reasoning or deliberation—a "mechanism" that is itself reasons-responsive.[50] But this would preclude responsibility for any spontaneous or capricious acts, and that would be implausibly restrictive. On my view, by contrast, responsibility for an action or omission requires that the action or omission reflect some quality of choice (see section 5.2). But so long as an agent retains the general powers of reflective self-control, it is not required that the choice for which the agent is held responsible is actually the result of deliberation on the basis of reasons at all. Thus, if I choose to hurt the person standing next to me on a lark or a whim, and proceed to stamp on his toe, it may be perfectly fair to hold me to blame for what I have done.[51]

49. It is sometimes said that no general abilities are exclusively unidirectional: if *s* has the general power to do *x,* then *s* must also have the general power to refrain from *x*-ing. (See Wolf, *Möglichkeit und Notwendigkeit bei Aristoteles und heute,* p. 356, for this suggestion.) Whether or not this is the case, it is the positive side of the powers of reflective self-control that matters, in connection with accountability.

50. See also Scanlon, "The Significance of Choice," p. 176: "What is required is that what we do be importantly dependent on our process of critical reflection, that that process itself be sensitive to reasons, and that later stages of the process be importantly dependent on conclusions reached at earlier stages." Construed literally, this condition—which Scanlon calls "intrapersonal responsiveness"—would seem to make the actual exercise of critical reflection a condition of responsibility.

51. Fischer and Ravizza might contend that this kind of choice would constitute a reasons-responsive "mechanism," since there presumably exists some alternate sequence in which there is sufficient reason to do otherwise, the agent chooses to act, and the agent acts otherwise as a result of this choice. But reasons-responsiveness is supposed to be compatible with the lack of alternate possibilities presented by "Frankfurt-style" cases, and it is not clear that the actual operation of choice satisfies this condition. Given the presence of a "nefarious neurosurgeon," it may be that every alternate sequence in which the agent chooses to act is one in which the agent chooses precisely as she does in the actual sequence. The strategy of trying to isolate a distinct, reasons-responsive "mechanism" actually at work in "Frankfurt-style" cases requires one to identify a "mechanism" that would be disengaged by the nefarious neurosurgeon in every sequence in which

A further point concerns the question of why the general powers of reflective self-control should matter to moral responsibility. Those who have urged the importance of powers of rational control have generally not attempted to explain why these powers are so important to responsibility, but have instead largely been content to assert that these powers are morally important.[52] An example of this tendency is (again) Hart, who suggests that it is virtually analytic of the concept of morality that the powers of reflective self-control should be taken to be conditions of moral responsibility. Regarding those powers, he notes that "a system or practice which did not regard the possession of these capacities as a necessary condition of liability, and so treated blame as appropriate even in the case of those who lacked them, would not, as morality is at present understood, be a morality."[53] This seems correct so far as it goes, but one wants to know why the general powers of reflective self-control have this kind of importance to moral responsibility. I have tried to answer this question by relating these powers to the account of the practice of holding people morally responsible developed in the earlier chapters of this book. In holding people morally responsible, I have suggested, we expect that they will comply with moral obligations that we accept, where this stance exposes them to the risks of harmful moral sanction; in addition these obligations are supported by reasons, which explain our own compliance with the obligations, and which could motivate compliance on the part of others. But it would be unreasonable to hold people to obligations that are supported by reasons in this

---

it would lead the agent to do otherwise, but that, if not disengaged, would (sometimes) lead the agent to do otherwise in the presence of a sufficient reason to do so (see Fischer, "Responsiveness and Moral Responsibility," pp. 85–86). Choice does not satisfy these constraints, since it would not necessarily be disengaged by the neurosurgeon (the surgeon might manipulate one's choices directly—see Fischer's own lifesaver example, on p. 94 of "Responsiveness and Moral Responsibility"). Indeed, I doubt whether there is any way of specifying the actual "mechanism" that satisfies the constraints. The intuitive candidate would be, as I suggest in the text, an actual process of reasoning or deliberation. But what if the nefarious manipulator were not a neurosurgeon but an artist in countersuggestion, who would directly alter the course of an agent's practical reasoning in all cases in which it might lead the agent to do otherwise, by uttering some mesmerizing phrase? (Fischer's discussion of the individuation of reasons-responsive "mechanisms," on pp. 93–95 of "Responsiveness and Moral Responsibility," suggests an awareness of these difficulties.)

52. An exception here is Scanlon, who explains the importance of the powers of reflective self-control in terms of a contractualist account of moral requirements; see "The Significance of Choice," lecture 1. The explanation I have offered is not tied so closely to a particular account of the nature and source of moral requirements, but draws on more general features of what we are doing when we hold people to moral obligations that we accept. My account of these features is, I hope, *compatible* with contractualism as Scanlon understands it, but it may also be compatible with other theories of the nature and source of moral requirements (or with the denial that there is a unified source of the requirements of moral rightness).

53. Hart, "Postscript: Responsibility and Retribution," p. 230.

way unless they possess the general powers of reflective self-control: the power to grasp and apply moral reasons, and to control their behavior in accordance with them. This helps to explain the moral significance we take these powers to have, tracing that significance to a basic principle of fairness (as reasonableness) in which we have the utmost confidence. By showing the relevance of that principle to the stance of holding people accountable, we gain insight into why a system that did not take the powers of reflective self-control to be conditions of accountability would only dubiously be a moral system at all.

Note finally that the account I have offered largely takes for granted the notion of a general power. That is, I have not attempted to provide a philosophical analysis of this concept; rather I have relied on informal characterization, supplemented by appeal to examples, to indicate what I mean when speaking of such general powers. It seems to me that this combination of informal characterization and appeal to examples is sufficient to locate a concept of general power that ought to be familiar to all of us, and that no attempt to explicate this concept in terms of more basic psychological or nonpsychological notions, or in terms of causal conditionals, is likely to succeed. From what I have shown, for instance, it is clear that the general powers in question admit of degrees. Furthermore, the failure to exercise a general power on a particular occasion is compatible with the continued possession of the power on that occasion. Indeed, isolated failures are compatible with continued possession of a general power, even on occasions when the agent had both the motivation and the opportunity to exercise the power (a skilled outfielder might occasionally drop a very "catchable" ball). Similarly, isolated success at doing something does not necessarily entail the general ability to do that sort of thing (the unskilled novice at darts might score a lucky bull's-eye).[54] We ascribe these kinds of power to people all the time, when (say) we credit them with the ability to speak French, or to play the guitar, or to juggle billiard balls. For purposes of understanding responsibility, the first task for philosophy is not to analyze the basic notion of a general power—as if our grip on this notion would become insecure in the absence of an account of its

54. On these points and the basic idea of ability or power more generally, see Michael Ayers, *The Refutation of Determinism: An Essay in Philosophical Logic* (London: Methuen, 1968), especially chaps. 2 and 6–8; Hampshire, *Freedom of the Individual,* chap. 1; A. M. Honoré, "Can and Can't," *Mind* 73 (1964), pp. 463–479 (especially the remarks about "'can' [general],"); Locke, "Natural Powers and Human Abilities"; and Ursula Wolf, *Möglichkeit und Notwendigkeit bei Aristoteles und heute,* secs. 25–26.

necessary and sufficient conditions. It is, rather, to explain why accountability should be interpreted in terms of such powers, and to specify
the kinds of powers that matter.

The most popular compatibilist analysis of the abilities that make us
morally responsible is, of course, the conditional analysis. This analysis
is now associated principally with G. E. Moore, though the basic
strategy is recurrent in the empiricist tradition and can be traced at least
back to Hobbes.[55] It holds that moral responsibility requires the ability
(in some sense) to do otherwise, and that *s* had the ability to do
otherwise, in this sense, if *s* would have done otherwise, had *s* chosen
(or intended or decided or wanted) to do otherwise. Now, this conditionalist approach seems to me to be flawed both in principle and in
detail. In principle, it goes wrong in conceding that responsibility
requires the ability to do otherwise, for as I explain in Appendix 2, any
compatibilist account that grants that alternate possibilities matter to
moral responsibility is apt to be vulnerable to incompatibilist counter-
attack. Crudely put, if alternate possibilities are really what matter, then
s's responsibility will plausibly depend not merely on whether *s* would
have done otherwise if *s* had chosen to do otherwise, but also on
whether *s* could have chosen to do otherwise in the first place.[56] The
incompatibilist can mount a persuasive case that this latter ability cannot
be reconciled with determinism. In matters of detail, the conditionalist
account has been found to diverge at a number of points from our
considered convictions about the conditions of responsibility. Thus if *s*
does something under the influence of hypnosis, or behavioral conditioning, or mental illness, it might well be true that *s* would have done
otherwise had *s* chosen to do otherwise; but we would nevertheless
consider it unfair to hold *s* morally responsible under these conditions.[57]

55. See G. E. Moore, *Ethics* (London: Oxford University Press, 1912), chap. 6; Hobbes, "Of
Liberty and Necessity."

56. This is the gist of Roderick Chisolm's well-known objection to the conditional analysis:
see, for example, his "Human Freedom and the Self," as reprinted in Watson, ed., *Free Will*,
pp. 24–35, at pp. 26–27. In "Freedom to Act," in Ted Honderich, ed., *Essays on Freedom of Action*
(London: Routledge and Kegan Paul, 1973), pp. 137–156, Donald Davidson responds to Chisolm's
objection by suggesting that the antecedents of the conditionals should be specified in terms of
psychological concepts about which the question of freedom does not in principle arise, such as
desire (rather than, say, choice or decision). But if this avoids Chisolm's objection, it does so by
making the conditional analysis even more remote from the kinds of freedom that matter to us.
What is morally important is not that our actions should be counterfactually responsive to our
desires, but that they should be responsive to our choices.

57. For recent discussions of the conditional analysis, see Watson, "Free Action and Free Will,"
pp. 153–154, 157–159, and Wolf, *Freedom within Reason*, pp. 97–100.

For my present purposes, however, I am less interested in the points at which the conditional analysis diverges from our considered judgments about responsibility than in the points at which it conforms with them. The conditional analysis would hardly have gained any following at all unless it seemed at least roughly to track what really matters for moral responsibility. On the account I have offered, what matters for responsibility are the general powers of reflective self-control, and the absence of specific excusing conditions, and I think we can see in terms of this account why the conditional analysis has some initial plausibility. The powers of reflective self-control involve the ability to step back from one's desires, to make choices on the basis of one's grasp of moral reasons, and to control one's behavior in accordance with these choices. But if someone has these abilities, and if the normal excuses (such as physical constraint) are absent, it will generally follow that the person would have done otherwise if she had chosen to do otherwise. Indeed, for a wide range of central cases the counterfactual dependence of action on choice, singled out by the conditional analysis, will track almost exactly the conditions in which an agent retains the general powers of reflective self-control.

This helps to explain, I would suggest, the persistent appeal of the conditional analysis, by showing that the analysis picks out a condition that is generally correlated with the factors that really matter to responsibility. Of course, even if the conditional analysis often gives the right answer to the question of whether someone is morally responsible, it does not follow that it gives this answer for the right reason. Even when it is true both that s is morally responsible for what she has done, and that s would have done otherwise had she chosen to do otherwise, it is not the fact that this conditional is true that makes s morally responsible; indeed, it is not the fact that s had alternate possibilities in *any* sense. What makes it fair to hold s responsible are rather the different kinds of facts that I have tried to characterize in this chapter and the preceding one—facts about the content of the choices expressed in s's actions, and about s's general powers of reflective self-control.

7

The Lure of Liberty

×⊘×

In the preceding chapters I considered and rejected the attempt to anchor incompatibilist principles of fairness in our concrete judgments of excuse and exemption (the generalization strategy). How else might incompatibilism be defended? I have suggested that any serious case for a subordinate principle of fairness must appeal to our considered convictions. Once the generalization strategy has been dispatched, there are two kinds of considered convictions that the incompatibilist might attempt to call upon: our concrete judgments about particular cases distinct from the standard excuses and exemptions (including, perhaps, hypothetical cases), and our more abstract judgments about the conditions that make it fair to hold people responsible. I address these possibilities in this chapter.

On the account I have offered, it is a hallmark of the stance of holding people responsible that the targets of the stance are subject to sanctioning treatment, where this treatment in turn serves to express the reactive emotions. The connection with sanctions is what brings the stance within the scope of moral principles, making it possible to raise the question of the fairness of holding people responsible in the absence of freedom of will. But in answering this question so far, I have considered the sanctioning aspect of responsibility primarily in relation to the reactive emotions, focusing on the obligations with which those emotions are bound up, and on the reasons that support them. In this chapter I shift my focus to look directly at the sanctioning behavior to which the stance of holding people responsible disposes us. Such behavior is potentially harmful to those at whom it is directed, and the exposure to harm may be a source of incompatibilist concern, independent of the connection of such harm with the reactive emotions. Thus it can seem unfair to expose people to harmful sanctions if they lack the ability to avoid the actions to which the sanctions are a response. I develop and refine this idea in section 7.1, formulating a principle of avoidability that has some surface appeal, and that seems to express an abstract conviction about the conditions that make it fair to hold people responsible.

Do we have good reason to accept this incompatibilist principle? Our confidence in it wanes, I believe, once we are clear that the principle is not needed to account for our concrete judgments of exemption and excuse. Its status is then analogous to that of the principle of alternate possibilities, after it has been shown that we do not require that principle to account for the accepted excuses. As I said in section 5.4, there may remain a residual tendency to endorse the principle of alternate possibilities even after we have seen that the principle is not anchored in our concrete judgments of excuse; but the availability of a diagnostic explanation of this tendency deprives it of normative force for purposes of moral theorizing. A successful diagnostic explanation would similarly undermine the incompatibilist's reliance on the principle of avoidability, and I therefore devote sections 7.2 and 7.3 to providing such a diagnosis; specifically, I trace the residual appeal of the principle of avoidability to natural confusions surrounding the notions of opportunity and difficulty.

Our attraction to the principle of avoidability is a reflection in moral consciousness of the phenomenon I have referred to as the seductiveness of incompatibilism. The principle captures our sense that responsibility would be especially threatened by determinism in cases in which an agent does something morally wrong. A successful diagnosis of this principle will therefore help to account for the deep pull that images of freedom have on our thinking about moral responsibility, without conceding to those images any genuine normative force. In this way, it should also help to increase our confidence in the compatibilist interpretation of responsibility developed in the preceding chapters—a point I explain in section 7.4.

7.1   Avoidability and Harm

I am looking for considered convictions, distinct from those of ordinary exemption or excuse, that might give some comfort to the incompatibilist. One potential source of such convictions is a venerable class of hypothetical cases that reliably evokes considered judgments about fairness. The cases in question are ones in which an agent acts intentionally, but the motive on which the agent acts has been insinuated into the agent's psyche in some unorthodox manner. The classic variation has it that the motive is implanted in the agent's psyche by a demonic neuroscientist,[1] but it will do just as well to imagine a demon who operates by supernatural rather than scientific means, or to suppose that the motive is due to a brain tumor. In all these cases, we tend to judge that it would be unfair to hold the agent responsible for acting on the suspect motive, and it can seem that these concrete judgments are best explained in terms supportive of incompatibilism.

Thus it is a notable feature of the cases that the agents in them act on motives for which they themselves are not directly responsible. This has been taken to be the feature that explains our reluctance to consider the agents in the cases responsible, suggesting the principle that it would be unfair to hold a person responsible for an action if the action is due to factors for which the agent is not directly responsible.[2] But if we accept this principle, it is doubtful whether moral responsibility could be reconciled with determinism. The principle would be satisfied only by actions that are caused exclusively by motives for which the agents themselves were responsible, and this in turn would seem to require that the actions should at some point be cut off from the surrounding causal nexus, being due to motives that are not in turn caused by preceding events or states. But determinism presumably would not tolerate the existence of causally isolated actions of this sort.

We do not, however, really require the incompatibilist principle to account for our moral judgments about the imaginary cases. To see this, note that the imaginary cases must involve more than the mere implantation of a motive in the agent's psyche—that alone would no more undermine responsibility than the influence of (say) television or peer pressure on the genesis of our desires. The imaginary cases must therefore be ones in which some further factor is present, and this factor seems to be that the implanted motive is supposed to lead to action in a way that (temporarily) disables the agents' ordinary powers of reflective self-control. Thus if a tumor or a demonic manipulator causes me to be subject to a certain desire, but I retain the power to control my behavior in accordance with moral obligations despite the presence of

---

1. See John Martin Fischer, "Introduction: Responsibility and Freedom," in John Martin Fischer, ed., *Moral Responsibility* (Ithaca, N.Y.: Cornell University Press, 1986), pp. 9–61, at p. 9.

2. See Martha Klein's defense of the "U-condition," in her *Determinism, Blameworthiness, and Deprivation* (Oxford: Clarendon Press, 1990), chap. 4. Klein contends that the incompatibilist intuitions evoked by the cases in question are independent of the principle of alternate possibilities (which she rejects).

the desire, the implantation of the desire would hardly constitute an exemption from responsibility.[3] This shows that the crucial feature of the imaginary cases is not the fact that the actions in them are caused by motives for which the agents are not themselves responsible. It is, rather, the assumption that the insinuated motives effectively lead to action in a way that disables the agents' normal powers of reflective self-control. But as I argued in the previous chapter, when we believe that an agent is led to act in a way that disables those powers, we exempt that agent (at least locally) from moral accountability; this is, for instance, the reason why we ordinarily suppose that hypnotism would constitute an exempting condition. Once they are carefully developed, then, the imaginary cases turn out not to support the idea that it is only fair to hold people responsible who are directly responsible for the motives on which they act.[4] Those cases are simply variations on a familiar kind of exempting condition, already acknowledged within moral life, in which a compatibilist principle of fairness is at work.

A more promising strategy for the incompatibilist would be to call attention to the harmful effects of the stance of holding people responsible. That stance is essentially defined in terms of the reactive emotions of indignation, resentment, and guilt, where these emotions in turn find their natural expression in sanctioning behavior: censure, reproach, denunciation, avoidance, and so on. But sanctioning behavior tends to cause harm to the person who is its target, and this connection with harm may point toward a further condition of responsibility. Thus it can seem unfair to expose people to the harms attendant on holding them responsible if they lack the ability to avoid the actions that ordinarily incur those harms.[5] I wish to explore this idea, to see if it can be developed in a way that supports the incompatibilist's conclusion.

The first thing to note is that, on the view developed in the preceding chapters, there is a sense in which accountable agents are able to

3. Klein's own consideration of compatibilist responses to the imaginary cases strangely neglects to consider this aspect of them; see *Determinism, Blameworthiness, and Deprivation*, pp. 70–75. My treatment of these cases has affinities with Daniel C. Dennett's treatment of cases of implanted belief, in his "Mechanism and Responsibility," as reprinted in Gary Watson, ed., *Free Will* (Oxford: Oxford University Press, 1982), pp. 150–173, at pp. 166–170.

4. When an agent retains the powers of reflective self-control, there may be a different sense in which she is "responsible" for the motives on which she acts: she is not causally responsible for having those motives, but is responsible for determining whether the motives will be acted on.

5. I am grateful to Gary Watson for encouraging me to think about the issues discussed in this section in terms of avoidability and harm.

avoid the harmful effects of blame even if determinism should be true. As I have shown, accountability requires the general powers of reflective self-control, powers that would not necessarily be undermined in a deterministic world. Someone in possession of these powers will have the general ability to grasp moral reasons and to regulate his behavior accordingly, and this amounts to a general ability to avoid the harms of blame and moral sanction. Indeed, the idea that the powers of reflective self-control provide a general capacity to avoid the harms of moral sanction played a large role in my discussion of why it is reasonable to hold accountable only people who possess those powers (section 6.1). By holding accountable only agents who have the general powers of reflective self-control, then, we already ensure that those who are exposed to the harms of blame and moral sanction have a reasonable opportunity to avoid them, insofar as they are competent to control their behavior by the light of moral reasons. The incompatibilist will have to contend that this is not enough: that fairness requires not just the general power to avoid the kinds of harms associated with blame and moral sanction, but also the specific ability to exercise that power on particular occasions of action.

One way to support this contention draws on an interpretation of the harms that are caused by blame and moral sanction. It has been taken to be essential to those harms that they are *personally* earned or deserved by the wrongdoer whom they befall, where the condition of personal desert can be satisfied only if the wrongdoer had the specific ability to avoid those harms by acting otherwise at the time of the impermissible deed.[6] But this interpretation of the harms associated with moral responsibility seems exaggerated. As was discussed in section 3.1, our practice of holding people responsible may sustain a retributivist interpretation, but it is a mistake to build such an interpretation into the self-understanding of participants in the practice. Perhaps we suppose that wrongdoers deserve moral sanctions, where these are understood essentially expressionistically, as ways of communicating the reactive emotions and articulating the moral obligations with which those emotions are connected. This is not necessarily to suppose, however, that wrongdoers have personally earned suffering per se; that suggests the questionable thought that their suffering is an intrinsically

6. See Ulrich Pothast, *Die Unzulänglichkeit der Freiheitsbeweise: Zu einigen Lehrstücken aus der neueren Geschichte von Philosophie und Recht* (Frankfurt am Main: Suhrkamp Verlag, 1987), pp. 370–381.

good thing, and conjures an image of the responsible agent as the sole ("personal") cause of his actions. If we are tempted by thoughts and images such as these, it is not simply because we view wrongdoers as having personally earned the harms that they endure.

But there are ways of developing the incompatibilist's concern that do not rely on such a tendentious interpretation of the harms caused by blame and moral sanction. Note, for instance, that the practice of holding people responsible has a comparative dimension. It can be thought of as a system for distributing the benefits and burdens of human favor, leaving some people—the wrongdoers—notably worse off than others, insofar as they are subjected to the harms of censure, reproach, avoidance, withdrawal of esteem, and the like. This way of distributing benefits and burdens may seem unfair, if determinism is true. Compare the positions of a winner and a loser in the distribution of these benefits and burdens. We are apt to think that, if determinism is true, then the winner would have acted precisely as the loser did, had she been in the loser's situation. This in turn would seem to make it unfair to prejudice the loser in the distribution of burdens, solely on account of his wrongdoing. The appropriate response on the part of the winner should not be one of satisfaction at the outcome of the distribution—still less, of active contribution to those outcomes through her own efforts to sanction the loser—but rather the thought, "There but for the grace of God go I."[7]

This verdict rests on a subtle confusion, however. There is a perspective from which it makes perfect sense for the winner to say, "There but for the grace of God go I." This is the perspective from which the winner acknowledges that it is a matter of luck that she has the basic moral powers she does, or (perhaps) that she has not found herself in situations in which those powers have been severely tested. These things are not the winner's own doing, and if they had been otherwise, then either she would not have been an accountable agent at all, or—like the loser—she might have acted in such a way as to incur serious moral sanction. But these reflections are quite different from the thought that, in a deterministic world, the winner would have acted exactly as the loser did had she been in the loser's situation. On any plausible construal of determinism, the notion of a "situation" that figures in this thought would have to be so interpreted that two agents

---

7. This interesting line of thought was suggested to me by an anonymous reader of an early draft of this book.

can be in the same situation only if they are themselves exactly identical in their physical and psychological states.[8] But of course on this interpretation, it does not make sense to suppose that the winner might have occupied the loser's situation. For her to occupy the loser's situation would be for her literally to *become* the loser, and this leaves us with no basis for a comparison between the winner's behavior and that of the loser.

Thinking of moral responsibility as a system for distributing the benefits and burdens of human favor, we can imagine distributive outcomes that we would not consider fair. It would seem unfair, for instance, if those who lose out in the distribution did not have the powers of reflective self-control to begin with, or if their educational or social conditions were such as to inhibit the normal development of those powers. People who lack these powers are deprived of the general capacity to avoid the kinds of action that incur moral sanction, and so they are relevantly disadvantaged in the processes that result in the distributive outcomes.[9] But of course these judgments do not rest on any new, comparative principle of fairness, nor do they support the thought that determinism would threaten responsibility. The judgments can be explained in terms of the independent principle that it is unreasonable to hold people accountable if they lack the powers of reflective self-control; and as I have shown, determinism would not undermine such general powers across the board.

Still, reflecting on the harms of moral sanction, there is a residual tendency to think that the general capacity to avoid the actions that incur such harms is not enough. Even when people have that general capacity, it may seem unfair to expose them to the harms of moral sanction if they lacked the specific ability to exercise their general powers in the circumstances of action, for that would mean that they were unable to avoid those harms. I will refer to this thought as the principle of avoidability. If accepted, this principle would provide at least a foothold for the incompatibilist's conclusion. Consider a case in which agent *s* fails to exercise her general powers to grasp and comply with the moral obligations we hold her to, thereby incurring the responses of moral sanction, and suppose in addition that determinism

8. Compare Daniel C. Dennett, "I Could Not Have Done Otherwise—So What?" *Journal of Philosophy* 81 (1984), pp. 553–565. Dennett suggests that once we are clear about this point, we will lose our interest in the question of whether we ever could have done otherwise.

9. This suggests that political and social conditions can have a bearing on the degree to which people attain the status of moral accountability—a theme I return to briefly in Chapter 8.

is true. It would follow that it was physically impossible for *s* to exercise her general powers of reflective self-control on this occasion. That is, it was not possible for *s* to exercise those general powers in such a way as to avoid moral sanctions, given the prior facts and the laws of nature.[10] But if it was not physically possible (in this sense) for *s* to exercise her general powers of reflective self-control on this occasion, we may conclude that *s* then lacked the specific ability to exercise those general powers. Given the principle of avoidability, it follows that it would be unfair to hold *s* responsible for her morally impermissible action. Determinism, in short, would be incompatible with responsibility for actions that violate the moral obligations that we accept.

In response to this argument, many compatibilists would challenge the inference from the claim that it was not physically possible for *s* to exercise her general powers to the conclusion that *s* lacked the specific ability to exercise those powers. They will insist that there is a sense in which *s* was able to exercise such powers, in the circumstances, even though it was physically impossible for her to do so.[11] As I explain in Appendix 2, however, arguments of this form seem to place implausibly heavy normative weight on rather precious modal distinctions. Without denying the opacity and complexity of claims about an agent's specific abilities, I shall therefore assume that the physical impossibility of *s*'s exercising her general powers would at least threaten to undermine *s*'s specific ability to exercise those powers. Accepting the principle of avoidability, this in turn would make determinism a threat to moral responsibility.

Note, however, that determinism would not necessarily threaten responsibility in all cases. So far I have considered scenarios in which an agent who possesses the general powers of reflective self-control fails to exercise them in accordance with our moral expectations, thereby incurring the harms of moral sanction. In situations of this sort, determinism threatens responsibility by making it physically impossible for

10. In the language of possible worlds, an event *e* will be physically possible in the actual world at time *t* if there is some possible world, indiscernible from the actual world in the facts up to *t*, and agreeing also in the natural laws that obtain, in which *e* occurs. In asserting that determinism would make it physically impossible, in this sense, for us to exercise those general powers that we do not exercise in fact, I assume that such an exercise would involve a change in the physical description of the world.

11. Thus it might be suggested that we can exercise our unexercised general powers, if determinism is true, in just the sense in which we can do something that entails, but does not itself constitute or cause, a violation of the laws of nature (a "local miracle"). For this distinction, see David Lewis, "Are We Free to Break the Laws?," *Theoria* 47 (1981), pp. 112–121.

the agent to exercise his general powers of self-control, where that in turn deprives him of the specific ability to exercise those powers, and so to avoid moral sanctions. But what if the agent does in fact exercise the powers of reflective self-control in accordance with the obligations we hold him to? Assuming that this condition is really satisfied, it is hard to see how the truth of determinism could possibly have any bearing on the question of whether the principle of avoidability is or is not satisfied. From the fact that s actually *does* avoid moral sanctions by exercising his powers of reflective self-control, we are surely entitled to infer that s has the specific *ability* to exercise those powers on that occasion. To draw this inference is to suppose that does entails can, and though this assumption is not always warranted, it seems a safe assumption in the present context.[12] In the sort of case I am considering, determinism would undermine the ability to exercise our general powers of reflective self-control only if it gave us reason to think that the agent did not really exercise those powers in the first place. As I have shown, however, it is very doubtful that determinism per se would give us such a reason. If we believe, independently of knowing whether determinism is true, that s has complied with our moral obligations because he grasps the moral reasons for doing so, how might this belief be undermined by the discovery that determinism is true? What difference would such a discovery make?

This line of thought suggests that the principle of avoidability would at most make responsibility selectively incompatible with determinism. If we accept this principle, then determinism might well undermine responsibility for morally impermissible actions, by depriving us of the specific ability to exercise our general powers of reflective self-control. But it does not appear that determinism would deprive us of this ability in cases where we exercise our general rational powers in accord with the moral obligations to which we are subject, and so the principle of avoidability would not be violated in these cases.

The idea that determinism should be only selectively incompatible with responsibility may at first seem strange. After all, any effect determinism would have on one class of actions (for instance, the morally

---

12. The contexts in which the assumption does not hold are ones in which it makes sense to suppose that one might have done something by luck or chance: thus from the fact that s hits a hole in one, or throws a bull's-eye, we are not necessarily entitled to infer that s had the ability to do these things (see sec. 6.4). But I do not think it makes sense to suppose that luck might play a similar role in explaining s's grasping moral reasons and complying with the moral obligations they support; one cannot do these things by luck or chance.

impermissible ones), it would seem to have equally on all other classes of actions (such as those that conform with our moral obligations). But this is not in fact true at all levels of description. Accepting the principle of avoidability, determinism becomes a threat to responsibility just insofar as it impinges on the specific ability to exercise the powers of reflective self-control and thereby to avoid the harms of moral sanction. As I have suggested, however, determinism seems to have this effect only on occasions when we actually act impermissibly, and hence incur blame and moral sanction.[13] Indeed, once we reflect on the ideas of avoidability and harm, it makes good intuitive sense to suppose that determinism should pose a special threat to responsibility in cases in which we act impermissibly. I have suggested that it is the exposure to harm that brings the stance of holding people responsible within the scope of moral principles of fairness in the first place. We should accordingly expect there to be a risk that determinism will violate such principles primarily in cases in which people expose themselves to the harms of moral sanction by doing something that at least appears to be morally wrong. Thus the version of the principle of alternate possibilities that I had occasion to consider in section 5.4 was a principle of *blameworthiness*, postulating a condition for the fairness of blame and moral sanction; it says that people do not deserve blame and moral sanction if they could not have done otherwise, and this leaves completely open the question of whether responsibility for permissible or obligatory performances similarly requires the availability of alternate possibilities. Hence the principle of alternate possibilities, like the principle of avoidability, does not even seem to be violated by determinism in cases in which people succeed in complying with the obligations we hold them to.[14]

But are we really committed to the principle of avoidability? To

13. Compare Susan Wolf, *Freedom within Reason* (New York: Oxford University Press, 1990), chap. 4, and her "Asymmetrical Freedom," as reprinted in Fischer, ed., *Moral Responsibility*, pp. 225–240. On the "reason view," which Wolf endorses, the ability that matters to responsibility is not the ability to do otherwise or the ability to be the sole source of one's actions, but rather the ability to act in accordance with reason. As Wolf points out, determinism—to the extent that it is a threat to this sort of ability—threatens it only in cases where the ability is unexercised.

14. Consider the Kantian claim that ought implies can. This claim has often been taken to support an incompatibilist conclusion. Even if one accepts such an interpretation, however, it follows that determinism is only selectively incompatible with responsibility. For our *ability* to do what we ought to do is threatened by determinism only in cases in which we do not in fact do what we ought to do. On this point, see Harry Frankfurt, "What We Are Morally Responsible For," as reprinted in his *The Importance of What We Care About: Philosophical Essays* (Cambridge: Cambridge University Press, 1988), pp. 95–103, at pp. 95–96. (In sec. 7.4 I propose a different way of understanding the idea that ought implies can.)

show that we are, one would need to establish that the principle is required to account for some class of considered moral convictions. It might be thought, for instance, that the principle of avoidability provides an account of our ordinary judgments of excuse that is superior to the other accounts I have considered. Excuses, after all, are conditions that make it unfair to subject a person to the harms of moral sanction. I have traced the force of these conditions to the principle of no blameworthiness without fault, and in defending this account I have argued that it explains our judgments of excuse better than the principle of alternate possibilities does. But I did not consider in this connection the different and more nuanced principle of avoidability. Perhaps it would better locate the force of the excuses to treat them as conditions in which we are unable to exercise our powers of reflective self-control in such a way as to avoid the kinds of actions that normally incur moral sanction.

But the excuses cannot plausibly be explained in terms of the principle of avoidability. This is because, on closer inspection, it emerges that the terms the principle sets out do not even apply extensionally to the ordinary cases of excuse. The principle maintains that it is unfair to expose people to the harms of moral sanction if they lack the specific ability to exercise the powers of reflective self-control in the circumstances, and thereby to avoid those harms. If my survey of the excuses is correct, however, it is simply false to say that people lack the ability to exercise their powers of reflective self-control in this way, when the excusing conditions obtain. People who have a valid excuse have not in fact done anything wrong. But someone who has not done anything morally wrong will either not have intentionally done anything at all (as in cases of inadvertence or automatic muscular contraction), or (as in cases of physical constraint and coercion) the agent will actually have exercised the powers of reflective self-control in such a way as to avoid the actions that normally incur moral sanction. In neither kind of case is it accurate to say that the excuses make moral sanctions unavoidable by rendering one unable to exercise one's rational powers, even if some excusing conditions (such as physical constraint) do present obstacles to the successful translation of one's choices into action.[15] Thus the ordi-

---

15. In such cases we might say that one is unable *fully* to exercise the powers of reflective self-control. But one is not unable to exercise those powers at all, and indeed one does exercise them sufficiently to choose to act as one ought, thereby avoiding a blameworthy quality of will. (The person stuck in an unanticipated traffic jam on the way to meet her friend at the airport has in fact chosen to act in accordance with her promise to pick up the friend, and so she has avoided the kind of choices that properly incur moral sanction.)

nary excuses offer no real foothold for the principle of avoidability, despite their being cases in which it is unfair to subject people to harmful moral sanctions. In this respect, the principle of avoidability contrasts with the principle of alternate possibilities. As I said in section 5.4, at least some of the excuses can truly be described as conditions in which an agent could not have done otherwise in some sense (consider, again, cases of physical constraint or reflex bodily movement). This remains the case even if we accept that the excuses are also conditions in which an agent has not done anything wrong, and it gives us a basis for comparing my account of the excuses with a competing account, in terms of the principle of alternate possibilities. But there is no such basis of comparison in the case of the principle of avoidability.

Beyond our judgments of excuse, I can think of no further class of concrete moral convictions that we might be tempted to explain in terms of the principle of avoidability. This leaves one remaining possibility to explore: that the principle of avoidability gives direct expression to an abstract moral conviction of ours, a conviction not immediately about concrete cases in which it would be unfair to hold people responsible, but about the kinds of considerations that make this stance unfair.[16] To accept the principle on such grounds, while agreeing both that it is not applicable to ordinary cases of excuse or exemption, and that it supports a (selectively) incompatibilist conclusion, would be to treat it as a "one-off" principle of fairness (in the terms proposed in section 4.4). The principle would apply in the single case in which determinism is true, without having a bearing on any other cases in which we judge people not to be responsible; so that the reason determinism would give us to refrain from holding people responsible would be different in kind from the reasons why people are not responsible when (say) the excuses and exemptions obtain.

Now it seems to me that we should accept the principle of avoidability on these terms only if we are independently very confident of the normative significance of the considerations isolated by the principle. But this is not the case. The principle tells us that the fairness of holding people responsible depends on their having the specific ability to exercise their general powers of reflective self-control, and thereby to avoid the harms of moral sanction. Once this principle is clearly

---

16. The principles of desert and reasonableness to which I appealed in Chapters 5 and 6 were of this sort, though (as I showed) they could also be brought to bear to account for our concrete judgments of exemption and excuse.

isolated from our concrete judgments of excuse, however, our confidence in it wanes dramatically. Its status can then be seen to be akin to that of the principle of alternate possibilities, once it was established that that principle is not anchored in our concrete judgments of excuse. We may retain a residual tendency to find something attractive in both principles, but neither of them can be said to express one of our most serious considered moral convictions. I have suggested that situations of this sort call for a diagnostic explanation. Provision of such an explanation deprives the principles in question of their normative authority, for purposes of moral theorizing, by tracing our residual tendency to accept the principles to natural confusions in our thinking about ordinary cases. In doing this, a diagnostic explanation also helps to account for the seductiveness of incompatibilism, where the delivery of such an account is a crucial ingredient in any plausible treatment of moral responsibility.

In section 5.4 I offered a diagnostic treatment of the principle of alternate possibilities, tracing the residual attraction of that principle to a false generalization from ordinary cases of excuse. The availability of this explanation goes some way toward accounting for the persistence of incompatibilist tendencies in our thinking about responsibility. But the seductiveness of incompatibilism is a complex phenomenon that has several discrete roots in our practice of holding people responsible. It will help us better to understand this phenomenon if we can also provide a diagnostic explanation of the principle of avoidability, which has its own residual appeal, and which therefore represents a potentially independent basis for the incompatibilist conclusion. I address this task in the sections that follow, isolating two natural mistakes that may lead us to find the principle of avoidability attractive.

7.2 Opportunity and Possibility

The account of the conditions of responsibility I have developed to this point has emphasized certain general powers of reflective self-control: the power to grasp and apply the reasons that support moral obligations, and the power to govern one's behavior by the light of such reasons. Though there is disagreement about the content of the general powers that matter to responsibility, many compatibilists would agree that some general abilities of this sort are basic conditions of responsibility. As I noted in the preceding chapter, however, those who acknowledge the importance of general abilities traditionally do so in the context of a bipartite account of the conditions of responsibility. According to such bipartite accounts, what matters to responsibility is not only the possession of the requisite general ability, but also the *opportunity* to exercise that general ability in the particular circumstances of action.[17] As I hope to show in this section, if we follow such accounts in admitting that responsibility requires opportunity as well as general ability, we will have powerful grounds for accepting the principle of avoidability. We will also have a locus for diagnosing the intuitive appeal of that principle.

To begin, suppose that responsibility requires not just the general powers of reflective self-control, but also the opportunity to exercise those powers on a specific occasion. Suppose, further, that determinism is true. If a given agent *s* in fact exercises the general powers of reflective self-control by complying with the moral obligations we hold her to, there would of course be no reason to suppose that *s* lacked either the ability or the opportunity conditions of responsibility. From the fact that *s* exercised the general powers of reflective self-control, we may surely conclude both that *s* possessed those general powers and that *s* had the opportunity to exercise them—and this, regardless of whether determinism is true. But what if *s* did not exercise the general powers of reflective self-control, instead doing something morally impermissible? As I showed in section 7.1, it would follow from the assumption that determinism is true that it was physically impossible for *s* to exercise her general rational powers, on the occasion of the impermissible act. That is, *s* could not have exercised those powers, given the facts about the past and the laws of nature. But if it was physically impossible, in this sense, for *s* to exercise her general powers of reflective self-control, may we not conclude that *s* then lacked the opportunity to exercise

17. For this bipartite schema, see, for instance, H. L. A. Hart, "Negligence, *Mens Rea,* and Criminal Responsibility," as reprinted in his *Punishment and Responsibility: Essays in the Philosophy of Law* (Oxford: Clarendon Press, 1968), pp. 136–157, at pp. 149–157, and his "Punishment and the Elimination of Responsibility," as reprinted in *Punishment and Responsibility,* pp. 158–185, at pp. 181–183; Jonathan Glover, *Responsibility* (London: Routledge and Kegan Paul, 1970), chaps. 3 and 4; Anthony Kenny, *Freewill and Responsibility* (London: Routledge and Kegan Paul, 1978), pp. 30–34; and Wolf, *Freedom within Reason,* chap. 5. (Wolf does not explicitly refer to opportunity as a condition of responsibility, but the "negative" condition she discusses on pp. 101–102 seems to come to the same thing.) Note that the notion of opportunity, as it figures in the bipartite schema, is a technical notion, indicating the absence of any condition that might prevent or interfere with the exercise of one's general powers. In its colloquial use, the notion of opportunity is narrower, signaling the presence in one's environment of the kinds of objects that the exercise of a given general power may require. In this more colloquial sense, one does not lack the opportunity to play basketball if one is bound, but only if one has no basketball, or court, or teammates. (Thanks to Gary Watson for reminding me of this.)

those powers? If so, we could begin to see how the specific ability to exercise our general rational powers, singled out by the principle of avoidability, might be thought to be a condition of responsibility.

The argument just sketched turns on the idea that the physical impossibility of exercising our general rational powers would deprive us of the opportunity to exercise those powers. For the argument to go through, it is not necessary that physical impossibility should be the only kind of opportunity-defeating condition. We could admit that other kinds of conditions deprive people of the opportunity to exercise their general rational powers, so long as it is granted that physical impossibility is also an opportunity-defeating condition. But there are philosophers who would not be willing to grant this last point. Susan Wolf, for instance, contends that we are deprived of the opportunity to exercise our general powers only when a condition is present that "prevents" or "interferes with" the exercise of those powers.[18] Thus, a lack of light would prevent us from exercising our general powers of vision, being chained to the floor would interfere with our exercise of the general ability to walk, and so on. But, Wolf suggests, determinism would not entail that one of these preventive or interfering conditions is present whenever we neglect to exercise our general powers, and so it would not by itself deprive us of the opportunity to exercise those general powers.

About this suggestion, we may agree that the conditions that standardly deprive us of the opportunity to exercise our general powers do so by interfering with or preventing the exercise of those powers. But it is not clear that this undermines the incompatibilist position I have been developing. The incompatibilist wishes to claim that determinism would universally deprive us of the opportunity to exercise those of our general powers that we do not exercise in fact. True, determinism would not necessarily entail that something always *interferes* with the exercise of our unexercised powers. But why should we not say that it would *prevent* us from exercising those powers, by making it physically impossible for us to do so? Wolf apparently assumes that a condition should count as preventing the exercise of our general powers only if it is sufficiently like such paradigm cases as those involving physical constraint, paralysis, or automatic muscular contraction. And this is certainly a fair move to make. But the incompatibilist will ask why the

18. See Wolf, *Freedom within Reason*, pp. 111–112. Compare the similar line of argument in Ursula Wolf, *Möglichkeit und Notwendigkeit bei Aristoteles und heute* (Munich: Wilhelm Fink Verlag, 1979), pp. 389, 392.

physical impossibility of exercising our general powers is not sufficiently like these paradigm cases to be counted an opportunity-defeating condition as well.

By Wolf's own account, the central cases count as cases in which we lack the opportunity to exercise our general powers because they are cases in which we are prevented from exercising those powers. It seems plausible, though, that the physical impossibility of exercising such a power would just as effectively prevent us from exercising it. Against this, the compatibilist might borrow the modal distinction mentioned earlier, to try to show that the physical impossibility of doing something would not prevent us from doing it. Thus, it might be argued that even if determinism makes it physically impossible for us to exercise our general powers on certain occasions, there remains a sense in which we are able to exercise the powers on those occasions, and in this sense we would not be prevented from exercising our general powers by the truth of determinism. Once again, however, it seems unpromising to bring the whole weight of the compatibilist position to bear on so fine and elusive a distinction. Our intuitive convictions about the ordinary concept of prevention simply do not seem nuanced enough to leave us satisfied by an argument that turns entirely on such a precious distinction. For this reason, once it is granted that responsibility requires the opportunity to exercise our general rational powers, it seems to me very difficult to resist the conclusion that determinism would at least be a threat to responsibility.

Moreover, the kind of threat that determinism would pose is just the kind suggested by the principle of avoidability. According to that principle, responsibility requires not only the general powers of reflective self-control, but also the specific ability to exercise those general powers, and so to avoid the harms of moral sanction. To account for the apparent appeal of this principle, one must explain why it seems so plausible to suppose that someone's inability to exercise his general rational powers should make it unfair to hold the person responsible. But the argument I have just sketched suggests an explanation. The reason that the specific inability to exercise his general powers seems to make it unfair to hold a person responsible is that such an inability would deprive the person of the opportunity to exercise those powers. As I have shown, if it is physically impossible for s to exercise his general rational powers on a given occasion, it is extremely plausible to suppose that s therefore lacks the opportunity to exercise those powers. Given the further common assumption that responsibility requires both general powers and the specific opportunity to exercise them, we can begin to understand the intuitive attraction of the principle of avoidability. That attraction can be traced to the assumption that the opportunity to exercise our general rational powers is among the basic conditions of responsibility.[19]

But is this assumption itself plausible? Not if the account of the excuses and exemptions offered in the preceding chapters is correct. According to that account, responsibility does indeed require the general power to grasp the reasons that support moral obligations, and to regulate one's behavior by the light of those reasons. But it does not require the opportunity to exercise those general powers on the occasion of the action for which the agent is held responsible. Neither the excuses nor the exemptions function by depriving us of the opportunity to exercise our general rational powers. To explain adequately the intuitive appeal of the principle of avoidability, then, it is not enough to derive it from the assumption that responsibility requires opportunity as well as general rational ability. One must also account for the intuitive appeal of this assumption—explaining why, for instance, compatibilists have so commonly endorsed bipartite accounts of responsibility, making room for an opportunity condition in addition to the condition of general ability. Only with such an explanation in place will we be equipped with a diagnosis of the principle of avoidability.

My discussion of Wolf's position suggests that we should seek such an explanation in a misunderstanding of the standard excusing conditions. Paradigmatic examples of conditions that are said to involve lack of opportunity are conditions that prevent or interfere with the exercise of our general abilities, such as paralysis, physical constraint, and automatic muscular contraction. But when these conditions are cited in the context of ordinary moral life, it is generally in the guise of excuses. This suggests that the widespread appeal of the assumption that opportunities matter to responsibility may lie in a misinterpretation of the excusing conditions. Recognizing that such conditions as paralysis and physical constraint are excuses, and assuming that they also deprive one of the opportunity to exercise one's general powers of reflective self-control, it is natural to infer that the fact that they deprive one of such opportunities is what makes these conditions excuses. But this inference is mistaken. As I said in Chapter 5, what really accounts for the force

19. In effect, this would treat the principle of avoidability as a corollary of the more basic principle that it is fair to hold people to an obligation only if they have the opportunity to exercise their powers of reflective self-control in accordance with the obligation.

of the excusing conditions is the fact that when those conditions obtain, the agent will not have done anything morally impermissible in the first place. The person who fails to keep a promise to meet a colleague for lunch because the subway car he is traveling in derails has not violated the duty of promise keeping, for his omission does not express a choice to do something other than what he was obligated to do.[20] And where an agent has not in fact violated the moral obligations we hold him to, it can hardly be fair to hold him responsible for such a violation. This is what explains the normative force of the excusing conditions, and it has nothing to do with the idea that the excusing conditions deprive us of opportunities to exercise our powers of reflective self-control.

So, one route to the conclusion that opportunities matter to responsibility is via a false generalization from the ordinary excusing conditions. It is assumed that these conditions deprive us of the opportunity to exercise our general rational powers, and this feature is then singled out as being what accounts for the normative force of the excuses. But the assumption from which this generalization begins is itself false, so its acceptance involves a prior and more subtle mistake. Excuses would deprive one of the opportunity to exercise the general rational powers if they prevented one from grasping moral reasons and regulating one's behavior accordingly. As was shown in the preceding section, however, it is not the case that the excuses completely prevent one from doing these things. Even in such cases as paralysis, external constraint, and automatic muscular contraction, the agent is sufficiently able to exercise the general rational powers to avoid having a blameworthy quality of will; this is presupposed by the conclusion that people have not really done anything wrong when the excusing conditions obtain.[21] What can truly be said about such conditions as physical constraint and automatic muscular contraction is that they sometimes interfere with the fully *successful* exercise of the powers of reflective self-control, insofar as they may prevent the translation of an agent's choices into actions. Focusing on this aspect of the cases, it is natural to draw the conclusion that they completely prevent the agent from exercising his rational powers, thereby depriving him of the opportunity to exercise those powers. But

20. Assuming, as before, that moral obligations regulate the choices that are expressed in action.

21. Indeed, there is something peculiar in the very idea of a condition that directly constrains or interferes with the operations of the will, as opposed to preventing one from translating one's choices into actions; on this point, see Rogers Albritton, "Freedom of Action and Freedom of Will," *Proceedings of the American Philosophical Association* 59 (1985–86), pp. 239–251.

this inference is too hasty and represents a second mistake on which the postulation of an opportunity condition may rest.

The mistakes I have identified are both extremely natural ones; indeed, it only becomes apparent that they are mistakes when one tries to work out a systematic account of all the excusing conditions, as I attempted to do in Chapter 5. One then realizes that some of the standard excuses do not seem to involve any deprivation of opportunity at all. Consider in this connection cases of inadvertence, coercion, or duress: if I step on the hand of another inadvertently, or because someone is threatening to torture me if I fail to do so, then my stepping on the person's hand would generally not be considered blameworthy; and yet, with excuses of this type, it would be strange to say that I am in any way deprived of the opportunity to exercise my general powers of reflective self-control in accordance with moral obligations. There is, for instance, nothing that strictly prevents or interferes with my exercise of those general powers in a case in which I tread on the hand of another inadvertently. Furthermore, even in cases such as physical constraint and automatic muscular contraction, in which it may seem that an agent lacks the opportunity to exercise the general rational powers, this turns out not really to be the case. As I have argued, the agents in these cases are sufficiently able to exercise their powers of reflective self-control to avoid having done anything morally wrong. This is what accounts for the force of these forms of excuse, and serves to unify them with the other excusing conditions. But we will not be in a position to grasp this point if—as is of course customary in ordinary life—we essay to make generalizations about the excusing conditions without having undertaken a systematic investigation of them.

A final objection suggests itself, however. I have argued that although it is natural to suppose that excuses function by depriving us of opportunities to exercise our general powers, this is not what it is about them that really accounts for their excusing force. Even if this conclusion is accepted, however, it does not necessarily follow that opportunities are not genuine conditions of responsibility. It follows only that they are not the conditions of responsibility that are defeated by the acknowledged excuses. This leaves open the possibility that there are other moral practices, besides our acknowledgment of excuses, that betray our commitment to the view that it would be unfair to hold people responsible if they lack the opportunity to exercise their general powers of reflective self-control. And here it will perhaps be remarked that opportunities have a clear moral significance quite independent of whether the acknowledged excuses function by defeating them. For instance, the fact that someone has suffered deprivation as a child—involving, say, physical abuse or the lack of emotional encouragement, support, and attention—can make us question the fairness of holding the person morally accountable as an adult, without yet constituting a straightforward excuse. But someone who has endured such deprivation could quite naturally be described as having lacked the kinds of opportunities that a more supportive childhood would have provided. Does this not suggest that opportunities are independent conditions of responsibility?

It may—but only if opportunity is understood in a different sense from that which we have heretofore considered. When we say that deprivation involves the lack of a normal range of opportunities, we mean, I think, that it diminishes the opportunity to develop one's basic powers in the first place. This seems relevant to moral assessments, because, as I have argued, such powers are important conditions of accountability. But to acknowledge the importance of opportunities in this sense gives no support to an incompatibilist interpretation of responsibility. The opportunities whose importance the incompatibilist should want to establish are not opportunities to develop the powers of reflective self-control, but rather opportunities to *exercise* those powers once they are possessed. Only if opportunities of this latter kind are shown to be conditions of responsibility do we have the beginnings of an argument for the incompatibilist's conclusion. The situations that encourage us to think that these sorts of opportunities matter, however, are situations in which people who possess the general rational powers are nevertheless not held to blame for what they have done. That is, they are cases of acknowledged excuse, and I have already shown that, despite appearances, these cases do not really support the conclusion that the opportunity to exercise one's general rational powers is a condition of responsibility.

7.3   Difficulty and Control

In this section I would like to offer another account of the attraction of the principle of avoidability. Rather than tracing the attraction of the principle to a misunderstanding of the acknowledged excuses, however, this second account appeals to the acknowledged exemptions, and to the misunderstandings they naturally invite. The exemptions, it will be recalled, indicate the absence of an A-condition of responsibility; they make it unfair, not to blame an agent for some specific moral wrong, but rather to hold the agent morally accountable in the first place. On the account of the exemptions that I have offered, these conditions function by impairing the general powers of reflective self-control that are basic prerequisites of accountability. Examples of such exemptions from accountability include childhood, insanity, addiction, posthypnotic suggestion, psychopathy, behavior control, and the effects of stress, deprivation, and torture.

Consider now a subset of these conditions: say, cases of addiction, or cases involving the effects of extreme physical deprivation. I have suggested that in cases of this sort, an agent's basic power to control her behavior by the light of moral obligations may be substantially impaired. Thus, people addicted to crack cocaine might have a substantially reduced ability to grasp, apply, and follow moral reasons, and the obligations they support, in the areas of conduct that are affected by their addictive drives. Similarly, people who are starving, or suffering from extreme sleep deprivation, would also seem to have a substantially impaired power to control their behavior in accordance with moral reasons. But this is not the only way we might describe such cases. Alternatively we could perhaps say that those suffering from addiction or physical deprivation are not deprived of the general powers of reflective self-control, but that they find themselves in conditions that make it extremely *difficult* for them to exercise the general powers they continue to possess.

On the surface, there seems to be very little to choose between these alternative descriptions. If s's general abilities in a given area of activity are substantially impaired, then s will be able to engage in those activities only with great difficulty; by the same token, if it is very difficult for s to engage in a given range of activities, his abilities in that area could surely be said to be reduced or impaired. Moreover, both of these descriptions seem to capture what is normatively significant about the kinds of exempting condition at issue. The basic principle of fairness implied by the exemptions, I have suggested, is that it is reasonable to hold a person to a demand only if the person possesses the general power to grasp and comply with the reasons that support the demand. But it would seem similarly unreasonable to hold a person to a demand if the person could grasp and follow such moral reasons only with extraordinary difficulty. If we accept this alternative description of cases such as addiction and deprivation, however, it may begin to look as if determinism would represent a general exempting condition, in a way that accords with the principle of avoidability.

Thus, suppose it would be unfair to hold people responsible when they are in conditions that make it difficult for them to exercise their general rational powers in conformity with moral obligations. It can very easily seem to follow from this assumption that determinism would render it unfair ever to hold people accountable when they fail to exercise their rational powers in this way. For if determinism is true, it would always be extremely difficult for people who do not in fact comply with moral obligations to do so. Indeed, not only would this be extremely difficult for people, it would be *physically impossible*. That is, if determinism is true, then given the laws of nature and the facts about the past, it is never so much as possible that people who failed to exercise their powers of reflective self-control in accordance with moral obligations should have done so. Moreover, this line of argument for incompatibilism lends some support to the principle of avoidability. According to that principle, responsibility requires the specific ability to exercise the powers of reflective self-control on the occasion of the act or omission for which one is held responsible. The question I have been asking about this principle is, in effect: why does the specific ability to exercise these general powers appear to matter to responsibility? The argument just sketched suggests an answer to this question. The specific possibility of exercising one's general rational powers matters to responsibility, because in the absence of that possibility it will in the strongest conceivable way be difficult for one to exercise one's general rational powers, where this sort of difficulty represents an exemption from accountability.

Like the other incompatibilist arguments I have considered, this argument trades in modal notions that are far from being clear or well-understood. The crux is the assimilation of the technical concept of physical impossibility with the more intuitive concept of difficulty—in particular, the assumption that the physical impossibility of exercising a general power would be the most extreme case of the general type of situation in which it is difficult to exercise such a power. This kind of assimilation seems to be suggested by the following line of thought. Intuitively we would think it difficult to exercise some general ability if doing so were (so to speak) at the outer limit of the range of competences defined by the ability. Thus for me—though not for, say, an Olympic middle-distance runner—it would be extremely difficult to run one mile in less than five minutes; achieving this time would be at the outer limit of my general athletic powers. As we consider the prospects for my doing a mile in ever shorter times, however, we will eventually be describing feats that are clearly beyond the range of my general athletic abilities, indeed beyond the range of any set of athletic abilities that can be ascribed to a normal human organism. These feats—such as running a mile in less than thirty seconds, to take a clear case—are not so much as possible for human beings to achieve; it is simply not possible for humans (and a fortiori, for me) to perform these feats, given the laws of nature and the empirical facts about the basic constitution and capacities of the human body. This suggests that the cases in which it is impossible for someone to perform a certain feat stand at the extreme end of a continuum of cases, with less extreme points on the continuum being occupied by cases about which we would intuitively say that it is difficult for the person to perform the feat.

But this suggestion should be resisted. The notion of impossibility that I have just shown to be continuous with that of difficulty is the notion, roughly speaking, of what it is not possible for a person to do, given the laws of nature and the facts about the basic constitution and capacities of the person. A given feat will be impossible for a person, in this sense, only if it is clearly beyond the person's general powers. However, this is not the notion of *physical* impossibility that figures in the incompatibilist argument sketched at the start of this section. That argument aimed to show that the physical impossibility of exercising one's general rational powers might threaten accountability in the same way that the difficulty of exercising those powers would. But the notion of physical impossibility that figures in this argument is the notion of what it is not possible for a person to do, given the laws of nature and the facts about the past, whereas the notion of impossibility that I have just shown to be continuous with difficulty is the notion of what is not possible for a person to do, given the natural laws and the facts about the person's constitution and capacities. These are two very different modal notions.

To see the difference between them more clearly, consider something that we would intuitively take it to be very easy for me to do—say, walking a mile in thirty minutes. Being clearly within the range of my general powers, this feat would not be impossible for me to perform, in the sense in which impossibility is on a continuum with difficulty. It is clearly possible for me to walk a mile in thirty minutes, given the natural laws and the facts about my constitution and capacities. But if determinism is true, this very same feat may turn out to be physically impossible for me, in the sense originally relevant to the incompatibilist argument. For if I have not in fact walked a mile in thirty minutes, on a given occasion, and if determinism is true, then it will not have been possible for me to perform the feat on that occasion, given the laws of nature and the facts about the earlier states of the world.[22]

Again, if determinism is true, then *anything* that I do not in fact do will be physically impossible for me to do, in the sense I have been considering. Thus if at a given moment I omit to do something fairly simple (say, perform a single push-up), then it must be counted physically impossible for me to have done a push-up at that moment—even if, only seconds later, I go on to perform a series of twenty push-ups. The notion of physical impossibility is in this way quite radically relativized to particular times. But the notion of impossibility that connects with the intuitive concept of difficulty is not temporally restricted in this way. The more intuitive notion collects the class of feats that lie clearly beyond the range of an agent's general powers. A feat that is clearly outside the range of an agent's general powers at one moment, however, cannot be a feat that the agent actually goes on to perform at the next moment.[23] We could make sense of this suggestion only on the supposition that the agent's general powers are constantly subject to wild fluctuation from moment to moment. To make this supposition, however, would simply be to abandon the familiar notion of a general power or ability, and with it the intuitive concept of difficulty that is the whole basis for the incompatibilist argument I have been considering. For that concept is intimately connected with the familiar notion of a general ability or power; it is, roughly speaking, the notion of what is at the outer range of the competences encompassed by one's general powers.

The incompatibilist argument sketched earlier in this section thus seems to rest on a modal confusion. The argument started out from the assumption that the difficulty of exercising one's general rational powers would exempt one from accountability, and tried to show that this same

22. Consideration of examples such as this is what led G. E. Moore to conclude that the word "could" may be ambiguous; see his *Ethics* (London: Oxford University Press, 1912), pp. 88–90.

23. This is not to deny that I may be prevented from exercising a general ability at one moment that I actually go on to exercise at the next moment. For instance, while temporarily chained to the floor I might be prevented from hopping into the air, though I in fact go on to do so (out of joy) as soon as I am released from the chains. But this is not a case in which my general powers radically change from moment to moment; only my opportunity to exercise those powers changes.

kind of exemption would generalize if determinism is true. The idea
was that it would always be difficult to exercise one's unexercised
general powers, if determinism is true, because determinism would
make it physically impossible to exercise those powers. But it turns out
that the sense in which determinism would make it physically impossible to exercise one's general powers is not the sense in which impossibility is continuous with the intuitive notion of difficulty. At the same
time, given the complexity and elusiveness of our modal notions, this
kind of confusion is one that we are quite easily susceptible to. But to
the extent that the confusion in question is a natural one, we can
perhaps understand in terms of it the appeal of the incompatibilist
argument I have been considering, and so the appeal of the principle
of avoidability. That appeal may stem in part from the understandable
confusion that surrounds the notions of difficulty and impossibility.

This section has been concerned with misunderstandings to which
cases of acknowledged exemption from accountability are easily susceptible. In conclusion, there is one further such misunderstanding that I
should like at least briefly to mention. This concerns the notion of
control, which figures prominently in the conditions of accountability
as I have interpreted them. To be a morally accountable agent, I have
suggested, is to possess the general powers of reflective self-control: the
power to grasp moral reasons, and to control one's behavior accordingly. Acknowledged exemptions have been shown to be conditions
that impair these basic powers, in one way or another. On behalf of
the incompatibilist, however, it might now be said that the importance
I have thus placed on control threatens to undermine accountability in
a different way, if determinism should be true.

To be a morally accountable agent, one needs to have the power to
control one's behavior by the light of moral reasons. But can we really
be said to have the power to control our actions in this way, if
determinism is true? Some philosophers have advanced accounts of
control that would make this seem doubtful. On John Martin Fischer's
view, for instance, we can be said to control what we do only if there
are alternate possibilities open to us at the time of our action, in some
fairly strong sense.[24] As I explain in Appendix 2, Fischer suggests that

---

24. John Martin Fischer, "Responsibility and Control," as reprinted in John Martin Fischer,
ed., *Moral Responsibility* (Ithaca, N.Y.: Cornell University Press, 1986), pp. 174–190, at pp. 181–
182. It should be noted that Fischer does not himself endorse the claim that control (in his sense)
is a genuine condition of responsibility; on the contrary, he thinks that "Frankfurt-style" counterexamples (of the sort discussed in Appendix 2) tell decisively against this claim.

control over an action of a given type requires the possibility of performing an action of a different type, as the result of a choice to do so.
If this is right, however, then determinism would seem to render
control impossible by depriving us of alternate possibilities for action.
On the position I have advanced, this, in turn, would seem to threaten
moral responsibility by undermining the power of reflective self-control
that I have described as a basic condition of accountability. Furthermore, the threat that determinism would pose to responsibility would
not arise only on occasions when an agent fails to exercise the general
powers of reflective self-control; it would not be a selective threat, but
a universal threat, undermining our moral responsibility whenever we
act.

The line of argument supporting this conclusion, however, seems to
be multiply mistaken. Consider first a case in which someone successfully exercises the powers of reflective self-control. To satisfy this
description, it would seem sufficient that one grasp the reasons that
support moral obligations, and that one act in conformity with such
obligations *because* one grasps these reasons. Reflective self-control, of
the sort I have been concerned with, is thus entirely a matter of the
factors that actually contribute to the explanation of what one does,
depending in particular on the explanatory role that is played by one's
grasp of moral reasons. But whether or not these factors actually contribute to explaining what one does is completely independent from
questions about the alternate possibilities that may have been open to
one, at the time when one acted. Reflective self-control, of the kind I
have shown to be relevant to responsibility, thus does not seem to
depend on the availability of alternate possibilities. Note, further, that
the position I have developed does not depict the successful exercise of
reflective self-control as a condition of responsibility for what one does.
It says, rather, that accountability requires the general power to control
one's behavior rationally, by the light of the reasons that support moral
obligations. If the successful exercise of such powers does not require
alternate possibilities, it seems clearer still that alternate possibilities do
not bear on the question of whether one possesses these general powers
in the first place.

I conclude that the powers of rational control that I have shown to
be conditions of accountability are not plausibly understood as requiring
alternate possibilities, in any sense. Even if there is an intuitive concept
of control, according to which one can be said to control what one
does only when it is open to one to perform a different type of action,

that is not the concept of control that has been shown to be relevant to moral accountability. But I doubt, anyway, that we have an intuitive concept of control that clearly requires the availability of alternate possibilities. Fischer's proposal, for instance, is not grounded in a careful and systematic study of the contexts in which we rely on the notions of control and self-control, and there is good reason to suppose that such a study would undermine the claim that control requires alternate possibilities in any sense.[25] For these reasons, confusions about control do not seem to me to be the most fruitful place to look for a diagnosis of incompatibilist tendencies in our ordinary thinking about responsibility. I mention them, nevertheless, because the notion of control does figure prominently in the interpretation of the conditions of accountability I have been developing. Hence the philosophical distortions to which the notions of control and self-control have been prone threaten to carry over to my interpretation of accountability, and so provide a further possible source of confusion about the conditions that that interpretation sets out.

7.4   Oughts and Cans

The discussion to this point has brought to light at least three separate loci of confusion in our thinking about responsibility and its conditions. One of these, already addressed in Chapter 5, concerns the relevance of alternate possibilities to responsibility. Many of the acknowledged excuses are conditions that deprive an agent, in some sense, of alternate possibilities, and this fact may encourage the false generalization that the availability of alternate possibilities is a condition of responsibility. Here we have an obvious and potent source of incompatibilist images. A second aspect of the acknowledged excuses is the fact that many of them deprive an agent of the opportunity to exercise successfully the powers of reflective self-control. Generalization from this fact leads to the common and erroneous supposition that such opportunities are an independent condition of responsibility, and this supposition in turn suggests that determinism would be at least selectively incompatible with responsibility. A third source of incompatibilist confusion can be located in a misunderstanding of the acknowledged exempting condi-

---

25. On this point, see Daniel C. Dennett, *Elbow Room: The Varieties of Free Will Worth Wanting* (Cambridge, Mass.: MIT Press, 1984), chap. 3; Dennett argues persuasively that determinism would not undermine the various kinds of control and self-control that actually matter to us.

tions. Some of the exemptions can be described as conditions that make it difficult to exercise the general powers of reflective self-control, but modal confusions surrounding the notions of difficulty and possibility can lead us to think that this difficulty condition would (selectively) generalize, if determinism is true. Together, these three diagnostic explanations undermine the principles of alternate possibilities and avoidability; they allow us to concede the residual attraction of these principles, while denying that this aspect of moral consciousness has probative force for purposes of normative reflection.

But my interest in a diagnosis of incompatibilist elements in our thinking has not been motivated exclusively by the need to undermine the principles of avoidability and alternate possibilities. Quite independent of whether we have specific incompatibilist alternatives such as these, it seems to me that compatibilists need to offer some account of the widespread tendency to think about responsibility in incompatibilist terms. That tendency is not plausibly treated as a prejudice to which philosophers alone are subject. It does not, for instance, result solely from the distortions induced by the sorts of "intuition pumps" that regularly feature in distinctively philosophical discussions of freedom and responsibility.[26] This point should be familiar to anyone who has had occasion to teach an undergraduate course on freedom of the will: students are frequently drawn to incompatibilism as a kind of default position and tend to view compatibilist arguments with suspicion, as attempts to talk them out of something that is virtually obvious outside of the classroom. This strongly suggests that the roots of incompatibilist thinking lie deep in our ordinary understanding of responsibility and its conditions. The compatibilist should acknowledge that this is the case, by tracing incompatibilist ideas to aspects of the accepted excuses and exemptions that are quite naturally subject to confusion and misunderstanding. Only when we are equipped with a diagnosis of this sort can we begin to accept that compatibilists have not simply left something out in their reconstruction of our views about responsibility and its conditions. For only such a diagnosis can convince us that what has been left out of the compatibilist reconstruction does not really belong there in the first place.

Conventional compatibilist accounts would seem to be well positioned to deliver diagnoses of the sort I have taken to be required, even

---

26. For the expression "intuition pump"—and the general strategy of accounting for incompatibilist ideas by appealing to such philosophical devices—see Dennett, *Elbow Room*.

if their proponents have not always appreciated this advantage. Compatibilists typically grant that alternate possibilities matter to responsibility, or that responsibility requires not only certain general abilities, but also the opportunity to exercise such general abilities. Granting these points, they then proceed to develop their own analyses of the central concepts of alternate possibility or opportunity, analyses that are meant to protect the central concepts from being threatened if determinism should be true. If this is the form that the compatibilist position takes, it ought to be very easy to explain the tendency to think about responsibility in incompatibilist terms, for it is extremely natural to understand the concepts of opportunity and alternate possibility in a way that would make them incompatible with determinism. Indeed, so natural are such interpretations that compatibilist alternatives tend to seem ad hoc and implausible. As I have suggested repeatedly, once compatibilists grant that responsibility requires opportunities or alternate possibilities, they may already have given the game away. They are then compelled to rest the case for compatibilism on distinctions between different senses of opportunity or alternate possibility that seem too fine-grained and technical to do the normative work required of them.

My compatibilist position, by contrast, does not concede the relevance of alternate possibilities or opportunities to responsibility. Instead it interprets the conditions of accountable moral agency as involving the general power to grasp moral reasons, and to control one's behavior by the light of those reasons. To put the point in familiar Kantian terms, we may endorse the thought that ought implies can; in doing so, however, we must be clear that the "can" that matters to responsibility is not the "can" of opportunity or alternate possibility, but the "can" of general rational power.[27] To be a morally accountable agent—the sort of agent who stands under moral obligations, and who can be held accountable for meeting or violating such obligations—requires the general power to grasp the reasons that support such obligations, and to control one's behavior accordingly. Provided it can successfully be carried through, this way of proceeding ought to represent a strategic advance, since it does not saddle the compatibilist with any concepts that clearly call for treatment in terms of freedom of the will. As I stressed in Chapter 6, and as clear-minded incompatibilists themselves have acknowledged, the possession of general psychological powers such as those of reflective self-control does not even appear to be

27. Compare secs. 6.3 and 6.4.

threatened by the thesis of determinism. Incompatibilist arguments begin to have plausibility only when it is conceded that responsibility requires the opportunity to exercise one's general abilities, or the availability of alternate possibilities for action. By denying these common assumptions, the account I have advanced thus deprives incompatibilism of its foothold in our understanding of the legitimate conditions of responsible moral agency.[28]

In doing this, however, the account also transforms the project of explaining the persistence and appeal of incompatibilist images. No longer can these images be traced to misunderstandings to which the genuine conditions of responsibility are subject; we have seen that responsibility does not really require the availability of alternate possibilities, or the opportunity to exercise one's general powers of reflective self-control. The task of diagnosing incompatibilist tendencies in our thinking about responsibility becomes instead the task of explaining why we are tempted to postulate the additional conditions of opportunity or alternate possibility in the first place. To discharge this task, I have found it necessary to consider the acknowledged excuses and exemptions, and to question what it is about them that invites us to suppose that opportunities or alternate possibilities are conditions of responsibility. It turns out that these conditions can often truly be described as depriving one of alternate possibilities, or of the opportunity to exercise one's general rational powers fully and successfully. The question then becomes: can we account for the normative force of the excuses and exemptions in terms of these facts, or does something else about them explain their normative force?

No doubt it is hard to get a handle on this question if it is not pursued systematically, in the context of an attempt to arrive at an overall interpretation of the excuses and exemptions. This accounts in large measure for the seductiveness of incompatibilist ideas, which are generally accepted prior to systematic philosophical inquiry, rather than being offered as the result of such inquiry. Even those who proceed philosophically tend to neglect the issue of how our moral judgments of exemption and excuse are to be explained. Compatibilists and in-

---

28. I have conceded that the *difficulty* of exercising one's general rational powers might be considered an exempting condition, and as I showed in the preceding section, the concept of difficulty naturally invites an incompatibilist treatment. But the tendency to construe the concept of difficulty in incompatibilist terms seems to me to rest on a modal confusion that becomes fairly obvious, once one reflects systematically on the concept. By contrast, incompatibilist interpretations of the concepts of opportunity and alternate possibility seem extremely plausible; if *they* are confused, the confusions have not yet been uncovered and explained.

compatibilists alike usually assume that responsibility requires alternate possibilities, or the opportunity to exercise one's general abilities; the locus of philosophical argument is then centered on the question of whether these conditions can be satisfied if determinism is true. Against this way of proceeding, I have tried to shift the locus of philosophical argument onto the prior question of whether responsibility really requires alternate possibilities or opportunities in any sense. This question can be answered only with a systematic interpretation of the excusing and exempting conditions that identifies what these conditions have in common, and explains why what they have in common is the source of their excusing and exempting force. The preceding chapters provide a systematic interpretation of this sort; with this interpretation in place, we can see why the conditions of opportunity and alternate possibility represent *false* generalizations from the acknowledged excuses and exemptions.

This suggests that philosophical reflection about responsibility may have not only a diagnostic but also a therapeutic role to play. By offering a systematic interpretation of our practices of excusing and exempting people from responsibility, such reflection helps us to understand why the pervasive incompatibilist elements in our thinking about responsibility are mistaken. But in doing so, it may also help to release us from the grip of incompatibilist pictures, providing a kind of protection against the admittedly powerful lure of liberty.

8

Conclusion

The normative argument of the preceding chapters has yielded the following conclusions: it is reasonable to hold agents morally accountable when they possess the powers of reflective self-control; and when such accountable agents violate the obligations to which we hold them, they deserve to be blamed for what they have done. Given the normative interpretation of the debate sketched in Chapter 4, it follows that neither accountability nor blameworthiness is to be understood in terms of strong freedom of will. Rather, accountability is a matter of one's general powers of reflective self-control, and questions of blameworthiness turn on whether accountable agents have really done anything morally wrong.

Against this, it will perhaps be objected that my normative argument has failed to capture some of our most strongly held moral views about responsibility and blame. Thus when an accountable agent has done something wrong, there is a tendency to think that the agent positively deserves to suffer the harms of moral sanction; we may suppose that it would be an intrinsically good thing for the agent to suffer those harms and take ourselves to have a duty to see to it that such harms are administered. It is not clear that the principles of fairness I have endorsed license these strong but familiar moral conclusions. Moreover these conclusions seem to encourage the idea that responsibility requires freedom of the will. We can be tempted to suppose that offenders would not really have earned the harms of moral sanction—construed as an intrinsic good that we have a positive duty to administer—unless they not only acted wrongly but also had the freedom to choose otherwise.[1]

---

1. I do not necesssarily mean to endorse this normative conclusion—it is not obvious to me that the conditions for the fairness of retributive sanctions are stronger than those for the kind of sanctions discussed in this book; on the other hand, I have not offered an argument against it.

It is true that I have not provided a basis for the strong conclusion that wrongdoers positively deserve to suffer the harms of moral sanction in this way. I have repeatedly urged against building such a retributivist interpretation into the very stance of holding people responsible (see sections 3.1 and 7.1). Furthermore, the principles of fairness I have articulated provide no support for these retributivist conclusions. Those principles are negative in form, identifying basic necessary conditions for the fairness of holding people responsible. They say that it is not reasonable to hold someone accountable who lacks the powers of reflective self-control, and that people do not deserve the responses of blame and moral sanction if they have not done anything wrong. It follows from these principles that wrongdoers who possess the powers of reflective self-control deserve the responses of blame and moral sanction, in the sense that it would not be unfair to respond to them in these ways. We may say that no moral complaint can be lodged against such treatment, on grounds of fairness, if the conditions of accountability and blameworthiness I have identified are fulfilled. But this is weaker than the conclusion that we have a positive moral obligation to inflict suffering on wrongdoers, or that such suffering would be an intrinsic good.

No doubt we are sometimes tempted by this stronger retributivist conclusion, but I can find a secure basis for it neither in our practice of holding people responsible nor in the moral principles of fairness that have a clear bearing on the assessment of that practice. Perhaps the strong conclusion rests on a misinterpretation of the urgency with which the reactive emotions are sometimes experienced. Confronted with a clear moral atrocity, we are apt to feel such emotions as resentment and indignation to an intense degree, and these intense emotions can adequately be expressed only through the sanctioning responses of reproach, denunciation, avoidance, censure, and the like; this provides a positive impetus to undertake these sanctioning responses, and helps to explain the peculiar satisfaction they may bring (a satisfaction that may also accompany the administration of official punishment by the state). Thus there is a kind of expressive logic of the reactive emotions that can drive us to engage in sanctioning behavior, but this expressive logic should not be mistaken for a moral imperative, to the effect that we have a duty to administer such sanctions or that the harms they occasion are an intrinsic moral good.

Some will continue to insist that these stronger moral claims form an essential part of our pretheoretical understanding of responsibility and desert.[2] I do not find this a plausible assertion—it has the peculiar consequence, for instance, that Gandhi and King acted wrongly in adopting the stance of presumptive forgiveness discussed in section 3.2. On the other hand, I do not know what more to say to someone who is not satisfied by the account of responsibility and desert offered in earlier chapters of this book. Suppose, for the sake of argument, that such a critic is correct. I would then be content to be offering a modestly revisionist interpretation of what we are doing in holding people responsible, and of the principles of fairness that bear on the assessment of that practice. As I suggested in section 3.1, part of the appeal of the economy of threats account has been a suspicion that our ordinary practice of holding people responsible is tainted with primitive retributivist associations that are no longer morally defensible. At the very least, the argument of this book should help to show those who share this suspicion that we do not need to throw the baby out with the bath water. The reactive account of responsibility defended in Chapter 3 captures far more of what we are doing in holding people responsible than the conventional economy of threats approach. And the principles of fairness identified in later chapters give us a way to make sense of claims that wrongdoers deserve the responses of blame and moral sanction, without committing ourselves to the problematic conclusion that we have a positive duty to respond in these ways or that the harms they may cause are intrinsically good. I believe these interpretations capture everything that is essential to our practice of holding people responsible and to the principles of fairness relevant to the assessment of that practice. Their availability certainly goes to show that the compatibilist can recover far more of the traditional territory of responsibility and desert than previous compatibilist accounts may have led one to suppose.[3]

A different line of objection to my argument will focus not on its

---

2. Kant may be an example here; see his notorious remarks about the duty to punish criminals in the *Metaphysics of Morals*, "Doctrine of Right," pt. 2, in the discussion of criminal law following sec. 49.

3. To this extent, my argument may be considered a contribution to rehabilitating the notions of responsibility and desert, in response to the kind of liberal skepticism about these notions described in Samuel Scheffler, "Responsibility, Reactive Attitudes, and Liberalism in Philosophy and Politics," *Philosophy and Public Affairs* 21 (1992), pp. 299–323. (In reconstructing this skeptical attitude toward the ordinary conception of responsibility, Scheffler seems to me to run together two quite different issues: [1] the role of desert in connection with moral responsibility, and [2] the role of desert as providing a preinstitutional basis for political claims about social justice. Liberals may affirm a role for ideas of desert in the former context, even if they deny desert a role in the latter context.)

normative details, but on its metaphysical conclusion. Some will think that I have not fully come to terms with the appeal of incompatibilist views because I have restricted my focus to the issue of fairness (in accordance with the normative interpretation sketched in section 4.1). These critics may agree that it could be fair to hold people responsible in the absence of strong freedom of will, but they will insist that we need such freedom all the same, arguing along the following lines. Our moral practices acknowledge a distinction between morally responsible agents and other kinds of creatures and things, a distinction that we have seen to be invested with great practical importance. But no such distinction could really be justified—metaphysically justified, one might say—if it does not correspond to a real difference in the objective world, a difference that is prior to and independent of our moral practices themselves. Only if morally responsible agents are radically unlike the other kinds of creatures and things in the world would it make sense for us to single them out for fundamentally special treatment in the way we do. For these purposes, however, nothing less than strong freedom of will would be enough; unless responsible agents are free in this sense, our differential treatment of them will lack the foundation in the nature of things that it requires.

This line of thought surely captures part of the attraction of incompatibilist interpretations of responsibility. It explains, for instance, the peculiar disappointment we are apt to feel when the indeterminacies of quantum theory are appealed to as a solution to our worries about freedom of will. The existence of indeterminacies in quantum mechanics may (or may not) be sufficient to refute determinism, but by themselves such indeterminacies do not give persons a privileged status in the world of natural objects, of the sort that would justify our special treatment of them as morally responsible. To speak adequately to this concern, it would be necessary to show not just that determinism is false, but also that what makes it false at the same time sets persons radically apart from other kinds of creatures and things. We should want to confirm, for instance, that persons are free choosers, capable of determining which out of a range of alternate possibilities is realized in particular situations of action, or that persons can be the uncaused originators of the things they do. Only if these pictures are true will the special treatment we accord morally responsible agents adequately reflect a genuine difference in the world.

This is, as I said, a familiar line of thought; but it also proves puzzling on closer inspection. The very idea of a metaphysical justification of our practice of holding people responsible is one that is hard to make sense of. Among other things, it does not seem to do justice to the special relevance that questions about freedom seem to have for our moral practices. If the point of the metaphysical justification is to ground our moral distinctions in real objective differences in the world, it is obscure why we should feel pressed to cash out these objective differences in terms of freedom. Why would it not be enough to show that all and only those agents who are morally responsible have (say) a certain distinctive chromosome? This would be an objective difference in the world, prior to and independent of our practices, yet I doubt the confirmation of this difference would leave us satisfied that our special treatment of responsible agents is adequately anchored in the nature of things. The objective differences that our practices track should be differences that we can recognize to be normatively significant; they should render it appropriate or warranted to treat responsible agents in the ways we do. This is the sort of consideration that led me to reject metaphysical interpretations of the debate about responsibility in Chapter 4, and to propose in their place a normative interpretation.

But the line of thought I have sketched is puzzling in other ways as well. The objection rests on the concern that our moral distinctions should track objective differences in the world. It is unclear, however, why this concern should lead us to prefer an incompatibilist account of responsibility to the approach I have developed. On that approach, the fundamental condition of accountable moral agency is not freedom of the will, but possession of the powers of reflective self-control. Whether this condition is or is not satisfied, however, is a perfectly objective matter of fact. Granted, it is a fact about how things stand within the manifest image of the world, not a microphysical or biological fact of the sort that could be characterized in the terms of the natural sciences. But the existence of free choosers, or uncaused initiators of action, would be equally ineffable in the terms of the natural sciences; to insist that our practices should be anchored in facts available within the scientific image of the world would be to set standards that no theory of responsibility could hope to satisfy, condemning those practices before a serious investigation of them has even begun.[4] A different complaint might be that the powers of reflective self-control are not prior to and independent of morality, insofar as they are construed

---

4. Compare Mark Johnston, "Reasons and Reductionism," *Philosophical Review* 101 (1992), pp. 589–618, at pp. 592, 618.

essentially in moral terms—they are the powers to grasp moral reasons, and to control our behavior by the light of them. But whether people have these powers is independent of our more specific practice of holding them morally responsible, at least in the sense that the fact that a given agent has these powers, at a certain time, is empirically and conceptually independent of whether she is then being held morally responsible.[5] This is independence enough to give content to the thought that our practice of holding people responsible tracks a real distinction in the world; beyond this, why should it matter whether the facts in question can be specified completely in nonmoral terms?

The important issue, I believe, is not whether the account I have offered gives our moral distinctions a real basis in the world, but whether it gives those distinctions the right kind of basis. In assessing the account, we need to ask whether the facts in terms of which it characterizes responsibility engage our genuine moral interests— whether they are the kinds of facts we ought to be concerned about insofar as we hold people morally responsible. I have tried to show that we do not really have reason to be concerned about whether people have freedom of will, in deciding whether they are morally responsible agents, whereas facts about their powers of reflective self-control have great normative significance for this purpose. This conclusion may be reinforced by considering, in conclusion, one kind of case that I have so far touched on only in passing: that of childhood deprivation.

It is well known that information about a person's childhood background can affect our disposition to hold the person morally responsible. We become reluctant to blame even those who have committed quite horrible crimes when we learn that they were subject to unusual deprivation in their youth.[6] Forms of deprivation apt to affect our judgments in this way include physical and verbal abuse, emotional neglect and inattention, withdrawal of love and concern, extreme arbitrariness and hypocrisy in the application of punishments and rewards,

---

5. It may be that the powers of reflective self-control are dependent on the practice of holding people responsible, in the different sense that people would not tend to develop those powers if they were not held morally responsible by others. Note too that, on my account, facts about *responsibility* are dependent on our practice of holding people responsible, insofar as they are specified in terms of that stance; they are facts about whether it would be fair to hold a person morally responsible. (See sec. 4.1 for further discussion of this point.)

6. See, for example, the remarkable presentation of the case of Robert Harris, in Gary Watson, "Responsibility and the Limits of Evil: Reflections on a Strawsonian Theme," in Ferdinand Schoeman, ed., *Responsibility, Character, and the Emotions: New Essays in Moral Psychology* (Cambridge: Cambridge University Press, 1987), pp. 256–286.

and an atmosphere of violence, insecurity, and hopelessness. The question is, why do conditions of this kind affect our judgments of responsibility? It is not a satisfying answer to suggest that such conditions deprive people of the relevant kind of freedom of will, committing them necessarily to later wrongdoing as adults. Partly this is because we have no more reason to think that childhood deprivation deterministically gives rise to adult wrongdoing than we have reason to think that an unusually conscientious and supportive upbringing deterministically causes adult virtue; and yet a childhood of the latter kind would hardly seem incompatible with responsibility.[7] More fundamentally, however, I believe we would continue to regard deprivation as a factor that inhibits responsibility even if we did not accept that it strictly necessitates adult wrongdoing. We might think it perfectly *possible* that someone with such a background should have stayed out of trouble as an adult, but we would still consider it unfair to treat the person as a fully accountable agent, and we would be reluctant to respond with ordinary moral blame when the person did something wrong.

The account I have developed makes it intelligible that we respond to deprivation in these ways. The account treats the powers of reflective self-control as the primary conditions of moral accountability. As I have stressed, however, these powers admit of degrees; like other general psychological and physical abilities, they can be more or less fully developed. Furthermore, it is extremely plausible to suppose that how far one's powers of reflective self-control are developed will largely be a function of the environmental and educational circumstances to which one is exposed in childhood and youth. If this is correct, then we can begin to understand the sensitivity of our judgments of responsibility to facts about childhood deprivation. Such conditions as verbal and physical abuse and emotional neglect, when they are chronic and extreme during a person's childhood, would seem to be exceptionally unfavorable to the development of a normal level of the powers of reflective self-control. People exposed to these conditions will often find it extremely difficult to take moral requirements seriously as independent constraints on what they do. They may be subject to a kind of pent-up, displaced anger much more insistent than the emotions most of us experience, and this may be a source of unusually strong incentives to

7. In response to this point, it might be suggested that psychological determination is incompatible only with responsibility for wrongdoing; see, for example, Susan Wolf, "Asymmetrical Freedom," as reprinted in John Martin Fischer, ed., *Moral Responsibility* (Ithaca, N.Y.: Cornell University Press, 1986), pp. 225–240.

antisocial behavior. Or their self-esteem may be so low that they feel themselves unworthy of the kind of relationship defined by the exchange of moral justification and criticism; they can then be driven to engage in behavior that confirms their sense of failure and worthlessness, and that is chosen precisely because it is in this way self-destructive.

Note that, on this account of it, childhood deprivation affects the adult's responsibility only insofar as it leaves continuing traces in the adult's psychological life.[8] This is as it should be—it would seem paradoxical to suppose that deprivation should interfere with responsibility independently of whether it has any continuing effects on the adult. Note too that the kinds of effects I have linked with childhood deprivation are not all-or-nothing effects, but rather matters of degree. I have described cases in which the impact of deprivation is unusually pronounced, leaving the adult in a condition that is in some ways like that of the psychopath.[9] But it is important to acknowledge that there will be other cases in which the residue of childhood experience in adult moral consciousness is less extreme, impairing the adult's powers of reflective self-control without altogether depriving the adult of those powers. Consider the fate of those raised in the pockets of desperate poverty and violence increasingly common in modern industrialized societies: people exposed to such conditions need not be deprived altogether of the powers of reflective self-control, but they are apt to find it much more difficult to take morality seriously than those whose formative circumstances and life prospects are more fortunate.[10] We may not wish to exempt such people altogether from accountability, and for legal purposes there may be good reason to punish them for their crimes much as we would fully accountable offenders. But morally it seems that we ought to take their social and developmental circumstances into account, recognizing those circumstances to be mitigating factors when the responses of blame and moral sanction are in question.

8. Thus appeals to childhood deprivation affect our judgments of responsibility by altering our perception of the motives and abilities of the wrongdoer as an adult; they make the adult wrongdoer's actions seem, not inevitable, but psychologically intelligible. On this point, see Watson, "Responsibility and the Limits of Evil," pp. 275–277.

9. In some cases, of course, deprivation may actually be the cause of psychopathy. But in the cases I have described, it was supposed that deprivation would impair the powers of reflective self-control not by depriving the adult agent of the ability to grasp and apply moral reasons (as in psychopathy), but by substantially diminishing the agent's capacity to control her behavior in accordance with such reasons.

10. Recall the point made in sec. 7.3, that conditions that render it difficult to exercise the general powers of reflective self-control could equally be said to diminish those general powers.

This is something that conventional approaches to moral responsibility have tended to obscure. Focusing as they do on questions of freedom of will, these approaches invite us to think of responsibility in absolute terms—as something one either has or lacks—and they suggest that the primary threats to responsibility are global hazards, such as determinism, posed by our common membership in the natural world. The approach I have defended suggests a different understanding of these matters. Once we see that accountability involves the powers of reflective self-control, we can begin to acknowledge the troubling intermediate cases where accountability is impaired without being altogether undermined. We can also begin to appreciate that the main hazards to accountability may be posed not by our physical and biological nature but by the social and political circumstances in which we develop and live. The conditions of responsibility I have identified in this book describe an ideal that is regulative of our social interactions, the ideal of a community of people capable of participating constructively with each other in the exchange of moral criticism and justification. No doubt many of the people we interact with conform to this ideal sufficiently to make it fair to hold them fully accountable; certainly, we have seen no reason to suppose that determinism would present a general obstacle to our achievement of this status. But approximation to the ideal is a matter of degree, and it is liable to be affected by such common phenomena as childhood abuse, psychological trauma, and the persistence of extreme poverty and violence in the midst of general affluence. If we take the ideal seriously, we should acknowledge the variety of ways that people can fall short of it, and be prepared to adjust our moral responses accordingly.

In practice, there will always be occasions that call for the reactive emotions. Confronted with the moral atrocities of modern life—the systematic rape and slaughter of civilians in the name of "ethnic cleansing," to take a very contemporary example—there is something bordering on the indecent in the suggestion that we should refrain altogether from indignation and blame; we need the reactive emotions if we are to take seriously the moral obligations we accept, as a basis for our common social life.[11] In holding people to these obligations, however, we should bear in mind that the powers of reflective self-control that justify this stance are a fragile achievement. This is equally a fact of moral life. To do justice to it, we must aspire to respond in

---

11. I speak here, obviously, as a member of a culture that makes the reactive emotions available.

ways that we can continue to regard as fair even after we have a full and accurate picture of the agents whose deeds we are judging. A willingness to adjust our reactions in this way would represent not a weakening of our commitment to holding people responsible, but rather the regulation of that commitment by the light of principles of fairness—an exercise of the very powers of reflective self-control that make us morally accountable ourselves.

Appendix 1

Further Emotional Vicissitudes

※※

In this appendix I look at some of the peculiar features of guilt, resentment, and indignation in more detail, starting with guilt. So far I have assumed that this emotional state is distinguished by its propositional content: one feels guilty for having violated an expectation that one holds oneself to, and so a particular occasion of guilt must be explained by the belief that one has in fact violated some such expectation. But the explanatory role of such beliefs, though the distinguishing mark of guilt, does not exhaustively characterize the state of guilt. It is often suggested, for instance, that the state of guilt is standardly associated with a syndrome of dispositions that help to set it apart from other emotional states (such as shame). Thus someone who feels guilty will normally tend to acknowledge wrongdoing, strive to avoid similar wrongdoing in the future, expect indignation and blame from others, and seek reconciliation through the acceptance of responsibility, as a basis of possible forgiveness; whereas shame tends to prompt one to expect disdain and contempt from others, and is prompted by beliefs of general inadequacy that cannot so easily be amended by the acknowledgment of any specific wrongdoing.[1]

This is correct, so far as it goes; but we must not suppose that the dispositions that characterize guilt in standard circumstances are necessary conditions for being in that emotional state. For instance, a feeling of guilt might dispose one not to accept responsibility for what one has done, but precisely to deny responsibility by way of repression.[2] In such a case, the feeling of guilt might be experienced as a form of contamination that is too awful to bear, and that prompts one to repress the drives that originally led one to violate some demand one holds oneself

1. See, for instance, John Rawls, *A Theory of Justice* (Cambridge, Mass.: Harvard University Press, 1971), sec. 73. I say a bit more about shame later in this section.

2. See Jonathan Lear, *Love and Its Place in Nature* (New York: Farrar, Straus and Giroux, 1990), pp. 65–68, 168–177, on the way in which holding oneself responsible might prevent one from accepting responsibility for one's drives, and hence lead to repression and neurosis.

to; here guilt would manifest itself not in action that aims to bring about forgiveness and reconciliation, but in neurosis and its symptoms. A still different course to which guilt might prompt one—which for obvious reasons we might call the "Macbeth syndrome"—would be to stop holding oneself to the demands whose violation led one to feel guilty in the first place. Here one does not overcome guilt by acknowledging its appropriateness and moving beyond it, but rather by getting rid of the susceptibility to guilt through a change in one's orientation toward the original demands: one abandons the quasi-evaluative stance of holding oneself to them.[3] This kind of response leads in the direction of criminality and amoralism rather than neurosis.

Thus the state of guilt should not be thought of exclusively in terms of the set of responses that it gives rise to under favorable conditions; there are other, far less constructive actions and symptoms that it can cause. What unifies these very different conditions, if I am correct, is the explanatory role of beliefs about the violation of demands. Now I have already suggested that the demands one believes to have been violated, when one is subject to the reactive emotions, need not be supported by distinctively moral reasons; in this way we may allow for the possibility of reactive emotions that are not strictly moral sentiments. In the case of guilt, this possibility shows up most clearly in cases in which one feels the emotion irrationally, on occasions when one does not believe oneself to have violated any moral demands that one genuinely accepts. Even when guilt is generated by the violation of demands one does accept, however, they need not be demands that one holds others to as well as oneself. In such cases guilt may be a moral sentiment in an extended sense, insofar as it is bound up with one's conception of how one should lead one's life; but the demands in question need not be supported by distinctively moral reasons, in the way characteristic of moral obligations. And even when the demands in question are justifiable in this way, their violation need not involve the infringement of the rights of others. For these reasons it is a mistake to suppose that in feeling guilt we must think of our actions from the perspective of other parties whom we have injured or whose rights we have infringed (as Rawls at one point suggests[4]).

---

3. See Gabriele Taylor, *Pride, Shame, and Guilt: Emotions of Self-Assessment* (Oxford: Clarendon Press, 1985), pp. 93–97, on Macbeth. The discussion of Lady Macbeth in these same pages illustrates the "neurotic" response to guilt that I have described.

4. Rawls, *A Theory of Justice*, pp. 445–446, 482, 484. A similar criticism of Rawls on this point can be found in Taylor, *Pride, Shame, and Guilt*, pp. 86–89.

Suppose, for instance, that we have moral duties to ourselves—say, following Kant, to develop our talents. If we take ourselves to be subject to such duties, both accepting them and holding ourselves to them, then their violation might well provoke a state of guilt, without any thought about the claims of others. Thus one might feel guilty for having watched television and consumed junk food and alcohol all weekend, instead of using the time to develop one's talents (by, for instance, reading Augustine to improve one's Latin, or going to the health club to work out). Granted, if this is a genuine case of a duty to oneself, then there will perhaps be a residual sense in which claims have been violated by one's action (namely, one's own claim to have well-developed talents and abilities), and the violation of these claims could legitimately occasion the indignation of third parties; all the same, the guilt on the part of the agent would not involve the thought that the claims of *others* had been infringed in any way.[5]

A different and perhaps less peculiar case might involve a "personal" morality or morality of supererogation. Such moralities are distinguished by the fact that they are idiosyncratic: one does not judge others by the standards of such a morality, and to this extent the morality does not provide a basis for resentment or indignation. Still, the injunctions of the personal morality might be taken by the agents who accept them, not merely as optional ideals, but as expectations to which they hold themselves, and hence as injunctions whose violation could occasion guilt. An artist, for example, might hold herself to the expectation that she should devote herself completely and uncompromisingly to the demands of her craft, to such an extent that she becomes susceptible to guilt for the slightest breach of those demands (spending an evening in mere relaxation at the movies, say).[6] And yet she need not hold other

5. It is notable that those who violate what they take to be duties to themselves, though they may be subject to guilt, do not tend to resent themselves. And yet, if there truly are moral duties to oneself, those who violate them would seem to be as much victims of the transgression of the duties (and so be candidates for resentment) as perpetrators of the transgression (and hence subject to guilt). Perhaps this illustrates the peculiarity of the whole notion of a moral duty to oneself. Note too that the parties to Rawls's original position do not acknowledge any duties to themselves (*A Theory of Justice,* p. 248). Thus in the context of the well-ordered society that is his primary concern, all violations of the principles of right will involve infringements of the claims of others. The possibility would remain, however, that one might feel guilt without believing oneself to have violated any principle of right at all; this is the possibility I go on to discuss, of guilt generated by the violation of some personal morality or morality of supererogation.

6. It has been suggested to me that we would not designate this form of bad conscience by the name "guilt," precisely because the demands in question are not socially enforced. I do not myself share this linguistic intuition, but it may be what leads Rawls to insist that guilt involves an infringement of the claims of others. I am less interested in what we would call these emotional

people to a similar expectation—she might think that even people who are as artistically talented as she is herself are under no requirement to perfect their abilities, and their failure to do so might not provoke indignation so much as sadness or disappointment (at the worst). The artist's acceptance of the demands to which she holds herself might in this way reflect a kind of personal commitment, rather than being based on a moral view about the general obligation to develop one's talents. In this case, too, an episode of guilt would not necessarily be bound up with thoughts about the infringement of others' claims.[7]

The possibility of cases of this sort, however, seems to render puzzling the distinction between shame and guilt. It has often been suggested that the same action can be the occasion for both shame and guilt.[8] This seems correct, but it raises the question of how the two emotions are to be distinguished. Presumably the distinction is to be drawn in terms of the different kinds of beliefs that give rise to the two emotions, suggesting that when one feels both shame and guilt about a single action, one is viewing that action in two different (though not incompatible) ways. But how is this difference to be characterized? In light of the preceding remarks, we cannot accept Rawls's proposal that shame involves thoughts about our own lack of excellences that we prize and aspire to possess, whereas in feeling guilt we take into consideration others who have been injured by our action or whose claims have been infringed. We cannot accept this proposal, because not all cases of guilt involve the infringement of *others'* claims at all. A better account, suggested by the picture of the reactive attitudes I have been developing, is the following: in feeling shame about an action, one thinks of the action as revealing the lack of an excellence that one values and aspires to possess; the basic evaluative stance here is that of desiring something as a good. By contrast, the stance involved in guilt is the

---

states than in the fact that they seem structurally very much like ordinary cases of guilt, even though they do not involve violations of the claims of others.

7. A personal morality of this sort would be peculiar, in that the artist would take certain reasons to generate demands in her own case, but not in the case of others to which they *seem* equally to apply (such as those who have comparable artistic talents). One way to understand a position of this sort is in terms of higher-order attitudes. The artist might accept and hold herself to first-order demands, together with higher-order attitudes that permit her (and others) not to hold themselves to those same first-order demands. This would capture the idea that the demands of a personal morality depend on an attitude of personal commitment on the part of the agent to whom the demands apply. For a related suggestion, see Allan Gibbard, *Wise Choices, Apt Feelings: A Theory of Normative Judgment* (Cambridge, Mass.: Harvard University Press, 1990), pp. 166–170.

8. See for example, Rawls, *A Theory of Justice*, p. 445.

quasi-evaluative stance of holding oneself to an expectation, so that in feeling guilty about an action one thinks of the action as violating some expectation. One and the same course of action (for instance, a weekend visit by the aforementioned artist to the beach, devoted mainly to debauchery) might of course be viewed in both of these ways at once, prompting guilt and shame together.

The difference between these stances is reflected in a further difference between the emotions of guilt and shame. It has been suggested that when one feels shame about an action, one typically sees oneself as being all of a piece, and thinks of oneself as being thoroughly degraded by the lack of an excellence that one desires to possess, whereas guilt is typically experienced as involving a split in the self: an "alien self" has emerged that stains or disfigures what one is.[9] This can naturally be accounted for on the supposition that guilt and shame involve different kinds of evaluative (or quasi-evaluative) stances. Shame, I have contended, presupposes desire for some good, and it is a basic feature of desire that one may desire something as a good without believing that the object of desire is in one's possession. Thus the excellences one desires to possess, and whose absence provides the occasion for shame, may be traits that one believes oneself quite fully to lack even while continuing to view them as goods; for this reason one may think of oneself as being all of a piece (as *completely* lacking the excellent traits) while feeling shame. In holding oneself to a demand, by contrast, one does not (merely) desire to conform to the demand, or view such conformity as good. To hold oneself to the demand is to assume the authority of the demand in judgment, and this necessarily involves one in adopting the "perspective" of the demand (at least so long as one is in the grip of the emotion[10]). Hence if one violates a demand that one holds oneself to, it will be very hard to think of oneself as all of a piece. In the very act of holding oneself to the demand, one at least temporarily commits oneself to it in thought, and so takes up a perspective from which one is set over against the part of oneself that perpetrated the wrongful act in the first place.

9. Taylor, *Pride, Shame, and Guilt*, pp. 92, 131–136.

10. Of course, as explained earlier, one may not fully accept the demands that generate guilt, insofar as one does not resort to them in practical deliberation and normative discussion. Still, in the grip of guilt there will be a sense in which one thinks of oneself from the perspective of the demands one holds oneself to. This is connected with the tendency of guilt, noted in sec. 2.4, to induce thoughts of harm and disfigurement of the self—even if one does not fully accept those thoughts.

This is presumably part of the appeal of the psychoanalytic account of the dynamics of guilt, which postulates a substructure in the self—the super-I—that is, or at least can be, set over against the delinquent I.[11]

A further issue that needs to be addressed concerns the pathologies to which guilt can give rise. I have already noted that guilt can be felt irrationally, on occasions when one does not really believe oneself to have done anything that violates demands that one accepts, and I have insisted (in section 2.4) that an account of guilt must allow for the possibility of cases of this sort, without depriving guilt altogether of its distinctive propositional content. A different set of pathologies are involved in the tendency to feel guilt in response to an antecedent desire to inflict suffering on oneself. Something like this tendency, I take it, is at work in what Nietzsche referred to as the "bad conscience," and a rather different version was discussed by Freud under the rubric of the "unconscious sense of guilt."[12] Someone under the influence of one of these pathologies will pursue guilt as a means of inflicting suffering on himself, not simply because he believes himself to have done something wrong, and the dynamic of this process will be unconscious to the agent himself—indeed, on Freud's view, the agent may even be unaware of feeling guilty at all, mistaking his guilt for *mere* illness when it is in fact the cause of his illness. Such pathologies raise two philosophical questions: how can guilt be unconscious to the agent in its grip? And how can guilt be caused by the desire to inflict suffering, without losing the connection with beliefs about expectations that gives it its propositional content?

The first question is relatively easy to answer. If, as I have maintained, guilt is explained by some belief about the violation of an expectation, then an episode of guilt might be unconscious if the belief that gives rise to it is unconscious to the agent who has it. This process seems to be presupposed in Freud's case studies of the role of guilt in neurosis and hysteria: the belief that one has violated some demand, being too horrible to contemplate, leads one to repress the desires that prompted one to violate the demand and thereby renders unconscious the belief

11. These remarks admittedly have a metaphorical quality; certainly they are not meant to provide a complete account of the difference between shame and guilt. For more on shame and guilt, and the (rather tangled) topic of the connections of both with self-respect and self-esteem, see Rawls, *A Theory of Justice*, secs. 67 and 73; Taylor, *Pride, Shame, and Guilt*, pp. 76–84, 130–141; and David Sachs, "How to Distinguish Self-Respect from Self-Esteem," *Philosophy and Public Affairs* 10 (1981), pp. 346–360.

12. See Friedrich Nietzsche, *On the Genealogy of Morals*, essay 2, and Sigmund Freud, *The Ego and the Id*.

that the demand has been violated in the first place.[13] Somewhat more puzzling is the idea that an antecedent desire to inflict suffering might be the motive for one's state of guilt. This suggests that the explanation for one's state is to be sought in the desire to suffer, whereas I have proposed that guilt is explained by the belief that one has violated a demand to which one holds oneself. The puzzle is solved, however, by noting that the two explanations need not be incompatible. The immediate explanation for an episode of guilt might be the fact that one believes, at some level, that one has violated a particular demand one holds oneself to. But the further explanation for how one has come to hold oneself to such a demand in the first place may cite a prior desire to inflict suffering on oneself.

Of course if Nietzsche and Freud are correct, there may be an element of self-directed aggression at work in all cases of guilt, even the nonpathological ones. What would then distinguish the pathological from the nonpathological cases? One difference may be located in the quality of the aggression. In the nonpathological cases, as I have interpreted them, the aggressive element is a tendency to sanctioning behavior (self-reproach, say, in the case of guilt), which serves an essentially *expressive* function, giving voice to the reactive emotion of guilt (see section 3.2, for example). By contrast, in the pathological cases the aggressive element seems to be an independent desire to inflict suffering on oneself that is prior to the episode of reactive emotion and so cannot similarly subserve an expressive function. A further difference is that, in the pathological cases, one's only sufficient motive for holding oneself to the demands is the desire for suffering: in the absence of that motive one would not hold oneself to the demands in question, because one does not genuinely accept those demands in the contexts of practical reasoning and criticism. By contrast, in the nonpathological cases we may suppose that one accepts the expectations to which one holds oneself, taking them to be supported by reasons that weigh with one in practical deliberation and normative discussion. When this condition is satisfied, one will have harnessed one's aggressive impulses in the service of demands with which one identifies, in a way that has no analogue in the pathological cases.

A final set of pathologies includes the phenomena of survivor guilt and vicarious guilt—the guilt felt, for instance, by the lone survivor of

---

13. See, for example, the discussion of the cases of Miss Lucy R. and Fräulein Elisabeth in Lear, *Love and Its Place in Nature,* chap. 2.

an accident, or by an American visitor to Hiroshima. These cases seem puzzling, on my account, since those subject to guilt of these kinds have generally not done anything at all to bring on their guilt; this makes it difficult to credit them with the belief that they have violated an expectation. Some of these situations may best be understood as situations in which one is not subject to a genuine state of guilt, but only to "residue guilt feelings" that are not strictly *about* anything at all.[14] What one experiences would then be the kinesthetic sensations familiar from genuine episodes of guilt—perhaps brought on by a traumatic event, such as an accident—but without the propositional objects that distinguish such genuine episodes. Experiencing sensations of this sort, one might seek some transgression on one's part that would rationalize them ("If only I had taken the car in to be serviced last week!"). In other cases there may be, in a stronger sense, something that one's guilt is about, but the content of the state will be specified by a proposition that one grasps in thought without genuinely accepting. Feeling oneself to be less worthy or accomplished than the others who perished in the accident, one may be haunted by the thought that one's very survival was a presumptuous transgression, even if one does not sincerely believe oneself to have done anything to violate a demand; or one might entertain the thought that, in virtue of one's nationality, the bombing of Hiroshima was something one had a hand in, even though one does not strictly accept that this is the case. Here, the propositional objects of guilt are fixed by cognitive states that may be considered beliefs only in a degenerate sense.[15]

This is hardly a complete account of the pathologies to which guilt can lead. My aim has been to say just enough to suggest how some of these pathologies might be explained in terms of the account of guilt that I have developed, for it seems a reasonable constraint on such an account that it should allow us to ascribe guilt in the full range of cases in which it seems to appear. With the other reactive emotions—resent-

---

14. The phrase "residue guilt feelings" is Rawls's: see *A Theory of Justice,* pp. 481–482. In sec. 2.4 I argued that we cannot plausibly treat all cases of irrational guilt in these terms, but the possibility was left open that we may sometimes be subject to residue guilt feelings of this kind.

15. The possibility of explaining some reactive emotions in terms of such degenerate beliefs was alluded to in Chapter 2; for an application of the strategy to the case of guilt, see P. S. Greenspan, "Subjective Guilt and Responsibility," *Mind* 101 (1992), pp. 287–303. On the phenomena of survivor guilt and vicarious guilt more generally, see also Herbert Morris, "Nonmoral Guilt," in Ferdinand Schoeman, ed., *Responsibility, Character, and the Emotions: New Essays in Moral Psychology* (Cambridge: Cambridge University Press, 1987), pp. 220–240.

ment and indignation—things are far simpler, for the possibilities of irrational or pathological syndromes are in these cases vastly reduced.

If my feeling guilt requires the belief that I have violated some demand to which I hold myself, resentment requires the belief that someone else has violated a demand to which I hold them. Further, the target of my resentment must have violated the demand by treating me in a certain way—or at least by treating in a certain way the members of a group with which I identify myself. (A British person might resent Germans not because they have done anything to her personally, but because she thinks they are condescending in their attitude toward her country and its people.) The demand in question need not be a demand specifically regarding oneself: the British person might think that nobody should treat the members of other groups with condescension, and resent the Germans only because she takes them to have violated this perfectly general demand in their attitude toward her own group. In this way—as observed earlier—resentment may have its basis in moral demands, even though it is felt only in cases in which the subject of resentment has (directly or indirectly) been affected by the violation of the demands.

A further complication is that one can be subject to resentment without resenting any particular individual or group of people. A teacher, for instance, might resent not only *her students* when they treat her with disrespect, but also *the fact* that she is paid so little for what she does. In the first case, it is easy to see how we can account for the propositional content of the resentment in terms of demands that she holds her students to: she expects them to show her at least a minimal amount of respect, and her resentment is about their flouting of this demand. But in the second case it may not be so obvious how the content of the emotional state might depend on holding people to demands, since there is no particular individual or group whom the teacher is said to resent.

Clearly, however, there are demands involved even in the second kind of case. The teacher resents the fact that she is paid so little, because she *expects* a level of compensation and respect commensurate with what she takes to be the value of her work and believes that this demand has not been met. (If she does not demand this, in the sense of holding people to the demand, but merely wants to be better paid, then she will hardly be subject to resentment in this case.) *Whom* does she hold to this demand for compensation? We might say: anybody in a position to affect her level of compensation and social respect. Thus the teacher's resentment might come to be focused on the school board, or on her senior colleagues, if she believes them responsible for what she takes to be her disproportionately low salary; or she might focus her resentment on the investment banker who has treated her dismissively at a reunion of her college class, taking him to have violated her generalized demand for respect. This suggests that in the cases in which resentment is not focused on a particular person or group, it is not because the subject of resentment does not hold people to demands; it is because, though she believes such demands to have been violated, she does not yet have a view about which particular people are responsible for violating them. In the limiting case, perhaps, she may believe that no particular individual or group could be responsible for violating the demands; she will then be apt to take "society" to be the target of her resentment, treating it (perhaps irrationally) as a kind of agent that can be held to demands.

Resentment, it seems plain, is not necessarily a constructive sentiment. Among its less happy manifestations may be counted the resentful temperament, where one has a basic and antecedent disposition to feel resentful toward the people with whom one interacts.[16] Such a disposition may lead one to imagine breaches of one's demands where no such breaches have occurred; in any case it will involve a self-obsessed vigilance about the way others have treated one that can encourage one to exaggerate and to fixate on such violations of one's demands as may in fact occur. In this there is a strong element of partiality, a tendency to treat oneself as exceptional. For even if one's demands are perfectly impartial, in the grip of a resentful temperament one will be far more assiduous about keeping track of other people's violations of them in their treatment of oneself than about attending to one's own violations of such demands, or the violations of them by third parties in their interactions with each other.

Often associated with the resentful temperament is a different phenomenon that is not really an example of resentment at all, as I have described it. This is the phenomenon Nietzsche referred to as *ressentiment,* the driving force in his account of the priestly character type and

---

16. See Joseph Butler, *Fifteen Sermons Preached at the Rolls Chapel,* reprinted as "Sermons" in Butler, *The Analogy of Religion, Natural and Revealed, and the Constitution and Course of Nature; to which are added, Two Brief Dissertations: On Personal Identity, and On the Nature of Virtue; and Fifteen Sermons* (London: George Bell and Sons, 1893), pp. 369–540, at p. 459, on the many cases in which "resentment has taken possession of the temper and of the mind, and will not quit its hold." (The quotation appears in sermon 8, "Upon Resentment.")

the slave revolt leading to morality.[17] *Ressentiment,* by contrast with resentment, essentially involves the evaluative thought that one lacks some characteristic that one values and wants very much to possess. The Nietzschean priests, for instance, value power and want to be powerful themselves, but in fact are impotent; and their recognition of this discrepancy between their nature and their values (however inarticulate that recognition may be) generates a habitual desire for revenge against the nobles, who have what they lack. Like resentment, *ressentiment* in this sense may involve demands: the priests, for instance, demand to be treated as powerful people. But *ressentiment* goes beyond ordinary resentment insofar as those subject to it take themselves to be deficient in respect of some important value (such as power).[18] Furthermore, the vengeful impulses that *ressentiment* generates are not directed exclusively toward those who have violated demands in their treatment of the person in its grip. Rather, they are directed at anyone who in fact possesses the traits which the person feeling *ressentiment* both values and lacks. For example, an athlete or a musician plagued by *ressentiment* may have vengeful impulses toward those who are more talented than she is, even if they actually treat her as an equal. We may summarize this comparison by saying that *ressentiment* is essentially *about* one's lack of some value or good, whereas resentment is *about* the breach of demands. Presumably the two emotions may overlap and reinforce each other—I take it this will often be the case with the resentful temperament I have described—but it is important to keep their defining features and objects distinct.[19]

17. See Nietzsche, *Genealogy of Morals.* The distinction I draw between resentment and *ressentiment* is not meant to reflect differences in the meaning of the English and French words "resentment" and "*ressentiment.*" Thus what I follow Nietzsche in calling *ressentiment* is sometimes what we mean when we speak of resentment in English. The point is that a central class of cases of resentment—those I have been concerned to describe—exhibits features very different from those involved in Nietzschean *ressentiment.* I distinguish between the two terms to keep track of the differences between these psychological phenomena.

18. Of course as a quasi-evaluative stance, resentment may involve some tendency to entertain evaluative thoughts of this sort (see sec. 2.4). But the resentful agent need not actually accept such evaluative thoughts, and even if she does, resentment—unlike *ressentiment*—is not essentially *about* the lack of some value.

19. An account of resentment that does not seem to do this is given by Jean Hampton in "Forgiveness, Resentment and Hatred," in Jeffrie G. Murphy and Jean Hampton, *Forgiveness and Mercy* (Cambridge: Cambridge University Press, 1988), pp. 35–87, at sec. 3. Hampton takes resentment to be essentially about a piece of "insulting" behavior or treatment, but builds into the emotion the (qualified) belief that one is degraded in rank or value. By contrast, I am suggesting that one may be subject to resentment without taking oneself to be degraded in rank or value; it is with *ressentiment,* rather than resentment, that such beliefs essentially come into play. On the general topic of Nietzschean *ressentiment,* see Max Scheler, *Ressentiment,* ed. Lewis A. Coser, trans. William W. Holdheim (New York: Schocken Books, 1972).

It has been suggested that resentment (as distinct from *ressentiment*) is an inherently moral sentiment. To express our resentment, we require moral demands, and a consistent egoist—one who held that the only reasons any agent can have for action are reasons stemming from that agent's own interests and (self-regarding) desires—could not be subject to resentment at all.[20] There is something right about this suggestion, even if (as the example of the resentful temperament illustrates) not all cases of resentment are morally justified; but we should be careful not to overstate the point. Suppose that, as an egoist, I try to hold other people to the demand that they treat me with special consideration, without believing that I possess any general trait, such as extraordinary accomplishment, that might require such special consideration in cases other than my own. Rather, I demand special consideration just because "I am I." If I could manage to hold other people to demands of this sort, then, despite being an egoist, I might feel resentment for the flouting of the demands. But it is very hard to see how a consistent and nondeluded egoist might hold people to such demands in the first place. In holding people to demands, what we expect of them is that they will comply with those demands in their behavior. But—barring the sudden emergence of a fetishistic concern on the part of others to satisfy my whims, just because they are mine—it is nearly inconceivable that any other person might ever come to have a motive to comply with my demand for special consideration, in the absence of some general reason for doing so that might at least in principle apply in other cases. It would therefore make no sense to hold other people to expectations of this sort, and this would deter a consistent and clear-eyed egoist from ever doing so.

Human psychology being what it is, it would seem to be a necessary condition for the possibility of conformity with a demand on the part of others that the demand be supported by general reasons, reasons that are formulable without indexicals or rigged definite descriptions, and that could therefore apply to others besides oneself. This is the kind of generality implicit in resentment, and it may be sufficient to render resentment inaccessible to the strict egoist (who takes it that only an agent's own immediate interests and self-regarding desires can provide that agent with reasons for action). By itself, however, it will not carry us to morality in all cases. A captain of industry, for instance, might

20. See Thomas Nagel, *The Possibility of Altruism* (Oxford: Clarendon Press, 1970), pp. 83, 85, 145, and Rawls, *A Theory of Justice,* p. 488.

demand special consideration from others on account of his great wealth and superior cultivation, acknowledging that others with similar traits would deserve comparable treatment, and the violation of this demand (by a colleague, or a headwaiter in a restaurant, say) might conceivably occasion resentment on his part. The demands that underlie resentment in this case are clearly not moral demands, and so we see that the kind of generality that resentment requires does not alone make it necessarily a moral emotion. What we can say is this: many of the central occasions on which we are subject to resentment are occasions when our demands are not supported by any claim to deserve special treatment that we ourselves would accept. If we resent the fact that our opponent has cheated at squash, we are apt do so simply because cheating is unfair; and our resentment is thus grounded in an appeal to reasons that, applied consistently, would require fair treatment from anyone (ourselves included). This is how we should construe the claim that resentment pushes us to acknowledge moral demands. It is not that resentment is necessarily a moral emotion, but that, in the central cases of resentment, our reasons for demanding certain forms of behavior from others would consistently require such behavior on our part as well. (Of course, even in these central cases we are often not consistent, worrying much more about other peoples' violation of the demands in their treatment of us than about our own violations of them—recall the resentful temperament).

Finally, to indignation: of the three reactive emotions I have distinguished, indignation is the one that seems most essentially to be a moral sentiment. This is because we are subject to indignation in cases in which we ourselves are not involved, but in which third parties violate the demands or expectations we hold them to in their interactions with each other.[21] For this to be possible, there must be a degree of disinterest in our application of the demands in question, and this is most likely to show up when those demands are moral ones. Still, there are borderline cases. For example, seeing a television clip of an enthusiastic American hugging Queen Elizabeth at a reception, a fan of the royal family might conceivably feel a wave of indignation at this breach of etiquette—not a clearly moral case.

Far more interesting is the tendency of indignation to take on a harsh and punitive character, a tendency that can lead to forms of emotional

21. We sometimes speak of indignation in cases in which the indignant agent is objecting to the way she has been treated by others. Used in this way, the word "indignation" emphasizes the distinctively *moral* quality of an episode of resentment.

irrationality. Indignation can be a way of channeling aggression onto others; indeed there may be an element of aggression present in all instances of indignation (and the other reactive emotions). If this is right, then we can see how (as with guilt) an antecedent aggressive impulse might be the original cause of one's indignation toward a person. Indignation requires the belief that the targets of the emotion have violated some demand that we hold them to, but the reason we hold them to this demand in the first place might be a prior feeling of hatred for which we seek a socially acceptable outlet. A racist, for instance, might come to feel indignant toward the blacks who live in his city for what he takes to be their slovenly habits, while the filth of the white workers' districts leaves him completely unmoved. Here, an antecedent hatred may be motivating him to hold blacks to demands that he (inconsistently) does not hold others to, and that he might not even accept (in the sense of "accepting a demand" distinguished in Chapter 2).

On the other hand, it is clear that indignation is often caused by the violation of demands that we do accept, that we consistently hold all people to, and that we strive to comply with, ourselves. I have devoted much of my attention in this appendix to the irrational and pathological manifestations of reactive emotion. My aim has been to test the account of the reactive emotions sketched in Chapter 2, by seeing whether it can illuminate the full range of cases that may arise. But it is also important to acknowledge that the reactive emotions make a positive contribution to the moral lives of normal, mature adults—a point I have tried to defend in this book by tracing the role of these emotions in our practice of holding people morally responsible.

Appendix 2

Alternate Possibilities

❧❧❧

Why have incompatibilists supposed that determinism would undermine moral responsibility? The answer is that they have generally taken responsibility to require alternate possibilities, and they have taken determinism, in turn, to deprive us systematically of alternate possibilities.[1] That is, incompatibilists traditionally present a two-step argument for the conclusion that responsibility requires strong freedom of the will. First, it is assumed to be a principle of fairness that people should be held responsible only if they have genuine alternatives open to them at the time when they act. Second, it is argued that if determinism is true, then it is never really open to an agent to do otherwise than what the agent in fact does.

Defenders and opponents of incompatibilism alike have focused most of their attention on the second step in this argument—and with good reason. Though it seems obvious that determinism would deprive us of alternate possibilities, in some sense, it is notoriously difficult to give a clear and intuitive account of exactly how determinism rules out alternate possibilities for action. I will understand determinism as the thesis

---

1. A possible exception to this generalization is John Martin Fischer, who concedes that alternate possibilities are not a genuine condition of moral responsibility, but suggests that determinism might still pose a threat to moral responsibility by rendering all of our actions compelled; see his "Responsibility and Control," as reprinted in John Martin Fischer, ed., *Moral Responsibility* (Ithaca, N.Y.: Cornell University Press, 1986), pp. 174–190, at pp. 182–190. It is extremely obscure, however, why we should think that deterministic causes constitute cases of compulsion, if we grant from the start that they do not compel us by making our actions necessary or inevitable. See also the "U-condition" discussed by Martha Klein, in *Determination, Blameworthiness, and Deprivation* (Oxford: Clarendon Press, 1990), chaps. 3–5. This condition is to the effect that a person's morally blameworthy choices should not be caused by factors for which the agent is not responsible, and Klein argues that it gives a foothold for incompatibilism that is independent of concerns about alternate possibilities. In sec. 7.1 I rebut her claim that we are committed to such a U-condition of responsibility.

that a complete physical description of the world at a given time, together with a statement of the laws of nature, entails every truth about the physical state of the world at later times.[2] I will also adopt the following further conventions:

b_t = a true proposition b entirely about the physical world prior to time t

a_t = a true proposition a entirely about the physical world at or after time t

L = a proposition completely stating the laws of nature

Then it follows from determinism that, for any a_t, there is a b_t such that L together with b_t entails a_t. The incompatibilist wishes to conclude from this that the events or states described by the proposition about the later time are inevitable, or necessary, so that where a describes a human action,[3] the agent no longer has an alternative open to her at the time when the action occurs. The difficulty is to define a notion of necessity or inevitability that will support this incompatibilist conclusion.

Incompatibilists have recently made admirable progress in responding to this difficulty.[4] They have argued that the sense in which determinism would make our actions necessary or inevitable is the sense (roughly speaking) in which it is not open to us or possible for us to do things that render false laws of nature or statements entirely about the past. Somewhat less roughly, I will understand the modal operator $O_{st}p$ to mean: it is open to agent s at time t to render proposition p false. Then, understanding a_t, b_t, and L as defined, and taking a to

2. This obviously glosses over many difficulties, concerning (for instance) the notion of a complete physical description of the world at a given time. For a discussion of some of these difficulties, see John Earman, *A Primer on Determinism* (Dordrecht: D. Reidel, 1986), chap. 2.

3. Human actions are not simply physical events or states, but rather intentional bodily movements. It will suffice, however, if we take a_t to describe the bodily movement made by an agent when the agent acts (or—since actions are often temporally extended—that segment of the complex bodily movement that takes place at time t).

4. See, for example, David Wiggins, "Towards a Reasonable Libertarianism," in Ted Honderich, ed., *Essays on Freedom of Action* (London: Routledge and Kegan Paul, 1973), pp. 33–61; Peter van Inwagen, *An Essay on Free Will* (Oxford: Clarendon Press, 1983), chap. 3; and Carl Ginet, *On Action* (Cambridge: Cambridge University Press, 1990), chap. 5. A useful overview of this strategy of incompatibilist argument is John Martin Fischer, "Introduction: Responsibility and Freedom," in Fischer, ed., *Moral Responsibility*, pp. 9–61, at pp. 32–40.

describe a human action, one can construct the following argument:[5]

1. $(L \ \& \ b_t) \rightarrow a_t$
2. If $((L \ \& \ b_t) \rightarrow a_t)$, and $O_{st}a_t$, then $O_{st}(L \ \& \ b_t)$
3. For any agent s, and any time t, not-$O_{st}b_t$
4. For any agent s, and any time t, not-$O_{st}L$
5. Therefore, for any agent s, and any time t, not-$O_{st}a_t$

The argument specifies a sense in which, for any action that is performed, it is never open to any agent—and, a fortiori, never open to the agent who performs the action—to render false a proposition that describes the action. The sense in which this is not open to the agent is precisely the sense in which it is not open to any agent to render false propositions entirely about the past, or to render false a proposition that completely states the laws of nature. But if it is not open to us, at or before the time when we act, to render false propositions that describe our actions, then we do not really have alternate possibilities; we cannot do otherwise.

Compatibilists have devised a variety of responses to arguments of this sort. Some have challenged the special modal inference rule on which the argument relies—premise (2) just listed (or a counterpart principle in different formulations of the argument).[6] Thus it has been argued that analogous principles fail for other modes of necessity, and for reasons that may carry over to the case of human will or ability,[7] and attempts have been made to devise direct counterexamples to the modal principles on which incompatibilists have relied.[8] But these arguments are inconclusive: the proffered counterexamples are controversial, and it may anyway be possible to reformulate the incompatibilist argument in ways that avoid the counterexamples.[9] Furthermore, from

---

5. I borrow freely here from Gary Watson's presentation of a version of the argument, in "Free Action and Free Will," *Mind* 96 (1987), pp. 145–172, at p. 155; compare van Inwagen's third (or modal) argument, in *An Essay on Free Will*, pp. 93–104.

6. Fischer calls this the "principle of transfer of powerlessness"; see "Introduction: Responsibility and Freedom"; compare van Inwagen's principle (β), in *An Essay on Free Will*, p. 94.

7. See Michael Slote, "Selective Necessity and the Free-Will Problem," *Journal of Philosophy* 79 (1982), pp. 5–24.

8. See David Widerker, "On an Argument for Incompatibilism," *Analysis* 47 (1987), pp. 37–41, and Kadri Vihvelin, "The Modal Argument for Incompatibilism," *Philosophical Studies* 53 (1988), pp. 227–244.

9. One of Vihvelin's counterexamples, for instance, relies on the idea that A lacks the power to make B leave a party, if A doesn't know that her showing up at the party would cause B to decide to leave (see "The Modal Argument for Incompatibilism," p. 237); but this might also be

the fact that principles such as (2) fail for some modes of necessity, it does not follow that there is no interpretation of necessity on which (2) is true.[10] The greater difficulty, in my view, is to show that such an interpretation of necessity also yields a plausible reading of premises (3) and (4) in the argument, premises that express what we would intuitively think of as the "fixity of the past" and the "inescapability of the laws." Take (4): this tells us that it is not open to any agent (at any time) to render false a proposition stating the laws of nature. It is meant to capture the intuitive idea that no proposition could count as expressing a law of nature if it were open to a person to falsify it. But it has effectively been argued that there is a stronger and a weaker way of interpreting operator O; the intuitive force of the idea that the laws are inescapable requires the stronger reading, leaving the weaker reading to define a sense in which determinism is after all compatible with alternate possibilities.[11]

On the stronger reading, to say that it is open to agent s to render proposition p false is to make a claim about s's causal powers. It is to say that s is able to do something that would either constitute the falsification of p, or cause an event that would constitute the falsification of p. It is on this strong reading, compatibilists have argued, that premiss (4) in the incompatibilist argument is true. That premiss, again, asserts that it is not open to any person to falsify a proposition stating the laws of nature; on the strong reading of O, this becomes the claim that it is not open to any person to perform an action that would either be or cause an event that falsifies a natural law proposition. And, the argument proceeds, this strong reading fully captures the intuitive force of the idea that it is not open to us to break natural laws, and explains all of our inferences in accordance with this idea. But that leaves available a weaker reading of O, on which premise (4) in the incompatibilist argument may be false. On this weaker reading, it is open to s to render law proposition p false if it is open to s to do something such that, if s did it, p would be falsified. This is a weaker reading, because it does not necessarily attribute to s any causal powers with respect to the

---

described as a case in which A doesn't realize that she has the power to make B leave the party. Ginet's most recent formulation of the argument attempts to avoid possible counterexamples by relying on a principle of inference weaker than the principle of transfer of powerlessness (or its equivalents); see *On Action*, pp. 103–104.

10. See Thomas P. Flint, "Compatibilism and the Argument from Unavoidability," *Journal of Philosophy* 84 (1987), pp. 423–440, at p. 430.

11. See David Lewis, "Are We Free to Break the Laws?" *Theoria* 47 (1981), pp. 112–121, and John Martin Fischer, "Freedom and Miracles," *Nous* 22 (1988), pp. 235–252.

falsification of law propositions: the possible worlds where *s* renders law proposition *p* false are worlds in which, though *p* is false, there is no action of *s*'s that constitutes or causes an event that falsifies *p*; rather, *s*'s action may be preceded by some other event—a "local miracle"— that constitutes the falsification of *p*. Equipped with this reading of premise (4), the compatibilist can accept that, if determinism is true, then we have alternate possibilities only if either (3) or (4) is false (reasoning in accord with the modal principle expressed by premise [2]). But such a compatibilist will argue that premise (4) *is* false: on the weak or noncausal reading, it is open to us to render false propositions that state laws of nature.

Is this a successful response to the incompatibilist argument? Doubts may be raised about the claim that the strong reading of premise (4) completely captures our inferential commitment to the inescapability of natural laws. Certainly it is intuitive to suppose that natural laws constrain us, not only in the sense that it is not open to us to cause events that would falsify them, but also in the sense that it is not open to us to do things that involve their falsification.[12] Even leaving these doubts aside, however, one may wonder whether the argument concedes too much to the incompatibilist. The argument grants that moral responsibility requires that we have alternate possibilities, but attempts to show that there is a sense in which we retain alternate possibilities consistently with the truth of determinism. Thus the compatibilist argues that it is open to us to do otherwise, if determinism is true, in just the sense in which it is open to us to do things that involve (rather than constitute or cause) the occurrence of a local miracle. But so long as we concede the importance of alternate possibilities to responsibility, doubts are bound to persist about whether this is really enough. In effect, the compatibilist ends up attributing great moral significance to a fine and rather technical modal distinction: not having it open to us to act otherwise in the strong or causal sense would not undermine moral responsibility, whereas responsibility would be undermined if it were not open to us to act otherwise in the weak sense. It is, on the face of it, hard to believe that so fine a distinction could bear such heavy moral weight.[13]

---

12. See Ginet, *On Action,* pp. 113–114, who produces an example to support the intuitive claim that natural laws place stronger limits on our freedom.

13. Compare Fischer, "Freedom and Miracles," p. 249, who sees it as a challenge to compatibilists to explain the importance attached to this distinction.

One way to respond to this challenge would be to investigate the moral basis of the principle of alternate possibilities. Perhaps if we knew more exactly why it is supposed to be a principle of fairness that moral responsibility requires alternate possibilities, we would see why the weak alternatives compatible with determinism would suffice to preserve our moral responsibility for what we do. But it would surely be a still more secure defense against incompatibilist concerns if we could reject the principle of alternate possibilities outright, thereby blocking the incompatibilist argument at the first stage. Suppose, that is, that moral responsibility does not require alternate possibilities at all. Then compatibilists could concede that the truth of determinism would leave it open to us to act otherwise only in a vanishingly thin sense (the sense, namely, in which it is open to us to do things that require or entail the occurrence of a local miracle). But they could insist that the absence of alternate possibilities, by itself, is not even a prima facie threat to our moral responsibility for what we do.

A position along these lines has influentially been defended by Harry Frankfurt.[14] Frankfurt formulates the principle of alternate possibilities ("PAP") as the principle that a person can be morally responsible for what she has done only if she could have done otherwise, and then proceeds to produce counterexamples to that principle. The essential feature of the counterexamples is the existence of circumstances that make it inevitable that an agent perform a given action, without actually bringing it about that the agent performs the action.[15] Thus, suppose that agent *s* does action *x*, after having deliberated carefully about the matter, and after having chosen to do *x* solely on the basis of her judgment of the merits of the case. Suppose, further, that—unknown to *s*—there is some different agent *r* who wants *s* to do *x*, and who would have ensured that *s* do *x*, as a result of choosing to do *x*, had *s*'s deliberation not by itself led *s* to do *x* (obviously we imagine *r* to be both clairvoyant and powerful). Alternatively, suppose *s* has a dor-

14. In Harry Frankfurt, "Alternate Possibilities and Moral Responsibility," as reprinted in his *The Importance of What We Care About: Philosophical Essays* (Cambridge: Cambridge University Press, 1988), pp. 1–10. Daniel C. Dennett also argues that we are not especially interested in alternate possibilities, in *Elbow Room: The Varieties of Free Will Worth Wanting* (Cambridge, Mass.: MIT Press, 1984), chap. 6; see also his "I Could Not Have Done Otherwise—So What?" *Journal of Philosophy* 81 (1984), pp. 553–565. But neither of Dennett's discussions considers in detail the relevance of the principle of alternate possibilities for moral responsibility.

15. Frankfurt, "Alternate Possibilities and Moral Responsibility," p. 9; compare his "What We Are Morally Responsible For," as reprinted in Frankfurt, *The Importance of What We Care About*, pp. 95–103, at p. 96.

mant addiction, of which she is unaware, that would have led *s* irresistibly both to choose to do *x* and to do *x,* had *s*'s deliberation not led her to choose to do *x* on its own.[16] In both scenarios the circumstances that make it inevitable that *s* will do *x*—namely, the existence and intentions of *r,* or the presence of a dormant addiction—do not actually bring it about that *s* does *x.* Frankfurt concludes that they do not undermine *s*'s moral responsibility for *x,* even though they deprive *s* of alternate possibilities. Thus *s* can be morally responsible for *x* despite the fact that *s* couldn't have done otherwise.

In discussions of this strategy for arguing against PAP, particular attention has been focused on the question of what exactly people are morally responsible for. Peter van Inwagen, for instance, accepts that Frankfurt's counterexamples tell against PAP, taking that principle to apply directly to responsibility for actions (where actions, in turn, are construed as universals).[17] However, he contends that what we really hold people morally responsible for are not their actions, but the consequences of their actions (or omissions).[18] Hence the principle of alternate possibilities should be reformulated to apply to responsibility for the consequences of action, and van Inwagen argues that when the principle is understood in this way, it turns out to be invulnerable to counterexamples of the sort that Frankfurt has devised.

Consider the claim that *s* is morally responsible for *x,* where *x* is the consequence of something that *s* has done, and where the situation is otherwise like that described in Frankfurt's original counterexamples to PAP. Van Inwagen suggests that *x* can be construed either as a particular (say, a particular event) or as a universal (for instance, a state of affairs).

16. Thus the existence of a second agent—a "nefarious neurosurgeon" (compare Dennett, *Elbow Room,* p. 8)—is not essential to the counterexamples. Note too that agent *r,* or the dormant addiction, would bring it about not merely that *s* performs the bodily movements involved in *x,* but that *s* does *x* intentionally. In this respect Frankfurt's examples are more sophisticated than the otherwise similar case of the person who chooses to remain in a locked room, described by Locke in *An Essay Concerning Human Understanding,* bk. 2, chap. 21, sec. 10.

17. Peter van Inwagen, "Ability and Responsibility," as reprinted in Fischer, ed., *Moral Responsibility,* pp. 153–173, at pp. 154, 170.

18. Van Inwagen, "Ability and Responsibility," p. 157. Van Inwagen also formulates and defends a version of the alternate possibilities principle that applies to acts one has omitted to perform: see his discussion of "PPA," in "Ability and Responsibility," pp. 155–157. But the example he deploys to this end really applies to our responsibility for the consequences of our omissions—a point made very forcefully by Frankfurt, in "What We Are Morally Responsible For," pp. 99–102. Hence the issues raised by van Inwagen's discussion of PPA do not seem to me essentially different from those raised by his other two principles, and I therefore confine my discussion to them.

Taking x as a particular event, he agrees that s can be morally responsible for x even in situations of the sort that Frankfurt describes, but
contends that those situations do not turn out to be ones in which x is
really inevitable.[19] For particular events are individuated by their causal
antecedents, and in the counterfactual case in which agent r, or the
addiction, brings about s's action, the consequences of the action will
have different causal antecedents from those at work in the actual case.
Agent r, or the addiction, can ensure that consequences of the same
type as x occur, but they cannot ensure that x itself, an event particular,
occurs. Hence Frankfurt's scenarios are not counterexamples to the
principle that s can be morally responsible for a certain particular event
only if s could have prevented it (what van Inwagen calls "PPP1"),
since even in those scenarios, s could have prevented x. Alternatively,
we may take x to be a universal state of affairs. In that case, Frankfurt's
scenarios do represent cases in which the consequences of s's action are
inevitable, since the presence of r or the dormant addiction ensures that
state of affairs x will result, whatever s decides on her own to do. But,
van Inwagen claims, precisely because state of affairs x is inevitable, we
would no longer hold s morally responsible for it.[20] That is, Frankfurt's
scenarios are not counterexamples to the principle that s can be morally
responsible for a certain state of affairs only if s could have prevented
it from obtaining ("PPP2").

  Frankfurt's own response to this argument is to deny van Inwagen's
claim that we hold people morally responsible for the consequences of
their actions rather than for the actions themselves.[21] What we are
morally responsible for, Frankfurt contends, are our (intentional) bodily
movements, including perhaps what is entailed by those movements,

---

19. Van Inwagen, "Ability and Responsibility," pp. 157–161.

20. Van Inwagen, "Ability and Responsibility," pp. 161–170. The intuition here is vividly
evoked by the following example. Suppose you find yourself floating down a river on a raft, and
you come to a fork in the river. You have enough control to determine which fork you take, but
the current is so strong and swift that you cannot make it to the bank. You decide to take the
right fork, believing that it will lead to a waterfall, which you wish to go over, and it does in fact
take you over the waterfall. But, unknown to you, the left fork would also have led to the same
waterfall. Here, van Inwagen would say, you were not responsible for the state of affairs that
consists in your going over the waterfall, since the same state of affairs would have obtained no
matter what you did. (Compare Fischer, "Introduction: Responsibility and Freedom," p. 52.)

21. Frankfurt, "What We Are Morally Responsible For," pp. 99–103. Compare Klein's discussion of van Inwagen's argument, in *Determinism, Blameworthiness, and Deprivation,* chap. 2, which
follows the different strategy of trying to show directly that van Inwagen's principles are false,
because they are counterintuitive. Klein's arguments in support of this strategy seem to me
inconclusive: the counterexample to PPP1 (pp. 42–43), for instance, is not sufficiently developed
to show that it is not really a case in which the agent could have prevented the particular event
of the dam's bursting, where this event is individuated by its causal antecedents.

but we are not responsible for the causal consequences of our movements. The causal consequences of our movements may affect how we describe the actions for which a person is morally responsible, but they cannot affect the fact of moral responsibility itself. Thus whether *s* is successful when he tries to kill his aunt will affect whether we describe the act for which *s* is morally responsible as an act of murder or attempted murder, but it cannot affect the degree or quality of *s*'s moral responsibility for the act. However, if it is acts rather than consequences for which we are morally responsible, then the relevant version of the principle of alternate possibilities is Frankfurt's original PAP, which applies to acts—and which van Inwagen himself concedes to be vulnerable to Frankfurt's counterexamples.[22] Thus van Inwagen's defense of PPP1 and PPP2 against similar counterexamples is simply beside the point.

On the question of what we are morally responsible for, van Inwagen may be correct about standard linguistic usage. Ordinarily we say that people are responsible for the consequences of their actions, rather than for their actions themselves—in most contexts, "He is responsible for her death" sounds more felicitous than "He is responsible for killing her."[23] But on the more fundamental point at issue, Frankfurt is surely right: as was discussed in section 5.2, the basic quality and degree of a person's moral responsibility even for the consequences of what he does seems to be determined essentially by those bodily movements that express the person's choices. Whether *s* is morally responsible for the death of his aunt—and hence whether we would *say* that *s* is morally responsible for her death—does not depend simply on whether her death resulted from something that *s* did, but on whether it resulted

22. See, again, van Inwagen's "Ability and Responsibility," p. 154, where he says he thinks "Frankfurt has made out a good case for the falsity of PAP."

23. See, for example, P. H. Nowell-Smith, "Action and Responsibility," in Myles Brand and Douglas Walton, eds., *Action Theory: Proceedings of the Winnipeg Conference on Human Action, Held at Winnipeg, Manitoba, Canada, 9–11 May 1975* (Dordrecht: D. Reidel, 1976), pp. 311–322, at pp. 315–316. As H. L. A. Hart reminds us, however, usage is not entirely uniform on this point; in both moral and legal contexts it is frequently said that a person is responsible for her actions, as well as for the things caused or produced by her actions. See Hart's "Postscript: Responsibility and Retribution," in his *Punishment and Responsibility: Essays in the Philosophy of Law* (Oxford: Clarendon Press, 1968), pp. 210–237, at pp. 224–225. Also relevant in this context is Hart's distinction between "causal responsibility," "moral liability responsibility," and "capacity responsibility"; see pp. 214–230. The (qualified) predilection for saying that people are responsible for the consequences of their actions rather than for their actions themselves suggests that the locution "*s* is responsible for *x*" is primarily used to report cases of causal responsibility. But this point of usage hardly settles the substantive issue of what people are morally responsible for (in, say, the moral liability sense).

from an intentional action of the right kind (for instance, *s*'s deliberately pulling the trigger with the intention of killing her). And if there is an intentional act of this kind, then *s* is morally blameworthy regardless of whether his act has the causal consequences he intended to produce by it. If this is correct, however, then the version of the principle of alternate possibilities that needs to be evaluated is Frankfurt's original PAP, applying directly to the actions that a person performs. And again, van Inwagen has apparently conceded that PAP is vulnerable to Frankfurt's counterexamples.

Ought van Inwagen to have conceded this point? There is, on the face of it, something puzzling about the suggestion that PAP might be vulnerable to counterexamples while PPP1 and PPP2 are not.[24] A counterexample to PAP would show that there are actions we are morally responsible for that we could not have prevented. An action, however, construed as an intentional bodily movement, must be either a particular or a universal, an event or a state of affairs; and so any counterexample to PAP ought to tell against either PPP1 or PPP2 (which concern our responsibility for particular events or universal states of affairs). But the connection between Frankfurt's and van Inwagen's formulations of the principle of alternate possibilities is a two-way street. That is, van Inwagen's strategy for defending PPP1 and PPP2 against Frankfurt's counterexamples, if effective, ought to be applicable to PAP itself, providing a way of protecting the principle against Frankfurt's objections. Thus, van Inwagen could concede that we are morally responsible principally for our intentional bodily movements, but argue that PAP is invulnerable to Frankfurt's counterexamples by an extension of the arguments he uses in defense of PPP1 and PPP2. The most natural way to do this, I suppose, would be to maintain that intentional bodily movements are particular events, and then to deploy the strategy used in defense of PPP1.[25] Frankfurt's counterexamples are scenarios in which *s* does *x* intentionally, but circumstances are present that both make it inevitable that *s* does *x* and play no role in the processes whereby *s* actually does *x*. But if we take *x* to describe a particular action, it may be doubted whether circumstances of the sort Frankfurt postulates (agent *r*, the dormant addiction) really do make *x* inevitable: if those circumstances were operative, they would produce an act that is in some sense of the same *type* as *x*, but they would not produce *x* itself (since the particular action they would produce would have causal

---

24. As Frankfurt remarks, in "What We Are Morally Responsible For," pp. 102–103, n. 5.

25. Van Inwagen maintains that it is hard to see how to construe actions as universals; see "Ability and Responsibility," p. 170.

antecedents different from *x*'s). Hence, even in Frankfurt's original scenarios, it remains possible for the agent to do otherwise, and PAP is preserved.

Now, there are various ways in which one might object to van Inwagen's argument, thus brought to bear on Frankfurt's alleged counterexamples to PAP. One might, for instance, challenge the principle for the individuation of particular events on which the argument relies. Frankfurt himself has apparently questioned this principle of individuation, insisting that one and the same action may have radically different causal antecedents.[26] But this strategy for defending the counterexamples would make their success hinge on the truth of controversial and to some extent counterintuitive positions in metaphysics and the philosophy of action. After all, it is not entirely arbitrary to suppose that an action that results solely from an addictive desire would be a different particular event from an action that results from the agent's careful deliberation—even if both actions involve indiscernible bodily movements.

It would therefore seem a more promising strategy to concede that Frankfurt's counterexamples do not undermine PAP, construed as applying to particular act-events, but to contend that PAP, so formulated, does not adequately capture what incompatibilists believe we require in the way of alternate possibilities. Suppose we take PAP instead to apply to actions, construed as states of affairs; do Frankfurt's counterexamples tell against this version of PAP? Well, even in Frankfurt's scenarios it turns out the agent *s* could have brought it about that he perform a different type of action. In the actual sequence that occurs, *s* brings about the state of affairs that *s* does *x* as a result of his own practical deliberation, whereas had *s* chosen to do otherwise, the state of affairs that would have obtained is that *s* does *x* as a result of the intervention of agent *r* (or the dormant addiction). What agent *s* could not have brought about is that an act of a different type was performed, as a result of a choice to produce an action of that type.[27] But perhaps this is the kind of alternate possibility that incompatibilists have taken to be im-

26. See Frankfurt, "The Problem of Action," as reprinted in his *The Importance of What We Care About*, pp. 69–79, at pp. 75–77.

27. If agent *r*, or the dormant addiction, had caused *s* to do *x*, then—though there is some kind, for example "intentionally *x*-ing," such that *s* would do an act of the same kind as the act *s* actually performed—there are also properties that *s*'s act would not share with the act *s* actually performed: for example, being causally influenced by *r*, or being causally influenced by an addictive desire. Hence there is a sense in which, in Frankfurt's scenarios, *s* could have performed an act of a different kind, but *s* could not have performed an action of this different kind as a result of his own choice to do so (since *s* does not choose to be causally influenced by agent *r* or the addiction, in the counterfactual situations in which those influences are effective).

portant: the ability to control one's actions by producing actions of a different type, as the result of a choice to do so. If so—as John Martin Fischer has maintained—then Frankfurt's counterexamples would, after all, be effective against the version of the alternate possibilities principle that really matters to the incompatibilist.[28] The counterexamples might not tell against PAP, but they undermine the stronger and more interesting principle of control (what Fischer dubs "PAP1★").

This response seems suspiciously ad hoc, however. After all, there is surely *some* sense in which the agents in Frankfurt's scenarios cannot do otherwise; it almost looks as if Fischer has singled out that sense and simply declared it to be the sense that matters to the debate. At the least, we need a convincing and principled reason for thinking that his formulation of the principle of alternate possibilities, PAP1★, is the one we ought to be assessing. Fischer suggests such a reason, proposing that alternate possibilities have mattered to people because they have taken responsibility to require control, and arguing that PAP1★ captures the sort of alternate possibilities we need if we are to be said to control what we do. But this suggestion requires much more defense and development than Fischer provides. First, it is not at all obvious that the importance of alternate possibilities lies in its connection with control. The incompatibilist might say that control is one thing, the ability to do otherwise another; each is nice in its own way, maybe even necessary for responsibility, but they are simply different issues. Second (what is perhaps a related point), Fischer's interpretation of the notion of control seems tendentious. He says, for example: "When we demand that an agent have control, we mean that there must exist an alternate sequence in which the agent chooses and acts as the result of his character or practical reasoning."[29] Is this really what we mean? If *s* deliberately and carefully drives his car over his aunt, as a result of his actual deliberation and reasoning, would we not say that he had control

28. See Fischer, "Responsibility and Control," pp. 181–182. (On pp. 180–181 of the same article, Fischer also questions the principle of event individuation on which van Inwagen's response to Frankfurt relies.)

29. Fischer, "Responsibility and Control," p. 181. Here and elsewhere, there seems to be an internal tension in Fischer's position. On the one hand, he wants to say that "we demand" a kind of control over actions that requires the truth of PAP1★. On the other hand, he agrees that Frankfurt's counterexamples show that we do not really require control, in this sense, as a condition of responsibility. To the extent that the counterexamples are effective, the claim that we demand control in this sense seems to be undermined. The incompatibilist might accept this, and maintain that what we really demand are simply alternate possibilities, in the sense captured by the original PAP, which is apparently not vulnerable to the counterexamples.

of what he did—quite independently of issues about which "alternate sequences" might "exist," and what goes on in those sequences? Answering these questions would require, at the least, a systematic examination of the concept of control, and of the reasons we demand control in contexts in which moral responsibility is at issue.[30]

What is beginning to emerge, I believe, is that Frankfurt's strategy is inadequate by itself to resolve the debate about the principle of alternate possibilities. His strategy is to try to refute the principle by producing counterexamples to it. But there is at least one version of the principle that may not be vulnerable to the counterexamples: the simple and straightforward PAP, applied to acts construed either as particular events or as states of affairs. To reject the relevance of alternate possibilities convincingly, we need to show that neither PAP nor any other version of the principle that might similarly escape the counterexamples states a genuine condition of moral responsibility. How to do this? One might attempt to devise further counterexamples, effective against PAP (and similar principles) in a way that Frankfurt's counterexamples are not. But even if one were to meet with initial success along this road, it would only invite still further attempts to formulate a principle of alternate possibilities that escapes the new counterexamples. In my view, it would be far more satisfactory if we could provide an *explanation* of why alternate possibilities are not a condition of moral responsibility in any sense. This in turn would require at least the following two things: (1) an explanation of what does matter to our judgments of moral responsibility, if not the availability of alternate possibilities; and (2) a diagnosis that accounts for the widespread tendency to take the availability of alternate possibilities to be a condition of moral responsibility.

In his original article and subsequent papers, Frankfurt himself begins to do both of these things. By way of explanation, he suggests that what really threatens moral responsibility for an action is not the mere fact that the action is unavoidable, but the explanatory role that unavoidability plays in bringing about the action. Specifically, moral responsibility for a given action is undermined if the action is performed only because the agent cannot do otherwise.[31] The reason for this is that when an action is brought about in this way, it will not be due to the

---

30. The concept of control is discussed in sec. 7.3.

31. See Frankfurt, "Alternate Possibilities and Moral Responsibility," pp. 9–10. Compare Klein, *Determinism, Blameworthiness, and Deprivation,* pp. 34–39, for an attempt to unpack the idea that people sometimes act only because they could not have done otherwise.

agent's higher-order commitments, where it is a necessary condition of moral responsibility that one's actions should express one's higher-order commitments.[32] On Frankfurt's view, then, the condition that makes us morally responsible for our actions is a condition of higher-order identification with them, and there is no reason to suppose that determinism would be a general threat to this condition. By way of diagnosis, Frankfurt conjectures that the original PAP derives its plausibility from reflection on cases of coercion; closer examination, however, reveals that genuine coercion of the sort that undermines responsibility occurs only when an action is brought about solely by the coercive forces that deprive the agent of alternatives.[33]

These are interesting proposals, but they do not by themselves amount to a satisfying account of the irrelevance of alternate possibilities to moral responsibility. The problem is that, even if Frankfurt is right to say that an agent is not morally responsible for an action when the action is performed only because it is inevitable, his explanation of this point is both questionable and undeveloped. It turns on the claim that higher-order identification with one's actions is a necessary condition of moral responsibility for them. But this claim seems dubious, on the face of it—we hold people to blame even when they act spontaneously, or negligently, or against their better judgment, and in none of these cases do their actions reflect their higher-order identifications.[34] Furthermore, Frankfurt fails to defend or develop this suggestion about the necessary conditions of responsibility, neglecting to explain *why* we should hold people morally responsible only for actions that express their higher-order identifications. Given the inconclusiveness of his counterexamples to it, the PAP (on one of its versions) is going to remain a serious contender so long as we do not have a systematic alternative account to hand, and Frankfurt does not provide such an alternative. For all he says, it remains possible that the "willing" addict is responsible not because her actions stem from her higher-order volitions, but because she really could have done otherwise, for the reasons I have given.

32. See Frankfurt, "Freedom of the Will and the Concept of a Person," as reprinted in his *The Importance of What We Care About,* pp. 11–25, at p. 24.

33. Frankfurt, "Alternate Possibilities and Moral Responsibility," pp. 2–5; compare his "Three Concepts of Free Action," as reprinted in Frankfurt, *The Importance of What We Care About,* pp. 47–57, at pp. 48–49, and his "Coercion and Moral Responsibility," reprinted in *The Importance of What We Care About,* pp. 26–46.

34. Frankfurt also contends that higher-order identification is sufficient for moral responsibility; I consider and reject this claim in sec. 6.2.

To put this suspicion to rest, it is not enough to cite some different factor (such as the absence of higher-order identification) that is alleged to be present whenever responsibility is undermined. We need to explain *why* the presence of that factor undermines responsibility—why, in the terms I have proposed, it would be unfair to hold a person responsible when the factor is present. That is what I try to do in Chapters 5 through 7 of this book. Together, those chapters show that the factors that we judge to undermine responsibility in moral practice include neither the absence of alternatives nor the lack of higher-order identifications, but quite different sorts of factors; and they explain, in terms of the reactive account of responsibility that I defend, why these different factors make it unfair to hold a person responsible when they obtain. They also develop a diagnosis of the persistent tendency to think that the availability of alternate possibilities is a condition of responsibility. My hope is that these explanations of our excuses and exemptions provide a more convincing response to incompatibilist concerns than the strategies of counterexample and analysis canvassed in this appendix.

Index

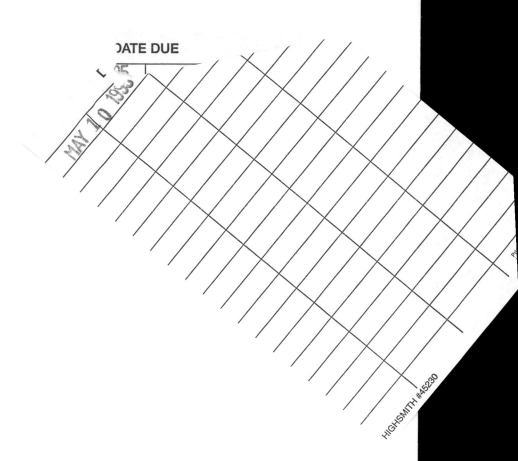

DATE DUE

MAY 10 1995

HIGHSMITH #45230